Get the eBooks FREE!

(PDF, ePub, Kindle, and liveBook all included)

We believe that once you buy a book from us, you should be able to read it in any format we have available. To get electronic versions of this book at no additional cost to you, purchase and then register this book at the Manning website.

Go to https://www.manning.com/freebook and follow the instructions to complete your pBook registration.

That's it!
Thanks from Manning!

Testing Angular Applications

JESSE PALMER

CORINNA COHN

MICHAEL GIAMBALVO

CRAIG NISHINA

with a Foreword by Brad Green

MANNING

SHELTER ISLAND

Manning Publications Co.
20 Baldwin Road
PO Box 761
Shelter Island, NY 11964

Development editors: Cynthia Kane and Toni Arritola
Technical development editors: Doug Warren and Nick Watts
Copyeditor: Carl Quesnel
Proofreader: Melody Dolab
Technical proofreader: Luis Carlos Sanchez Gonzalez
Typesetter: Happenstance Type-o-Rama
Cover designer: Marija Tudor

ISBN 9781617293641
Printed in the United States of America
1 2 3 4 5 6 7 8 9 10 – SP – 23 22 21 20 19 18

To my wife, whose love and support helped me get through many long nights and weekends while working on the book. Your accomplishments inspire me to do my best every day.
To my parents, who passed down to me their work ethic and provided me with opportunities to succeed in life, for which I am forever grateful.
—Jesse Palmer

To my dear friends, who encouraged me to keep writing!
—Corinna Cohn

To my wife, who has been consistently and limitlessly supportive over the many long nights these past few months.
—Michael Giambalvo

To my parents, whose hard work and sacrifice afforded me many opportunities, and to my wife, who supports me in all that I do.
—Craig Nishina

contents

foreword

I've known Jesse Palmer for many years as part of the Angular community, so I was excited when he told me he'd be writing a book specifically focused on testing for Angular projects. I've seen firsthand how hard it can be to do a great job at automated testing on some of the world's biggest applications. As a result, when I started the Angular project, I wanted to make sure everything we did contributed to making testing easier and even a joyful experience.

I was hired at Google primarily for my experience in testing, and my first roles here were in improving test techniques, infrastructure, and adoption of testing for products like Gmail, Google Calendar, and Google Docs.

At Angular's core, we've set the application architecture itself to be testable, with dependency injection, mocks, and API hooks for end-to-end testing. We've built tools like Protractor for easy, stable, and fast end-to-end tests. We built Karma for a great developer experience in unit testing. And there's still more to do!

This book picks up where we on the Angular team left off. It provides guidance on the overall strategy for how to think about testing on your projects to get the best return on your investment. It dives into specifics for testing different aspects of your applications. And it covers what are often regarded as advanced topics, such as setting up continuous integration for your tests and doing screenshot diff testing.

So here's my big thank you to Jesse, Corinna, Mike, and Craig for writing this book and helping to build a stronger, smarter Angular community.

And thanks to you for being part of the Angular community and taking the time to improve your skills.

Brad Green
Engineering Director for Angular at Google

preface

Back in 2013, I was working on a content management system that used AngularJS heavily, and the expectation was that we have 80% unit-test coverage. My team struggled . . . a lot. You couldn't find many materials on testing at the time. It was easy to find a blog post here and there, but it was hard to find something that guided you through everything you needed to know to be successful writing tests in a complete package.

I kept thinking to myself, *someone needs to write a book on this.* I knew it would be challenging to cover all of the potential use cases, but someone could at least give enough foundational knowledge to show people where to start. Plus, with the upcoming rewrite to Angular 2, there would be a need for quality content regarding testing. The idea for *Testing Angular Applications* was born.

One day in 2015, Manning Publications contacted me to review a proposal for another Angular book. I agreed, and they sent me a questionnaire to fill out. I was ecstatic to see a question at the end of the questionnaire asking if I had an idea for a book. Of course I did! This was my chance to pitch my book, and I was thrilled at the opportunity. Shortly after I pitched it, Manning gave me a contract to sign that marked the book's official beginning. Along the way, I was lucky enough to add three wonderful authors who helped bring tremendous value to the effort.

Now is a great time to get into testing Angular applications, if you haven't already. Since the early days of testing AngularJS applications, the platform has matured dramatically. The Angular CLI comes with numerous testing commands that make running tests a breeze. It also handles all installation of the testing tools, which saves time and prevents headaches as you set up your test suite. A lot of helpful tools available within Angular, like `TestBed` and `ComponentFixture`, aid in unit testing. Additionally, Protractor has matured and is stable, making end-to-end testing much easier.

In your hands or on your monitor, tablet, phone, or e-reader, or any other device, is everything you need to know to get started with testing Angular applications. My fellow coauthors and I have put a lot of time and effort into getting you up and running with testing. In many ways, we set out to write the book that we wished we had when we first started writing tests for Angular. We hope you enjoy reading and using the book as much as we did writing it.

Jesse Palmer

acknowledgments

We'd like to acknowledge the work of editors Cynthia Kane and Toni Arritola. Toni stepped into the process long after work on the book started, but she propelled us forward and to the finish line. It isn't an exaggeration to say that Toni is the reason you're able to read this book. Our technical proofreader, Luis Carlos Sanchez Gonzalez, was an invaluable help. Thanks also to the Manning reviewers, whose insightful comments helped make this book the best it could be: Bradley Suira, Desmond Horsley, Dinesh Arora, Jason Pike, Jim Schmehil, Nathan Roberts, Rafael Avila Martínez, Rainer Jeschor, Sergey Evsikov, Shobha Iyer, Siva Kumar Boyapati, Steve Atchue, Tahir Awan, and Zorodzayi Mukuya.

Jesse would like to acknowledge his former manager, Shawn Ward, who taught him the value of testing. Ward Bell also deserves credit for helping debug tests, writing the testing documentation on Angular.io, and insisting that he use the Angular CLI, which greatly changed the direction of the book for the better.

Heartfelt thanks go to Brad Green for getting Jesse interested in contributing to Angular in the first place and Peter Bacon Darwin for bringing him into the Angular organization. Finally, Jesse would like the thank his coauthors, Corinna Cohn, Craig Nishina, and Michael Giambalvo, for coming on board and helping to complete the book. The book wouldn't be what it is now without their valuable contributions.

Corinna would like to thank Samantha Quiñones, whose service to the developer community as a teacher and speaker inspired her to learn about unit testing, and who encouraged her to introduce testing practices to her organization. She also thanks Igor Minar and Miško Hevery for spending their time in person teaching newbie developers the basics of Angular and inspiring developers like Corinna to take a step into a larger world.

Craig would like to thank his previous team, Julie Ralph, Michael Giambalvo, and Sammy Jelin, for ramping him up on Protractor and reviewing all of his pull requests. He'd also like to thank Evan Harris, who years ago took him to his first Seattle Google Developers Group Meetup to learn about AngularJS.

Michael would like to thank Craig Nishina for bringing him in on this book. Special thanks to Julie Ralph, Sammy Jelin, and Craig Nishina for all the hard work they did on Protractor. Thanks to the Angular team for being consistently focused on creating a great community!

about this book

Testing Angular Applications exists to help developers better understand one of the trickier parts of using the power of Google's Angular framework: writing testable, reliable code. Angular departs wildly from the earlier AngularJS framework, introducing developers to a slew of new concepts not familiar from AngularJS or any other JavaScript framework. Writing unit tests and end-to-end tests requires a deeper knowledge of Angular than even the most heroic of tutorials can convey. Angular written for production should be backed by a set of reliable and useful tests, and with this book, we equip the reader with the knowledge to deliver those tests.

Who should read this book

Whether you're an experienced developer contributing to an enterprise-scale Angular application or new to Angular and hoping to gain a deeper understanding of the framework, this book will help you understand the fundamentals of writing testable code. Angular is evolving at a rapid pace, faster than the official documentation can match. Supplemental material such as this book goes beyond the online documentation by providing step-by-step examples that explain not only the how but also the whys of unit testing in Angular. This book assumes a comfortable knowledge of JavaScript and some knowledge of TypeScript, a superset of JavaScript that adds a variety of new language features.

This book reflects many hours of real-world experience understanding and applying the Angular framework for both unit and end-to-end tests. As authors, we've read the online documentation, delved into the Angular source code, upgraded Angular multiple times (along with the example application written for this book), applied multiple Angular testing APIs, and created realistic examples covering each major system of Angular.

If you need to write testable Angular code and want to take advantage of our experience of having already walked the path, this book will help you on your testing journey.

How this book is organized: a roadmap

The book has three parts that cover 11 chapters. Two appendixes include supplemental content:

- Chapter 1 provides a gentle introduction to testing Angular applications. It offers background information on TypeScript and touches on the differences between unit testing and end-to-end testing. It also gives you an overview of the different tools—Jasmine, Karma, and Protractor—you'll use throughout the book.

Part 1 covers the most common concepts that you'll need to understand to write unit tests for Angular:

- Chapter 2 will get your testing skills warmed up by writing basic tests. It discusses how to use key parts of the Jasmine framework, including beforeEach, afterEach, it, describe, and matcher functions. You'll also learn how to test classes.
- Chapter 3 discusses how to test the most fundamental concept in Angular: components. It introduces common testing classes and functions, and you'll learn the differences between shallow and isolated tests.
- Chapter 4 describes testing directives. You'll learn how to test two types: attribute directives and structural directives.
- Chapter 5 covers testing pipes. You'll learn about the transform function, which is essential learning for writing tests for pipes. You'll also learn about pure functions.
- Chapter 6 discusses how to test services. The chapter covers how to test services that use the Angular HTTP class, how to test services using promises and RxJS observables, and how to use stubs to create isolated unit tests. The chapter also covers dependency injection with unit tests for services.
- Chapter 7 goes deep into the subject of testing routing. Topics the chapter covers include configuring the router, testing components that use the router, and testing advanced router configurations.

Part 2 covers how to write end-to-end tests with Protractor:

- Chapter 8 covers how to get started with Protractor. You'll learn about how Protractor works, how to write your first Protractor tests, how to interact with elements, how to interact with a list of elements, and how to organize the tests with page objects.
- Chapter 9 discusses timeouts. It goes into detail about understanding the causes of timeout errors in Protractor and how to avoid them, waiting for specific changes in your app, and understanding flakiness with Protractor and how to eliminate it.
- Chapter 10 dives into advanced Protractor topics, like configuration files, screenshot testing, and debugging tests.

Part 3 is about continuous integration:

- Chapter 11 demonstrates how to set up a continuous integration server that will automatically run all the tests you've been writing. Doing so will help you find bugs as soon as possible.

Appendix A covers setting up the sample project, and appendix B includes additional resources for you to consider.

In general, you can read the book from front to back, or you can pick and choose which chapters you want to read. Most chapters use the sample app, which you can install using appendix A, so you may want to get that set up before skipping around the book.

About the code

This book contains many examples of source code, both in numbered listings and inline with normal text. In both cases, this code is formatted in a `fixed-width font like this` to separate it from ordinary text. Sometimes code is also in bold to highlight when it has changed from previous steps in the chapter, such as when a new feature adds to an existing line of code.

In many cases, we've reformatted the original source code; we've added line breaks and reworked indentation to accommodate the available page space in the book. In rare cases, even this wasn't enough, and listings include line-continuation markers (➥). Additionally, we've often removed comments in the source code from the listings when the code is described in the text, but code annotations accompany many of the listings to highlight important concepts.

You can find the accompanying code for the book on the book's webpage at manning.com (www.manning.com/books/testing-angular-applications) and also on GitHub at http://mng.bz/z22f. To execute the code, you need to have Node.js version 6.9.0 or higher and npm version 3 or higher. You can use a Windows, Mac, or Linux machine. We wrote the code for this book on a Mac, so your experience may vary slightly. You can find installation instructions in appendix A.

Book forum

Purchase of *Testing Angular Applications* includes free access to a private web forum run by Manning Publications where you can make comments about the book, ask technical questions, and receive help from the author and from other users. To access the forum, go to https://forums.manning.com/forums/testing-angular-applications. You can also learn more about Manning's forums and the rules of conduct at https://forums.manning.com/forums/about.

Manning's commitment to our readers is to provide a venue where a meaningful dialogue between individual readers and between readers and the author can take place. It is not a commitment to any specific amount of participation on the part of the author, whose contribution to the forum remains voluntary (and unpaid). We suggest you try asking the authors some challenging questions lest their interest stray! The forum and the archives of previous discussions will be accessible from the publisher's website as long as the book is in print.

about the authors

JESSE PALMER started programming back in the day when BASIC was still a thing. He spent much of his early childhood developing video games on his sweet Atari 400. Jesse started off his professional career by slinging ColdFusion, PHP, ASP.NET, and Java. Around 2013, he started his first contributions to AngularJS and thought that maybe this whole AngularJS thing had legs.

Jesse now finds himself as a Senior Engineering Manager at Handshake where he leads the Student Engineering organization. When Jesse isn't programming, you can find him playing video games or cheering on his beloved Virginia Tech Hokies. He lives with his wife, Elizabeth, and his two cats, Nicky and Gracie, in San Francisco.

CORINNA COHN is a web developer with more than 20 years of experience building websites and writing web applications. Corinna takes responsibility for having written ugly, unmaintainable code but is now working to bring the principles of clean code, unit tests, and high-quality refactoring into the realm of JavaScript web applications.

CRAIG NISHINA is a software engineer at Google working on Ads; he was previously on the Protractor team. In an earlier career, Craig worked as a civil engineer designing buildings, but he much prefers writing code to drawing building structures. When he's not contributing to open source projects like Protractor and webdriver-manager, he enjoys playing golf and traveling.

MIKE GIAMBALVO is a developer with a passion for creating testable, quality code. He is currently at Google working on the UI for Google Cloud Platform and has contributed to Angular and Protractor, the end-to-end test framework for Angular applications. He enjoys learning new things and helping others learn and is a cofounder of the Angular Seattle Meetup group. In his copious free time, he enjoys hiking and building crappy robots.

about the cover illustration

The figure on the cover of *Testing Angular Applications* is captioned "Habit of a Moor of Arabia." The illustration is taken from Thomas Jefferys' *A Collection of the Dresses of Different Nations, Ancient and Modern* (four volumes), London, published between 1757 and 1772. The title page states that these are hand-colored copperplate engravings, heightened with gum arabic.

Thomas Jefferys (1719–1771) was called "Geographer to King George III." He was an English cartographer who was the leading map supplier of his day. He engraved and printed maps for government and other official bodies and produced a wide range of commercial maps and atlases, especially of North America. His work as a map maker sparked an interest in local dress customs of the lands he surveyed and mapped, which are brilliantly displayed in this collection. Fascination with faraway lands and travel for pleasure were relatively new phenomena in the late 18th century, and collections such as this one were popular, introducing both the tourist as well as the armchair traveler to the inhabitants of other countries.

The diversity of the drawings in Jefferys' volumes speaks vividly of the uniqueness and individuality of the world's nations some 200 years ago. Dress codes have changed since then, and the diversity by region and country, so rich at the time, has faded away. It's now often hard to tell the inhabitants of one continent from another. Perhaps, trying to view it optimistically, we've traded a cultural and visual diversity for a more varied personal life—or a more varied and interesting intellectual and technical life.

At a time when it's difficult to tell one computer book from another, Manning celebrates the inventiveness and initiative of the computer business with book covers based on the rich diversity of regional life of two centuries ago, brought back to life by Jeffreys' pictures.

Introduction to testing Angular applications

This chapter covers

- Understanding Angular testing
- Getting a first look at TypeScript
- Understanding the basics of unit and end-to-end tests
- Introducing Jasmine, Karma, and Protractor

Poorly written code, buggy functionality, and bad refactoring practices can lead to unreliable applications. Writing good tests will help detect these types of problems and prevent them from negatively affecting your application. It's vital that you thoroughly test your application if you want to make it sustainable and supportable for years to come. A core purpose of writing tests is to help guard against breaking application functionality when you have to add new features or make bug fixes later on.

If you've developed an Angular application, you may know that Angular is a great framework for building testable web and mobile web applications. One of the goals in writing Angular was to make it a testable framework, and it shows.

Although testing Angular applications is of utmost importance, figuring out how to do that has been challenging until now. You may have been able to find a blog post or two, perhaps a video, but generally materials have been lacking to help guide you through all the different aspects of testing in one place. Well, you're in luck! In your hands (or on your screen), you hold the key to getting started with testing Angular applications.

This book will help you build a foundation for testing the most important parts of Angular applications with confidence. We assume that you have some familiarity with the Angular framework, TypeScript, and command-line tools. If you haven't written a test, this book will teach you enough fundamentals to get you started.

If you don't have experience with Angular, now is a great time to learn about the Angular applications. For newbies, we would encourage you to walk through the tutorials and introductory information you can find at https://angular.io.

In this first chapter, you'll get an overview of testing Angular applications, take a brief look at TypeScript, learn about the testing tools you'll use, and be introduced to unit and end-to-end (E2E) tests. Let's get started!

1.1 Angular testing overview

Most Angular testing you'll find out there involves two types of tests: unit tests and E2E tests. The bulk of this book will revolve around those two types.

This book is separated into two parts. The first part covers unit testing, which tests units of code. You'll learn how to create unit tests for components, directives, pipes, services, and routing—using testing tools like Karma and Jasmine—and run those tests using the Angular command-line interface (CLI). The following list breaks down each of the testable concepts we'll cover in part 1 of the book:

- *Components*—Chunks of code that you can use to encapsulate certain functionality that you can then reuse throughout the application. Components are types of directives (see next bullet), except they include a view or HTML template.
- *Directives*—Used to manipulate elements that exist in the DOM or can add elements to or remove them from the DOM. Examples of directives included with Angular are ngFor, ngIf, and ngShow.
- *Pipes*—Used to transform data. For example, say you want to turn an integer into currency. You would use a currency filter pipe to turn 15 into $15.00.
- *Services*—Although services technically don't exist in Angular, the concept is still important. You'll use services to fetch data and then inject it into your components.
- *Routing*—Allows users to navigate from one view to the next as they perform tasks in the web application.

In the second part of the book, we'll dive into E2E testing using the Protractor framework. You'll get practice writing tests that behave as if the interactions were coming from the user in a browser.

As for which version of Angular you'll be using, this book is written to be compatible with versions of Angular 2 and later. Angular 2 was a complete rewrite from AngularJS 1.x, so that's the base for the current version.

> **NOTE** It's just *Angular* now. In the past, people have referred to Angular as AngularJS, Angular 1, Angular 2, Angular 4, and so on. From here on out, we'll use AngularJS when we mean Angular 1.x, and Angular when we're talking about versions 2 and higher. To read more about the decision, check out this blog post: http://angularjs.blogspot.com/2016/12/ok-let-me-explain-its-going-to-be.html.

In the next section, we'll look at TypeScript, which is the language you'll use to write tests in this book.

1.2 *Getting friendly with TypeScript*

TypeScript is an open source language created at Microsoft in 2012 by Anders Hejlsberg, who also created C#.[1] The major problem that Hejlsberg attempted to solve with TypeScript is that JavaScript was never meant to be used with large-scale applications. The first version of JavaScript was created in 1995 in 10 days by Brendan Eich[2] and was meant to be used as a scripting language for adding interactivity to web pages.

Although you can build Angular applications with native JavaScript, we recommend you use TypeScript, because most of the examples, tutorials, documentation, code examples, and so on in the book will use TypeScript. In addition, the Angular framework itself is built with TypeScript.

TypeScript adds benefits needed for enterprise applications, such as annotations, static typing, and classical object-oriented features like interfaces and code encapsulation, while still providing the key features of JavaScript.

You'll find the syntax of TypeScript to be much like that of JavaScript, because TypeScript is a superset of JavaScript. Figure 1.1 shows how TypeScript's key features (outer circle) encompass the key features of the ES6 version of JavaScript (inner circle).

---

[1] See "TypeScript," Wikipedia, https://en.wikipedia.org/wiki/TypeScript.
[2] See "JavaScript," Wikipedia, https://en.wikipedia.org/wiki/JavaScript#Beginnings_at_Netscape.

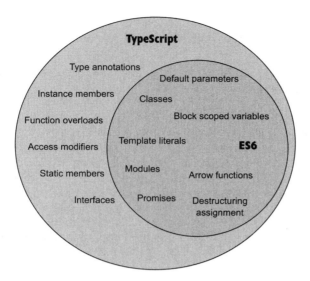

Figure 1.1   TypeScript is a superset of JavaScript version ES6, so they share much of the same syntax.

TypeScript includes most of the key ES6 features, so almost any valid ES6 or ES5 feature is also valid TypeScript. You could have a perfectly valid TypeScript file that uses only standard JavaScript syntax.

TypeScript compiles to JavaScript, and the Angular CLI will compile TypeScript automatically out of the box. If you're familiar with JavaScript and have some knowledge of object-oriented programming (OOP), you should be able to pick up TypeScript quickly. If you're new to OOP, that's fine. It may just take a little more work for you to get up to speed.

The following listing creates a simple class called `Cat` that demonstrates what a class looks like in TypeScript.

Listing 1.1   Simple TypeScript class example

_name is a private instance variable.   _name is set to an empty string by default.

```
export class Cat {
  private _name: string = '';

  constructor(name? : string) {
    this._name = name;
  }

  get name() : string {
    return this._name;
  }
}
```

The string types are added to specify return, variable, and parameter types.

The ? makes parameters optional.

```
  set name(name : string) {
    this._name = name;
  }

  toString() : string {
    return `This cat's name is ${this._name}!`;
  }
}
```

The string types are added to specify return, variable, and parameter types.

```
const cat = new Cat('Nicky');
```

This example demonstrates several features. The `class`, `get`, `set`, and `constructor` keywords, along with the template string found in the `toString()` method, are all part of the ES6 version of JavaScript, so those keywords aren't exclusive to TypeScript.

The features in the example that belong to TypeScript are the actual variable types, the `private` access modifier, and the `?` operator, which allows for an optional parameter.

In the `Cat` class, notice that the keyword `string` is sprinkled throughout the example. This is how you specify the expected types in TypeScript. You can specify return types, variable types, and parameter types within your code. The ability to specify types—type annotations—is the key advantage of using TypeScript, hence the name.

We'll be covering TypeScript throughout the book, but if you want to get your feet wet with TypeScript outside of that, visit www.typescriptlang.org. The website offers a Playground feature where you can write and test code.

Now that you've learned a bit about TypeScript, let's look at the different types of tests that you'll be writing in this book.

1.3 A closer look at test types

Unit tests and E2E tests are the two types of tests you'll see in the wild for testing Angular applications. In this section, we'll look a little more closely at those two types.

1.3.1 Unit tests

You write unit tests to test the functionality of basic parts or units of code. Each unit test should only test one responsibility of the source code. You can test functions, methods, objects, types, values, and more with unit tests. The advantages of using unit tests are that they tend to be fast, reliable, and repeatable, if you write them correctly and run them in the right environment.

Jasmine, a behavior-driven development framework for testing JavaScript code, is the framework you'll use in this book for writing unit tests. The following listing shows the code for a basic unit test written using the Jasmine framework.

Listing 1.2 Example of a simple unit test

```
describe('super basic test', () => {
  it('true is true', () => {
    expect(true).toEqual(true);
  });
});
```

Sanity check to see if true equals true

All you're doing in listing 1.2 is checking to see that the Boolean value `true` is equal to the Boolean value `true`. This test serves as a sanity check and nothing more. You can use a *sanity check* to see if all the parts of your testing environment are set up correctly, and you use it when you're only attempting to get a basic test to pass. You wouldn't want to add a test this simple to a production application.

The next listing shows a slightly more sophisticated unit test that tests getters and setters for the `name` instance found in the `Cat` class you created in listing 1.1.

Listing 1.3   Better example of a unit test

```
import { Cat } from './cat';

describe('Test Cat getters and setters.', () => {
  it('The cat name should be Gracie', () => {
    const cat = new Cat();
    cat.name = 'Gracie';
    expect(cat.name).toEqual('Gracie');
  });
});
```

Checks that the cat name is as you expected

Although unit tests tend to be reliable, they aren't the best type of test for reproducing real user interactions.

1.3.2   E2E tests

You use E2E tests to test the functionality of an application by simulating the behavior of an end user. For example, you might have an E2E test check if a modal correctly appears after a form is submitted or a page renders certain elements on page load, such as buttons or text.

E2E tests do a good job with testing applications from an end user's standpoint, but they can run slowly, and that slowness can be the source of false positives that fail tests because of timeout issues. E2E tests' timing issues make it preferable to write unit tests instead of E2E tests whenever possible.

For writing the E2E tests in this book, you'll use the Protractor E2E test framework developed by the Angular team.

The following listing shows a sample E2E test written using Protractor that checks the sample project's website and makes sure the title of the page is equal to `Contacts App Starter`.

Listing 1.4   Sample E2E test using Protractor

The describe block specifies the suite of tests that you want to run. In this case, the test involves the title of the test app you'll be using.

```
import { browser } from 'protractor';

describe('Contacts App title test', () => {
  it('Title should be correct', () => {
```

The logic of the test

```
const appUrl = 'https://testing-angular-applications.github.io';
const expectedTitle = 'Contacts App Starter';
browser.get(appUrl);
browser.getTitle().then((actualTitle) => {
  expect(actualTitle).toEqual(expectedTitle);
});
});
});
```

◄── The specific test case that
you're trying to prove as true

We'll explore unit tests and E2E tests in much greater detail throughout the book. If you understand these two types of tests, you'll understand much of Angular testing.

1.3.3 *Unit tests vs. E2E tests*

Unit tests and E2E tests have different advantages. We've discussed these advantages a little already, but in table 1.2, we summarize the pros and cons of the different types of tests.

Table 1.2: Advantages to using unit tests vs. E2E tests

Feature	Unit tests	E2E tests
Speed	Tend to be faster than E2E tests.	Tend to be slower than unit tests.
Reliability	Tend to be more reliable than E2E tests.	Tests can be flaky and fail because they may time out while executing.
Helping enforce code quality	Writing tests can help identify needlessly complex code that may be difficult to test.	Tests from the browser won't help write better code because you're testing the app as a whole from the outside.
Cost-effectiveness	More cost-effective because of developer time to write tests, execution of tests, and reliability.	Less cost-effective because it takes longer to write tests, execution of tests is slow, and tests can be flaky.
Mimicking user interactions	Tests can mimic user interactions but can be hard to use to check complex interactions.	Mimicking user interactions is E2E tests' forte and what they're made for.

Let's discuss each of these features one by one:

- *Speed*—Because unit tests operate on small chunks of code, they can run quickly. E2E tests rely on testing through a browser, so they tend to be slower.
- *Reliability*—Because E2E tests tend to involve more dependencies and complex interactions, they can be flaky, which can lead to false positives. Running unit tests rarely results in false positives. If a well-written unit test fails, you can trust that there's a problem with the code.
- *Helping enforce code quality*—One of the main benefits of writing tests is that it helps enforce code quality. Writing unit tests can help identify needlessly complex

code that may be difficult to test. As a general rule, if you're finding it hard to write unit tests, your code may be too complex and may need to be refactored. Writing E2E tests won't help you write better quality code per se. Because E2E tests test from the browser standpoint, they don't directly test your code.

- *Cost-effectiveness*—Because E2E tests take longer to run and can fail at random times, a cost is associated with that time. It also can take longer to write such tests, because they may build on other complex interactions that can fail, so development costs also can be higher when it comes to writing E2E tests.
- *Mimicking user interactions*—Mimicking user interactions with the UI is where E2E tests shine. Using Protractor, you can write and run tests as if a real user were interacting with the user interface. You can simulate user interactions using unit tests, but it'll likely be easier to write E2E tests for that purpose because that's what they're made for.

Both types of tests are important to have to thoroughly test your applications. You can test a lot of the functionality that a user would perform by writing unit tests, but you should test key functionality with E2E tests.

Generally, you want to have more unit tests than E2E tests in your project. A software developer named Mike Cohn created a testing pyramid to show how the different types of tests should be broken down. In figure 1.2, you can see approximate percentages for the different tests you should include in your project.

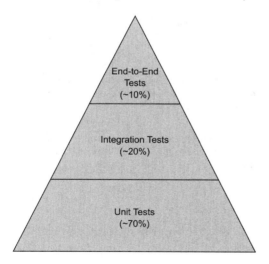

Figure 1.2   Testing pyramid of the recommended distribution for the different types of tests in your project

You may have noticed that the pyramid includes integration tests. Integration tests are used to test that a whole system works correctly. For our purposes, we'll roll the integration tests into E2E tests, because E2E tests test the entire UI system.

That gives you a basic background on Angular testing. In the next chapter, you'll get the chance to dive in to writing your first real tests.

Summary

- Angular provides a great framework for building testable web and mobile applications. It relies heavily on the concept of components for developing applications.

- You'll run across two types of tests when developing Angular applications: unit tests and E2E tests. You use unit tests to test the actual code, whereas you write E2E tests in a way that enables them to simulate user interactions.

- TypeScript is a language created by Microsoft that's a superset of JavaScript. Angular is built with TypeScript, and although you can use native versions of JavaScript (ES5 or ES6) or compile-to-JavaScript languages like CoffeeScript or Dart, we recommend you use TypeScript to write your code. Most of the coding examples, tutorials, and blog posts for this book will use TypeScript, so it's in your best interest to jump in and start using it.

- TypeScript comes with some nifty features not found in native JavaScript, such as the ability to assign types, declare private variables, and use object-oriented features, like interfaces.

- Protractor, Jasmine, and Karma are the primary tools that make the testing of Angular applications easy. These tools are written in JavaScript, and you'll configure them to run automatically while you write your tests and during your build process.

Part 1

Unit testing

In the almost 20 years since Kent Beck's *Test Driven Development*, software developers have taken more and more responsibility for writing automated tests for their applications. Whether you practice full TDD or write tests after the fact, having a robust automated test suite for your project is incredibly freeing. As Martin Fowler said, "Legacy code is untested code." It's risky to change untested code, especially if it was developed by someone else (or even by you months ago). People tend to work around untested code and avoid making changes to it. Having a robust suite of automated tests gives you the confidence to refactor your code and improve it, even while adding new features.

Angular is built from the ground up to be testable. Angular makes it easy to architect your application as a collection of loosely coupled components, and the TypeScript-based dependency injection makes it easy to mock dependencies. Unit tests in Angular can exercise your entire component, including the template and DOM. In the coming chapters, you'll learn how to write effective unit tests for Angular.

In chapter 2, we'll start by covering the basics of writing unit tests with Jasmine. If you've written unit tests in JavaScript and are familiar with ES6 classes, most of this chapter will be familiar to you.

Chapter 3 introduces the fundamental building blocks of Angular applications—components—and how to test them. If you're familiar with JavaScript testing but not testing Angular applications, this is a good place to start.

We discuss testing *directives* in chapter 4. Directives in Angular are different from AngularJS directives, and we explain those differences. Testing directives is a good example of how to write DOM-focused unit tests in Angular.

In Angular, *pipes* are simple functions that transform data in templates. Chapter 5 covers how to test them and, along the way, introduces some functional programming concepts.

Similar to AngularJS, you share data in Angular throughout your app via singleton objects called *services*. Chapter 6 explores testing services, including using dependency injection to provide mocks and handling asynchronous behavior with promises and RxJS observables.

Finally, the Angular *router* allows your application to switch between different views. Chapter 7 dives deep into using the router and testing its configuration.

Creating your first tests

2

This chapter covers

- Writing basic unit tests using Jasmine
- Using `beforeEach`, `afterEach`, `it`, `describe`, and matcher functions
- Testing classes

Now that you understand the basics of Angular testing, you'll get started writing tests. Before you continue, follow the project setup instructions in appendix A to install the sample project along with the necessary tools: the Angular CLI, Jasmine, Protractor, and Karma. You'll use the sample project throughout the book.

After you get the sample project up and running, you'll start writing basic tests using Jasmine, the behavior-driven JavaScript testing framework that you'll use throughout the book. We won't talk about any of the testing modules that come with Angular in this chapter. We'll save those for chapter 3 and the rest of the book.

We want to cover testing without the Angular test modules because at times you won't need help from Angular itself. For example, you might have a pipe that transforms dates or a function that performs a calculation that needs to be tested, and you could test them without any help from the Angular test modules. If you aren't familiar with pipes, don't fret. All you need to know for this example is that it's an Angular utility that can be used to transform data. Chapter 5 is dedicated to pipes.

In this chapter, we'll discuss testing classes without the help of the Angular framework. If you're comfortable with writing basic unit tests, you may want to skip this section and start on chapter 3, "Testing components." Otherwise, let's get started!

2.1 Writing tests using Jasmine

As we discussed in chapter 1, Jasmine is a behavior-driven development (BDD) framework that's a popular choice when testing JavaScript applications. BDD is a great methodology because you can use it to explain the why of things. The advantage of writing tests using BDD is that the test code you'll write will read close to plain English, as you'll see in the examples.

Though you can write Jasmine tests in JavaScript, you'll write all your tests (and all code in this book) using TypeScript to maintain consistency.

2.1.1 Writing basic tests

To write the first test, you'll create a sanity test like the one in chapter 1.

Essential Jasmine functions

There are several important Jasmine functions—`describe`, `it`, and `expect`—that you need to become familiar with. You'll use them often when writing tests in the real world and in this book.

describe

You use the `describe` function to group together a series of tests. This group of tests is known as a test suite. The `describe` function takes two parameters, a string and a callback function, in the following format:

```
describe(string describing the test suite, callback);
```

You can have as many `describe` functions as you want. The number of `describe` functions depends on how you want to organize your tests into suites. To organize your tests, you also can nest as many `describe` functions as you want.

it

You use the `it` function when you want to create a specific test, which usually goes inside a describe function. Like the `describe` function, the `it` function takes two parameters—a string and a callback function—using the following format:

```
it(string describing the test, callback);
```

You create a test inside an `it` function by putting an assertion inside the callback function. You create an assertion by using the `expect` function.

expect

The `expect` function comes into play in the code that confirms that the test works. These lines of code are also known as the assertion because you're asserting something as being true. In Jasmine, the assertion is in two parts: the `expect` function and the

(continued)

matcher. The `expect` function is where you pass in the value; for example, a Boolean value `true`. The matcher function is where you put the expected value. Matcher function examples include `toBe()`, `toContain()`, `toThrow()`, `toEqual()`, `toBeTruthy()`, `toBeNull()`, and more. For more information about matchers, check out the Jasmine documentation at https://jasmine.github.io.

Keep in mind that when you're writing your assertions, you should try to have only one assertion per test. When you do have multiple assertions, each assertion must be true for the test to pass.

In the first test, you'll use the `describe` function to group tests together into a test suite and use the `it` function to separate individual tests. All you're doing in this test is checking to see that the Boolean value `true` is equal to the Boolean value `true`. The `expect` function is where you want to prove your assertion, and you'll chain it together with a matcher, which in this case is `toBe(true)`.

This test serves primarily as a sanity check and nothing more. You may recall from chapter 1 that a sanity check is a test to see if all the parts of your testing environment are set up correctly.

You'll use the following naming convention for all your unit tests: `<name of file tested>.spec.ts`. Navigate to website/src/app and create a file named first-jasmine-test.spec.ts. You'll use this generic name here because this is a one-off test and you aren't testing a file. In the future, you'll include the name of the file that you're testing in the file name for your unit test.

You may have noticed that the file name includes the word `spec`, which stands for specifying. This means that the test is verifying that a specific part of the code base works as described in the test file. Generally, you'll see this format used for unit tests with Angular.

In your first-jasmine-test.spec.ts file, add the code shown in the following listing.

Listing 2.1   First Jasmine test

Groups tests into a test suite   Separates individual tests

```
describe('Chapter 2 tests', () => {
  it('Our first Jasmine test', () => {
    expect(true).toBe(true);
  });
});
```

Assertion (true) and matcher toBe()

To execute the unit tests in this book, you'll use the Angular CLI command `ng test`. If you enter `ng test` in the terminal, any file that ends in `.spec.ts` will run. Now, go ahead and enter `ng test` in the terminal window that you've been using for navigation.

A browser should open automatically, and you should see something similar to figure 2.1.

Figure 2.1   Your first passing test, confirming that true really is true

Now that your first test has passed, try an exercise to practice what you just learned.

EXERCISE

Write a test that proves that 2 + 2 equals 4 inside your previous `describe` function, but in a new `it` function.

SOLUTION

Now you should have two basic tests. Your test should look similar to the code in bold in the following listing.

Listing 2.2   Adding a second Jasmine test

```
describe('Chapter 2 tests', () => {
  it('Our first Jasmine test', () => {
    expect(true).toBe(true);
  });
                                        Second test
  it('2 + 2 equals 4', () => {    ←─────┘
    expect(2 + 2).toBe(4);
  });
});
```

Run `ng test`. When the browser window opens, you should see something like figure 2.2.

Figure 2.2 Your second passing test, proving that 2 + 2 = 4

Now that you have two passing tests, let's see what happens when you have a failing test. Change the `toBe` part of your assertion to something other than 4. After you change the value, run `ng test,` and you should see something like the screenshot in figure 2.3.

```
● X

2 specs, 1 failure

Spec List | Failures

Chapter 2 tests 2 + 2 equals 4

Expected 4 to be 5.

Error: Expected 4 to be 5.
    at stack (http://localhost:9876/base/node_modules/jasmine-core/lib/jasm
    at buildExpectationResult (http://localhost:9876/base/node_modules/jasm
    at Spec.expectationResultFactory (http://localhost:9876/base/node_modul
    at Spec.addExpectationResult (http://localhost:9876/base/node_modules/j
    at Expectation.addExpectationResult (http://localhost:9876/base/node_mo
```

Figure 2.3   A failing test showing what happens when the value is not what's expected

As you can see, when you come across a failing test, it'll be obvious that you have an error. You'll see the failing test along with a stack trace below the test. You can go through the stack trace line by line to debug the error. Each line in the stack trace will have a line number that you can visit to find the error. The last line of the stack trace is usually the line closest to the issue, so starting from the bottom up is a good way to debug the test. Change the `toBe` back to 4. Your result should again look like figure 2.2.

You won't be using this first test going forward, so you can delete it by running the following command:

```
rm first-jasmine-test.spec.ts
```

Now that you understand the basics behind writing tests using Jasmine, let's move on to testing classes.

2.2   *Testing classes*

Writing tests for a class is the easiest and quickest way to level up your testing skills without getting mired in some of the Angular framework's complexity. As we mentioned in the introduction, at times you'll need to test a normal class. Let's say you have a class that validates inputs from a form, and you want to check the inputs client-side before passing them along to the server. For that sort of check, you can write your tests as if the class was any other TypeScript code, without using Angular at all. In this section, you'll learn how to do that.

The first class you'll write tests for is named ContactClass. ContactClass will hold a person's contact information, which you'll be able to use with the sample application. You can use ContactClass to get and set a person's ID, name, email, phone number, country, and whether they are a favorite.

First, navigate to website/src/app/shared/models/. The code of the class that you'll write the test for, ContactClass, is in this directory in the contact.ts file, if you want to have a peek. In the same directory, create a file called contact.spec.ts. It's generally a good idea to keep your tests in the same directory as the module you'll be testing.

In test files, the first thing you typically want to do is import your dependencies. Because you'll be testing the ContactClass class from the contact module, add the following code at the top of the file:

```
import ContactClass from './contact';
```

Notice that although the module's file name is contact.ts, you can leave off the ts file extension in the code because it's optional in import statements.

Next, you'll create a test suite using the describe method. Call this test suite Contact class tests. Add a blank line after the import statement, and then the following lines of code:

```
describe('Contact class tests', () => {
});
```

Inside the describe function, you need to create a variable to hold your instance of the ContactClass and set it to null. Add this code inside the describe block:

```
let contact: ContactClass = null;
```

Now you need to initialize the contact variable. You often need to reset a variable every time you run a test. Resetting variables that have been manipulated inside a test helps make sure that each test runs independently and that previously manipulated variables don't interfere with any subsequent tests. Preventing such interference helps to avoid unwanted side effects. An example of a side effect could be changing a variable in one test and then accidently using the changed variable in another test.

The part of the tests where you set variables like this is known as the *setup*. In your setup, you'll use the beforeEach method to initialize your contact variable every time a test runs. Add a new line and the following code directly beneath the contact variable declaration that you previously added:

```
beforeEach(() => {
  contact = new ContactClass();
});
```

You'll use the beforeEach functions to set up your tests and to execute expressions before each one of your tests runs. In this case, you're setting the contact variable to a new instance of the ContactClass class each time you run your test.

Now you can write your test. If the test creates an instance of ContactClass success-fully, it will use the class's constructor to do so. You'll test this by seeing if the contact is not null. Add a new line directly below the beforeEach method that you previously added, and then add the following test case:

```
it('should have a valid constructor', () => {
  expect(contact).not.toBeNull();
});
```

Based on the test description part of your it function, should have a valid constructor, you can see that you're trying to test the ContactClass constructor. You do so by evaluating the expression expect(contact).not.toBeNull(). Because the ContactClass class does have a valid constructor, the matcher, not.toBeNull(), will evaluate to true, and the test will pass.

> **TIP** Should you start test cases with should? You may have noticed that all of the test cases so far have started with should. It's common syntax to start your test cases with should do x. If you do this consistently, it makes your test cases easier to read. But it's not a requirement—you should write your test cases in a way that makes the most sense to you and your team.

Finally, tests commonly have a *teardown* part in addition to the setup part. You can use the teardown part of the test to make sure instances of variables get destroyed, which helps you avoid memory leaks. In this case, you'll use the afterEach function to set the contact variable to null.

After the test you added, add a new line, and then add this code:

```
afterEach(() => {
  contact = null;
});
```

Your contact.spec.ts file should look like the code in the following listing.

Listing 2.3 contact.spec.ts—constructor test

Imports ContactClass from the contact module

Declares the contact variable as a ContactClass type

```
import ContactClass from './contact';

describe('Contact class tests', () => {
  let contact: ContactClass = null;

  beforeEach(() => {
    contact = new ContactClass();
  });

  it('should have a valid constructor', () => {
    expect(contact).not.toBeNull();
  });
```

Executes beforeEach function before each test case

Tests the contact not to be null

```
afterEach(() => {
  contact = null;
});
});
```

Executes afterEach function
after each test case

Run the new test by running the following command in your terminal window inside the testing-angular-applications/website directory:

```
ng test
```

In the Chrome window that's running your test runner, you should see something like figure 2.4.

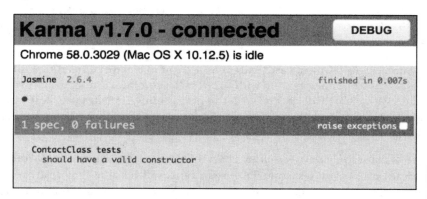

Karma v1.7.0 - connected   DEBUG

Chrome 58.0.3029 (Mac OS X 10.12.5) is idle

Jasmine 2.6.4   finished in 0.007s

•

1 spec, 0 failures   raise exceptions ▪

  ContactClass tests
    should have a valid constructor

Figure 2.4   Chrome window showing that the ContactClass constructor works

You've tested to see that creating an empty constructor works in an instance of the ContactClass. Let's see what happens when you try to test creating an instance of the ContactClass by passing a name to it. To see if the name property is set correctly, you'll also have to test the get method for the name properties. Add the new test in bold in the following listing to the contact.spec.ts file directly below the constructor test.

Listing 2.4   contact.spec.ts—constructor setter and getter name test

```
import ContactClass from './contact';

describe('ContactClass tests', () => {
  let contact: ContactClass = null;

  beforeEach(() => {
    contact = new ContactClass();
  });

  it('should have a valid constructor', () => {
    expect(contact).not.toBeNull();
  });
```

```
it('should set name correctly through constructor', () => {
    contact = new ContactClass('Liz');
    expect(contact.name).toEqual('Liz');
});

afterEach(() => {
    contact = null;
});
});
```

Tests for setting name using a constructor and testing the getter for name

If you left the test server running when you used ng test, the tests should update automatically after you add this code. If you need to restart the test server, run ng test again. You can check to see if the tests ran successfully by either looking at the test runner in the Chrome browser, as you've been doing so far, or by checking the terminal window you've been using to input commands. You should see two successfully run tests (figure 2.5).

```
05 11 2017 21:23:23.977:INFO [karma]: Karma v1.7.1 server started at http://0.0.0.0:9876/
05 11 2017 21:23:23.977:INFO [launcher]: Launching browser Chrome with unlimited concurrency
05 11 2017 21:23:23.985:INFO [launcher]: Starting browser Chrome
05 11 2017 21:23:29.206:WARN [karma]: No captured browser, open http://localhost:9876/
05 11 2017 21:23:29.327:INFO [Chrome 62.0.3202 (Mac OS X 10.12.6)]: Connected on socket MbDP2zN5opDkacmrAAAA with id 78653198
Chrome 62.0.3202 (Mac OS X 10.12.6): Executed 1 of 2 SUCCESS (0 secs / 0.012 secChrome 62.0.3202 (Mac OS X 10.12.6): Executed
 2 of 2 SUCCESS (0 secs / 0.013 secChrome 62.0.3202 (Mac OS X 10.12.6): Executed 2 of 2 SUCCESS (0.003 secs / 0.013 secs)
```

Figure 2.5 Two successfully run tests in a terminal window

2.2.1 Adding the rest of the tests

Next, you can test out the getters and setters for the id and name properties in your class. Add the two tests that are in bold in the following listing.

Listing 2.5 contact.spec.ts—adding getters and setters tests for id and name tests

```
import ContactClass from './contact';

describe('ContactClass tests', () => {
    let contact: ContactClass = null;

    beforeEach(() => {
        contact = new ContactClass();
    });

    it('should have a valid constructor', () => {
        expect(contact).not.toBeNull();
    });

    it('should set name correctly through constructor', () => {
        contact = new ContactClass('Liz');
        expect(contact.name).toEqual('Liz');
    });
```

```
it('should get and set id correctly, () => {
  contact.id = 1;
  expect(contact.id).toEqual(1);
});
```
Getters and setters for the id property

```
it('should get and set name correctly, () => {
  contact.name = 'Liz';
  expect(contact.name).toEqual('Liz');
});
```
Getters and setters for the name property

```
afterEach(() => {
  contact = null;
});
});
```

If you have your test server running, you should now see four passing tests in your terminal or in your browser. If you don't have your test server running, run ng test in your terminal to get it started and see your passing tests.

If you want to strive for 100% test coverage for a given module, you should have tests to cover every line in the module. To do this for the ContactClass, you need to complete an exercise.

EXERCISE

For this exercise, write the rest of the tests for ContactClass in the contact.ts file in the same directory as your test. These tests should be similar to the ones you've already written.

SOLUTION

Your final contact.spec.ts should look something like the bold code in the following listing.

Listing 2.6 contact.spec.ts—complete

```
import ContactClass from './contact';

describe('ContactClass tests', () => {
  let contact: ContactClass = null;

  beforeEach(() => {
    contact = new ContactClass();
  });

  it('should have a valid constructor', () => {
    expect(contact).not.toBeNull();
  });

  it('should set name correctly through constructor', () => {
    contact = new ContactClass('Liz');
    expect(contact.name).toEqual('Liz');
  });
```

```
it('should get and set id correctly', () => {
  contact.id = 1;
  expect(contact.id).toEqual(1);
});

it('should get and set name correctly', () => {
  contact.name = 'Liz';
  expect(contact.name).toEqual('Liz');
});

it('should get and set email correctly', () => {
  contact.email = 'liz@sample.com';
  expect(contact.email).toEqual('liz@sample.com');
});

it('should get and set number correctly', () => {
  contact.number = '1234567890';
  expect(contact.number).toEqual('1234567890');
});

it('should get and set country correctly', () => {
  contact.country = 'United States';
  expect(contact.country).toEqual('United States');
});

it('should get and set favorite correctly', () => {
  contact.favorite = true;
  expect(contact.favorite).toEqual(true);
});

afterEach(() => {
  contact = null;
});
});
```

Tests for getting and setting email

Tests for getting and setting number

Tests for getting and setting country

Tests for getting and setting favorite

Make sure that all your tests pass; you should have eight passing tests in total. At this point you should have a pretty good understanding of how to test classes in TypeScript using the Jasmine testing framework. We covered a lot in this chapter. You should feel confident that the information you've learned here will help you immensely on your journey to becoming an Angular testing master.

Summary

- Writing basic unit tests can come in handy when you don't need to use any of the Angular testing modules. Writing tests for simple functions, classes, and pipes doesn't require any testing dependencies outside of Jasmine, the behavior-driven development (BDD) framework. You can use Jasmine to write tests that read close to plain English.

- Most unit tests you'll write or see in production applications will cover a similar pattern. You usually have a section at the top for importing dependencies, a section to create the test suite, a section for setting up the tests, a section for the tests themselves, and a section to tear down the tests.

Testing components

Angular applications are built from components, so the most important place to start when testing an Angular application is with component tests. For example, imagine a component that displays a calendar. It might enable a user to select a date, change the selected date, cycle through months and years, and so on. You need to write a test case for each of these pieces of functionality.

In this chapter, we'll cover key testing classes and functions, such as `TestBed`, `ComponentFixture`, and `fakeAsync`, which help you test your components. You'll need a good grasp of these classes and functions to write component tests.

Don't worry if you've never heard of these concepts before. You'll practice using them as we go. By the end of this chapter, you'll understand what components are and know how to write tests for them. Let's kick off the chapter by looking at some basic component tests.

3.1 *Basic component tests*

The best way to get comfortable writing component tests is to write a few tests for a basic component. In this section, you'll write tests for the ContactsComponent component. ContactsComponent has almost no functionality and will be easy to test.

To get started, follow the instructions for setting up the example project in appendix A, if you haven't already. Then, navigate into the testing-angular-applications directory, create a file named contacts.component.spec.ts in the website/src/app/contacts/ directory, and open it in your text editor or IDE. (While you're there, if you want to take a peek at the source code for ContactsComponent that you'll be writing tests against, open the contacts.component.ts file.)

The first step in creating your test is to import your dependencies. This kind of test requires two dependencies. The first is ContactsComponent in the contacts.component module. At the top of the file, add the following line:

```
import { ContactsComponent } from './contacts.component';
```

The second dependency you need to import is the interface that defines a contact. Immediately after the first import statement, add the following line of code:

```
import { Contact } from './shared/models';
```

Now, you'll create the test suite that will house all your tests for ContactsComponent. After the import statement, add a describe block to create your test suite:

```
describe('ContactsComponent Tests', () => {
});
```

Next, you need to create a variable named contactsComponent that references an instance of ContactsComponent. You'll set the contactsComponent variable in the beforeEach block of your tests. Doing so will guarantee that you're generating a new instance of ContactsComponent when each test runs, which will prevent your test cases from interfering with each other. On the first line inside the describe callback function, add the following code:

Add a beforeEach function that sets the contactsComponent variable to a new instance of ContactsComponent before each test is executed:

```
beforeEach(() => {
  contactsComponent = new ContactsComponent();
});
```

Your first test validates that you can create an instance of ContactsComponent properly. Add the following code below the beforeEach statement:

```
it('should set instance correctly', () -> {
  expect(contactsComponent).not.toBeNull();
});
```

After adding this code snippet, your contacts.component.spec.ts file should look like the code in the following listing.

Listing 3.1   contacts.component.spec.ts

Declaration of the contactsComponent variable initialized to null

A new instance of ContactsComponent will be set before each test using the beforeEach method.

```
import { ContactsComponent } from './contacts.component';
import { Contact } from './shared/models';

describe('ContactsComponent Tests', () => {
  let contactsComponent: ContactsComponent = null;

  beforeEach(() => {
    contactsComponent = new ContactsComponent();
  });

  it('should set instance correctly', () => {
    expect(contactsComponent).toBeTruthy();
  });
});
```

The assertion where you test whether the component is set correctly

This is a simple test, and if the contactsComponent variable contains anything other than null, the test will pass.

Run ng test to run your first test. You'll see one passing test in the Chrome window (figure 3.1). If you get an error, examine the error messages to see where the test is failing.

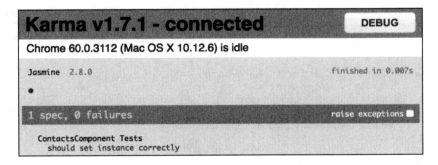

Figure 3.1   First passing unit test validating creation of ContactsComponent instance

You need to write a few more basic tests to finish the tests for `ContactsComponent`. For the next test, let's see what happens if the component contains no contacts. Without any contacts, the `contacts` array length should be zero, because the `contacts` array is empty by default. Add the following test to your test file:

```
it('should be no contacts if there is no data', () => {
  expect(contactsComponent.contacts.length).toBe(0);
});
```

For the last test, you'll make sure that you can add contacts to the list. To do this, create a new contact using the `Contact` interface and add it to an array called `contactsList`. Finally, set the `contacts` property of `ContactsComponent` to the `contactsList` array that you created. To do this, add the following code after the previous test:

```
it('should be contacts if there is data', () => {
  const newContact: Contact = {
    id: 1,
    name: 'Jason Pipemaker'
  };
  const contactsList: Array<Contact> = [newContact];
  contactsComponent.contacts = contactsList;

  expect(contactsComponent.contacts.length).toBe(1);
});
```

Your completed contacts.component.spec.ts test should look like the following listing.

Listing 3.2   Completed contacts.component.spec.ts file

```
import { ContactsComponent } from './contacts.component';
import { Contact } from './shared/models';

describe('ContactsComponent Tests', () => {
  let contactsComponent: ContactsComponent = null;

  beforeEach(() => {
    contactsComponent = new ContactsComponent();
  });

  it('should set instance correctly', () => {
    expect(contactsComponent).not.toBeNull();
  });

  it('should be no contacts if there is no data', () => {
    expect(contactsComponent.contacts.length).toBe(0);
  });

  it('should be contacts if there is data', () => {
    const newContact: Contact = {
      id: 1,
      name: 'Jason Pipemaker'
    };
```

Assertion to test that there should be no contacts by default

```
    const contactsList: Array<Contact> = [newContact];
    contactsComponent.contacts = contactsList;

    expect(contactsComponent.contacts.length).toBe(1);
  });
});
```

Assertion to test that if one contact is added, then the number of contacts in the contact array should be 1

If your test process is still running, you should see three passing unit tests in the Chrome test-runner window (figure 3.2).

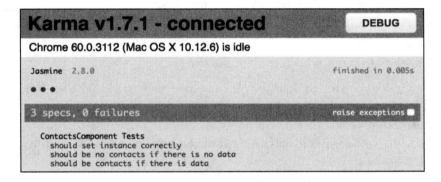

Figure 3.2 Three passing unit tests for `ContactsComponent`

If you see any errors, check your code against the GitHub repository at http://mng .bz/1BFL.

So far, your tests haven't needed any Angular-specific dependencies because `ContactsComponent` is a normal TypeScript class. When testing these types of components, you don't need any help from the Angular testing modules. These types of tests are known as *isolated* tests because they don't need any Angular dependencies and you can treat them like ordinary TypeScript files.

You might need to write this kind of test when a component has limited functionality. For example, let's say you've created a component for a new page, like a sign-up page, but you haven't implemented the logic yet. You could write a couple of isolated tests to make sure the component is created correctly.

You've warmed up your component testing skills a bit, so in the next section you can write tests for a component with more functionality.

3.2 Real-world component testing

In the real world, you'll need to test more complex components. For example, say you want to test a sidebar that contains a menu. You'd like to be able to test the sidebar without worrying about the menu. In such situations, you can use what are known as *shallow* tests. Shallow tests let you test components one level deep, ignoring any child elements that the element may contain; you can test the parent component in isolation.

In this section, you'll write shallow tests for the `ContactEditComponent` component. `ContactEditComponent` is similar to components used in real applications, so it's a good example to write tests against. Navigate to website/src/app/contacts/contact-edit in the project directory and create a file named contact-edit.component.spec.ts. You'll start by importing the necessary dependencies.

3.2.1 *Importing the dependencies*

Because `ContactEditComponent` is a fully functioning component, it requires a lot of dependencies. Your tests will reflect that in the number of import statements that you need. Let's consider the imports in the following order:

- Testing dependencies that come from Angular
- Dependencies that are included with Angular
- Dependencies that you created for this project

These dependencies are required for your test module to work. Let's see how to meet that requirement by diving into the Angular dependencies.

ANGULAR IMPORT STATEMENTS

The following list provides a walkthrough of the import statements you'll need for your tests:

- `import { DebugElement } from '@angular/core';`—You can use `DebugElement` to inspect an element during testing. You can think of it as the native `HTMLElement` with additional methods and properties that can be useful for debugging elements.
- `import { ComponentFixture, fakeAsync, TestBed, tick } from '@angular/core/testing';`
  - `ComponentFixture`—You can find this class in the `@angular/core` module. You can use it to create a fixture that you then can use for debugging.
  - `TestBed`—You use this class to set up and configure your tests. Because you use `TestBed` anytime you want to write a unit test for components, directives, and services, it's one of the most important utilities that Angular provides for testing. In this book, you'll be using the `configureTestingModule`, `overrideModule`, and `createComponent` methods, which you'll put to use later in the chapter. Because the API for `TestBed` is extensive, we only scratch the surface of the API in this book. If you want to see what else belongs to the `TestBed` API, we recommend visiting https://angular.io/api/core/testing/TestBed.
  - `fakeAsync`—Using `fakeAsync` ensure that all asynchronous tasks are completed before executing the assertions. Not using `fakeAsync` may cause the test to fail because the assertions may be executed without all of the asynchronous tasks not being completed. When using `fakeAsync`, you can use `tick` to simulate the passage of time. It accepts one parameter, which is the number

of milliseconds to move time forward. If you don't provide a parameter, `tick` defaults to zero milliseconds.

- `import { By } from '@angular/platform-browser';`—`By` is a class included in the `@angular/platform-browser` module that you can use to select DOM elements. For example, let's say you want to select an element with the CSS class name of `highlight-row;`. The element may look like the following HTML element:

```
<i class="highlight-row">
```

You would use the `css` method to retrieve that element using a CSS selector. The resulting code would look like this:

```
By.css('.highlight-row')
```

Note that you use a period to select the elements by CSS class name. In total, `By` provides three methods, which you can find in table 3.1.

Table 3.1 By methods

Method	Description	Parameter
`all`	Using all will return all of the elements.	None
`css`	Using a CSS attribute, you can select certain elements.	CSS attribute
`directive`	You can use the name of a directive to select elements.	Directive name

- `import { NoopAnimationsModule } from '@angular/platform-browser/animations';`—You use the `NoopAnimationsModule` class to mock animations, which allows tests to run quickly without waiting for the animations to finish.
- `import { BrowserDynamicTestingModule } from '@angular/platform-browser-dynamic/testing';`—`BrowserDynamicTestingModule` is a module that helps bootstrap the browser to be used for testing.
- `import { RouterTestingModule } from '@angular/router/testing';`—As the name implies, you can use `RouterTestingModule` to set up routing for testing. We include it with the tests for this component because some of the actions will involve changing routes.

NOTE There are several code changes in the following pages. If you need to cross check anything the listings at https://github.com/testing-angular-applications/testing-angular-applications/tree/master/chapter03 are also up-to-date. The final file is up-to-date at: https://github.com/testing-angular-applications/testing-angular-applications/blob/master/chapter03/contact-edit.component.spec.ts as well.

At the top of your contact-edit.component.spec.ts file, add the import statements from Angular shown in the following listing.

Listing 3.3   Completed contact-edit.component.spec.ts file

These dependencies are from the Angular core testing library.   **DebugElement will debug the elements you select.**   **Uses By to select elements**

```
import { DebugElement } from '@angular/core';
import { ComponentFixture, fakeAsync, TestBed, tick } from
    '@angular/core/testing';
import { By } from '@angular/platform-browser';
import { NoopAnimationsModule } from
    '@angular/platform-browser/animations';
import { BrowserDynamicTestingModule } from
    '@angular/platform-browser-dynamic/testing';
import { RouterTestingModule } from '@angular/router/testing';
```

Uses RouterTestingModule to test routing   **Uses NoopAnimationsModule to simulate animations**

We covered quite a bit in these import statements. You'll be using all of these statements and will find all of them useful, but pay special attention to the most important classes and functions: TestBed, ComponentFixture, and fakeAsync.

ANGULAR NONTESTING MODULE STATEMENT

You only need to import one Angular nontesting module—FormsModule. You need this module because the ContactEditComponent uses it for some Angular form controls. Right after the import statements that you added, add the following import statement:

```
import { FormsModule } from '@angular/forms';
```

REMAINING DEPENDENCY STATEMENTS

Now that we've covered the major classes and methods included in the Angular framework that you'll use, you can add the rest of the dependencies you'll need to finish the tests. Add the following lines of code after the existing imports:

```
import { Contact, ContactService, FavoriteIconDirective,
    InvalidEmailModalComponent, InvalidPhoneNumberModalComponent } from
    '../shared';
import { AppMaterialModule } from '../app.material.module';
import { ContactEditComponent } from './contact-edit.component';

import '../../../material-app-theme.scss';
```

Verify that your imports section looks like the code in the following listing before continuing.

Listing 3.4 contact-edit.component.spec.ts imports section

The top six lines contain the Angular testing dependencies.

```
import { DebugElement } from '@angular/core';
import { ComponentFixture, fakeAsync, TestBed, tick } from
  '@angular/core/testing';
import { By } from '@angular/platform-browser';
import { NoopAnimationsModule } from
  '@angular/platform-browser/animations';
import { BrowserDynamicTestingModule } from
  '@angular/platform-browser-dynamic/testing';
import { RouterTestingModule } from '@angular/router/testing';

import { FormsModule } from '@angular/forms';

import { Contact, ContactService, FavoriteIconDirective,
  InvalidEmailModalComponent, InvalidPhoneNumberModalComponent } from
  '../shared';
import { AppMaterialModule } from '../app.material.module';
import { ContactEditComponent } from './contact-edit.component';
```

Angular nontesting dependencies

These last three lines are the dependencies created for this project.

Next, you'll set up the tests.

3.2.2 Setting up the tests

The first step in setting up your tests is to create the describe block that will house all your tests and declare the instance variables they need. Beneath the import statements, add the following code:

```
describe('ContactEditComponent tests', () => {
  let fixture: ComponentFixture<ContactEditComponent>;
  let component: ContactEditComponent;
  let rootElement: DebugElement;
});
```

The describe method creates the test suite that contains all your tests. As for the instance variables:

- fixture—Stores an instance of the ComponentFixture, which contains methods that help you debug and test a component
- component—Stores an instance of the ContactEditComponent
- rootElement—Stores the DebugElement for your component, which is how you'll access its children

DEFINITION   A test *fake* is an object you use in a test to substitute for the real thing. A *mock* is a fake that simulates the real object and keeps track of when it's called and what arguments it receives. A *stub* is a simple fake with no logic, and it always returns the same value.

FAKING CONTACTSERVICE

You'll use a test fake for ContactService because the real ContactService makes HTTP calls, which would make your tests harder to run and less deterministic. Also, faking ContactService allows you to focus on testing the ContactEditComponent without worrying about how ContactService works. Angular's dependency injection system makes it easy to instantiate a ContactEditComponent with a fake version of ContactService. The fake ContactService has the same type as the real one, so the TypeScript compiler will throw an error if you forget to stub out part of the interface.

Right after the last variable declaration, but still inside the describe block, add the code in the following listing to create the fake service named contactServiceStub.

Listing 3.5   Mock ContactService

```
const contactServiceStub = {          ┌─| The default contact object
  contact: {            ◄─────────────┘
    id: 1,
    name: 'janet'
  },
                                              ┌ Sets the passed-in object to the
  save: async function (contact: Contact) {   │ component's contact property
    component.contact = contact;     ◄────────┘
  },

  getContact: async function () {   ◄──┐  Method that sets the current contact to
    component.contact = this.contact;  └─ the component's contact property and
    return this.contact;                  returns that contact
  },

  updateContact: async function (contact: Contact) {   ◄──┐
    component.contact = contact;                           │ Method that updates
  }                                                        └ the contact object
};
```

THE FIRST BEFOREEACH

Now that you have a fake ContactService, add two beforeEach blocks, which will execute before each test. The first beforeEach sets up your TestBed configuration. The second will set your instance variables. You could have just one beforeEach, but your test will be easier to read if you keep them separate.

A lot needs to happen now, as you can see in listing 3.6, so let's break down the code a bit. The TestBed class has a method called configureTestingModule. You can probably guess its purpose, which is to configure the testing module. It's much like the NgModule class that's included in the app.module.ts file, which you can find at src/app. The only difference is that you only use configureTestingModule in tests. It takes an object that's in the format of a `TestModuleMetadata` type alias. If you aren't familiar with a type alias, for our purposes you can think of it like an interface. In the code listing, note the providers section:

```
providers: [{provide: ContactService, useValue: contactServiceStub}]
```

This is where you provide your fake contact service `contactServiceStub` in place of the real `ContactService` with `useValue`.

You use `overrideModule` in this case because you need the two modal dialogs to be loaded lazily. Lazy loading means that the dialogs won't be loaded until the user performs an action to cause them to load. Currently, the only way to do this is to use `overrideModule` and set the `entryComponents` value to an array that contains the two modal components that the `ContactEditComponent` uses—`InvalidEmailModalComponent` and `InvalidPhoneNumberModalComponent`.

Finally, the last line of this first `beforeEach` statement uses `TestBed.get(Contact-Service)` to get a reference to your fake `contactService` from Angular's dependency injector. This will be the same instance that `ContactEditComponent` uses.

After the code for `contactServiceStub`, add the code in the following listing as your first `beforeEach` statement.

Listing 3.6 First `beforeEach`

```
beforeEach(() => {
  TestBed.configureTestingModule({
    declarations: [ContactEditComponent, FavoriteIconDirective,
      InvalidEmailModalComponent, InvalidPhoneNumberModalComponent],
    imports: [
      AppMaterialModule,
      FormsModule,
      NoopAnimationsModule,
      RouterTestingModule
    ],
    providers: [{provide: ContactService,
      useValue: contactServiceStub}]     ◄─── This is where you use the contactServiceStub
                                               instead of the real service.
  });                                    ◄─── Configuring TestBed to
                                               be used in your tests

  TestBed.overrideModule(BrowserDynamicTestingModule, {
    set: {
      entryComponents: [InvalidEmailModalComponent,
        InvalidPhoneNumberModalComponent]
    }
  });                                    ◄─── You have to use overrideModule
});                                           because a couple of components
                                              will be lazily loaded.
```

You can see in the listing that `TestModuleMetadata` accepts four optional properties, which are described in table 3.2.

Table 3.2   `TestModuleMetadata` **optional fields**

Field	Data Type	Description
declarations	any[ ]	This is where you list any components that the component you're testing may need.
imports	any[ ]	You set `imports` to an array of modules that the component you're testing requires.
providers	any[ ]	Lets you override the providers Angular uses for dependency injection. In this case, you inject a fake ContactService.
schemas	Array<SchemaMetadata | any[ ]>	You can use schemas like `CUS-TOM_ELEMENTS_SCHEMA` and `NO_ERRORS_SCHEMA` to allow for certain properties of elements. For example, the `NO_ERRORS_SCHEMA` will allow for any element that's going to be tested to have any property.

THE SECOND BEFOREEACH

Now you'll add the second `beforeEach` statement. The `fixture` variable stores the component-like object from the `TestBed.createComponent` method that you can use for debugging and testing, which we mentioned earlier. The `component` variable holds a component that you get from your `fixture` using the `componentInstance` property.

But what is this `fixture.detectChanges` method that you haven't seen before? The `detectChanges` method triggers a change-detection cycle for the component; you need to call it after initializing a component or changing a data-bound property value. After calling `detectChanges`, the updates to your component will be rendered in the DOM. In production, Angular uses something called zones (which you'll learn more about in Chapter 9) to know when to run change detection, but in unit tests, you don't have that mechanism. Instead, you need to call `detectChanges` frequently in your tests after making changes to a component.

Directly after the first `beforeEach` statement, add in the following code:

```
beforeEach(() => {
  fixture = TestBed.createComponent(ContactEditComponent);
  component = fixture.componentInstance;
  fixture.detectChanges();
  rootElement = fixture.debugElement;
});
```

So far, so good. You've added the code to set up your tests. In the next section, you'll add the tests themselves.

3.2.3 Adding the tests

You're ready to write your tests. You want to test the `saveContact`, `loadContact`, and `updateContact` methods for `ContactEditComponent` because those methods hold most of the functionality of the component. The `ContactEditComponent` class has several more private helper methods, but you don't need those because testing the component's public API will exercise them. In general, you shouldn't test private methods; if a method is important enough to be tested, you should consider making it public.

TESTING THE SAVECONTACT METHOD

First, you should write a test for the `saveContact` method. Calling `saveContact` changes the component's state, which will be reflected in changes to the DOM. You'll use the `fakeAsync` method to keep the test from finishing until the component has finished updating.

Next, create a contact object and set the `component.isLoading` property to `false`. You need to do this manually; otherwise, all that will render is the loading-progress bar. Then you'll call the `saveContact` method to save the contact that's stored in the contact variable. Normally, `saveContact` would use the real `ContactService`, but because you configured the testing module to provide `contactServiceStub` earlier, the component will call the stub.

After you've called the `saveContact` method, you'll notice that you call `detectChanges`. As mentioned earlier, after you make changes to components, you need to call `detectChanges` so that those changes will be rendered, which allows you to test that changes to the component are reflected in the DOM.

After calling `detectChanges`, query `rootElement` using `By.css` for the `contact-name` class to get the input element that contains the contact name. Then call `tick` to simulate the passage of time so the component will finish updating. Notice that the `tick` method doesn't have a parameter for milliseconds, so it uses the default value of zero milliseconds. Finally, assert that the value of `nameInput` is equal to `lorace`.

Add the code in the following listing directly after the last `beforeEach` statement. Make sure you stay within the overall test suite (the top-level `describe` block).

Listing 3.7 `saveContact` method test

The contact object you'll save

```
describe('saveContact() test', () => {
  it('should display contact name after contact set', fakeAsync(() => {
    const contact = {
      id: 1,
      name: 'lorace'
    };

    component.isLoading = false;
```

Sets isLoading to false to hide the progress bar

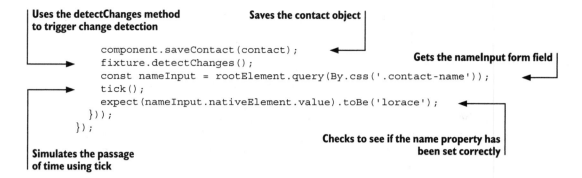

Uses the detectChanges method to trigger change detection

Saves the contact object

```
        component.saveContact(contact);
        fixture.detectChanges();
        const nameInput = rootElement.query(By.css('.contact-name'));
        tick();
        expect(nameInput.nativeElement.value).toBe('lorace');
    }));
});
```

Gets the nameInput form field

Checks to see if the name property has been set correctly

Simulates the passage of time using tick

TESTING THE LOADCONTACT METHOD

Next, you'll write a test for the loadContact method. This test is similar to the test in listing 3.7. The only difference is that you'll use the loadContact method instead of the saveContact method of the ContactEditComponent class. The loadContact method will load a contact for your testing purposes inside the contactServiceStub. The contact's name is janet, which is the value you'll use in the assertion.

Add the code from the following listing directly after the saveContact method test that you just created.

Listing 3.8   loadContact method test

```
describe('loadContact() test', () => {
  it('should load contact', fakeAsync(() => {
    component.isLoading = false;
    component.loadContact();
    fixture.detectChanges();
    const nameInput = rootElement.query(By.css('.contact-name'));
    tick();
    expect(nameInput.nativeElement.value).toBe('janet');
  }));
});
```

Executes the loadContact method

The default contact that's loaded has a value of janet for the name property.

Now we'll move on to testing the updateContact method.

TESTING THE UPDATECONTACT METHOD

By now, you've probably picked up on a pattern: this test is similar to the other two tests. This time, you first set a contact that has a name of rhonda and test that the component renders correctly. The major difference between this test and the other two tests is that it uses a second assertion. You want to check to see that the name updates when you call updateContact. To do this, call updateContact and pass it newContact.

You might notice that you call tick in the following listing with 100 as a parameter. You need this time because the updateContact method takes a bit longer to execute than the other methods that you've been testing. Add the code from the following listing after the previous test.

Listing 3.9 First `updateContact` method test

```
describe('updateContact() tests', () => {
  it('should update the contact', fakeAsync(() => {
    const newContact = {
      id: 1,
      name: 'delia',
      email: 'delia@example.com',
      number: '1234567890'
    };

    component.contact = {
      id: 2,
      name: 'rhonda',
      email: 'rhonda@example.com',
      number: '1234567890'
    };

    component.isLoading = false;
    fixture.detectChanges();
    const nameInput = rootElement.query(By.css('.contact-name'));
    tick();
    expect(nameInput.nativeElement.value).toBe('rhonda');

    component.updateContact(newContact);
    fixture.detectChanges();
    tick(100);
    expect(nameInput.nativeElement.value).toBe('delia');
  }));
});
```

Updates the existing contact to the newContact object

Triggers change detection.

Checks to see that the value in the nameInput form field has been changed correctly

Simulates the passage of time, in this case 100 milliseconds

Run ng t in your console (if you haven't already). You should see six passing tests. If you don't see six passing tests, go back to the code samples and make sure your code matches the code in this book.

You now have a test that will update a contact, but you need to test what happens when you try to update the contact with invalid contact data. First, see what happens when you try to update the contact with an invalid email address. The differences between listing 3.9 and 3.10 are highlighted in bold. The newContact variable now has an invalid email, and the last assertion doesn't expect the contact to change because the email is invalid. That's why both assertions expect the contact's name to remain chauncey. Add the code in the following listing directly after your first updateContact method test.

Listing 3.10   Second `updateContact` method test

```
it('should not update the contact if email is invalid', fakeAsync(() => {
  const newContact = {
    id: 1,
    name: 'london',
    email: 'london@example',          ◄─── Email is invalid
    number: '1234567890'
  };

  component.contact = {
    id: 2,
    name: 'chauncey',
    email: 'chauncey@example.com',
    number: '1234567890'
  };

  component.isLoading = false;
  fixture.detectChanges();
  const nameInput = rootElement.query(By.css('.contact-name'));
  tick();
  expect(nameInput.nativeElement.value).toBe('chauncey');

  component.updateContact(newContact);
  fixture.detectChanges();
  tick(100);
  expect(nameInput.nativeElement.value).toBe('chauncey');    ◄───
}));
```

> Because the email is invalid, the contact shouldn't be updated using the newContact object, so the contact name should be the same.

Now let's see what happens when you try to update a contact with an invalid phone number. Again, notice the bolded code in listing 3.11. The only difference between this test and the previous test is that the number now contains too many digits. Similar to the test before this one, the contact name is the same in both assertions.

Add the code in the following listing to the end of the second `updateContact` method test that you just wrote.

Listing 3.11   Third `updateContact` method test

```
it('should not update the contact if phone number is invalid',
  fakeAsync(() => {
  const newContact = {
    id: 1,
    name: 'london',
    email: 'london@example.com',
    number: '12345678901'          ◄─── Number is invalid
  };

  component.contact = {
    id: 2,
    name: 'chauncey',
    email: 'chauncey@example.com',
    number: '1234567890'
  };
```

```
component.isLoading = false;
fixture.detectChanges();
const nameInput = rootElement.query(By.css('.contact-name'));
tick();
expect(nameInput.nativeElement.value).toBe('chauncey');

component.updateContact(newContact);
fixture.detectChanges();
tick(100);
expect(nameInput.nativeElement.value).toBe('chauncey');
}));
```

**Because the number is invalid, the contact
shouldn't be updated using the newContact
object, so the contact name should be the same.**

Run `ng t` in your terminal again. You should see eight passing tests. If you see any errors, try checking your code against the version in the GitHub repository at http://mng.bz/Ud5b.

You've coded complete test coverage for a real-world component! You're likely to come across components out there that are more advanced, but what you've learned here gives you a foundation for writing tests that can handle that complexity. Components are one of the most—if not the most—important concepts in Angular, so you need a firm understanding of the component testing basics to be successful in writing tests.

Summary

- Isolated tests don't rely on the built-in Angular classes and methods. You can test them as if you were using normal TypeScript classes. Sometimes for your tests you'll have to render components one level deep without rendering child components. To accomplish that, you'll use shallow tests.
- Using the `fakeAsync` function, you can ensure that all asynchronous calls are completed within a test before the assertions are executed. Doing so prevents test from failing unexpectedly before all of the asynchronous calls are completed.
- Use the `ComponentFixture` class to debug an element.
- `TestBed` is a class that you use to set up and configure your tests. Use it anytime you want to write a unit test that tests components, directives, and services.
- You can use `DebugElement` to dive deeper into an element. You can think of it as the `HTMLElement`, with methods and properties added that can be useful for debugging elements.
- The `nativeElement` object is an Angular wrapper around the built-in DOM native element.

Testing directives

In this chapter, you'll learn how to test directives. Directives, like components, are a way to encapsulate parts of your application as reusable chunks of code. With regard to functionality, both directives and components allow you to add behavior to the HTML in your application.

For example, let's say your application has a table, and you want to change the background color of a row when the pointer hovers over it. You could create a directive named `HighlightRowDirective` that adds that row highlighting behavior and reuse it throughout your project.

Before you get started writing the tests for directives, you'll want to know a little more about them.

4.1   What are directives?

Angular provides three types of directives:

1 Components
2 Structural directives
3 Attribute directives

Directives and components are similar. Let's get started by exploring the differences and similarities between the two.

4.1.1   Components vs. directives

Components are a type of directive. The only difference between the two is that components contain a view (defined by a template). Another way to think about the difference is that components are visible in the browser, and directives are not. For example, a component could be a header or a footer, whereas a directive modifies the element it's attached to. A directive might append classes to an element or hide and show something based on a condition. Examples of directives built into Angular include ngFor and ngIf.

To expand your understanding, let's look at two of the decorators that are included with the Contacts app you've been working on. Decorators are a way to add behavior to a class or method, kind of like annotations in Java.

First, let's look at the @Component decorator for the ContactDetail component, which you can find at /website/src/app/contacts/contact-detail/contact-detail.component.ts:

```
@Component({
  selector: 'app-contact-detail',
  templateUrl: './contact-detail.component.html',
  styleUrls: ['./contact-detail.component.css']
})
```

You can customize the view using options such as templateUrl, styleUrls, and viewProviders.

Now, let's look at the @Directive decorator for FavoriteIcon, which you can find in /website/src/app/contacts/shared/favorite-icon/favorite-icon.directive.ts and will be testing later in this chapter:

```
@Directive({
  selector: '[appFavoriteIcon]'
})
```

You may notice that the selector has a different name, [appFavoriteIcon], than the name of the directive, which is FavoriteIcon. We prefixed the selector name with 'app' to namespace the directive. This is an easy way to differentiate between directives that we created versus ones that belong to Angular.

Notice that the FavoriteIcon @Directive decorator has a selector, like the @Component decorator, but no options for templateUrl, styleUrls, or viewProviders. Because directives have no views associated with them, they also have no templates to use, create, or style.

Now that we've looked at components and the difference between components and directives, let's review the difference between attribute and structural directives.

4.1.2 Different directives

Use *attribute directives* when you're trying to change the appearance of a DOM element. A good example of an attribute directive is the one we mentioned earlier where you were changing the background color of a row in a table to highlight it as a user rolled over the row.

Use *structural* directives to add or remove elements from the DOM—to change the structure of the page. Angular includes a few structural directives out of the box, like ngIf and ngShow.

In this chapter, you'll create tests for both an attribute directive and a structural directive. The attribute directive adds a gold star to a contact when it's marked as a favorite. The structural directive adds and removes contact tables depending on whether contacts are available.

You'll write tests for the attribute directive first; then you'll move on to the structural directive.

4.2 Testing attribute directives

To test an attribute directive, you get an instance of the directive, take some kind of action, and then check that the expected changes show up in the DOM. Before you get to the process of writing the tests, let's take a closer look at the attribute directive that you'll be testing.

4.2.1 Introducing the favorite icon directive

You'll be testing a directive that we created, named FavoriteIconDirective. Its source code is in /website/src/app/contacts/shared/favorite-icon/icon.directive.ts. You can add FavoriteIconDirective to an element to display a star when a contact is favorited. Let's see how to use it.

USAGE

Usage for FavoriteIconDirective looks like the following:

```
<element [appFavoriteIcon]="expression"></element>
```

The following is an example of `FavoriteIconDirective` being used from line 20 of the contact-list.component.html template at /website/src/app/contacts/contacts-list/ in the Contacts app source code:

```
<i [appFavoriteIcon]="contact.favorite"></i>
```

In this example, you can see that you set `[appFavoriteIcon]` to the `contact.favorite` expression, which can be either `true` or `false`. If the expression evaluates to `true`, meaning that the contact is a favorite, a gold star will be displayed, as in figure 4.1.

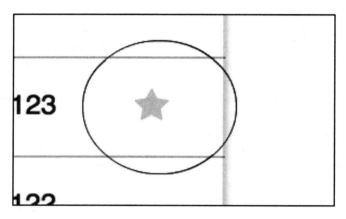

Figure 4.1   `[appFavoriteIcon]` **set to** `true`, **displaying a gold star**

> **TIP** What's the deal with those square brackets? Glad you asked! In this case, you use the brackets to bind an expression to your directive. You can use brackets a couple of different ways to bind in Angular. Check out the binding syntax in the Angular docs at http://mng.bz/w8u4 for more information.

Figure 4.2 shows what happens when `[appFavoriteIcon]` is `false`. The star becomes white, which makes it invisible against the white background.

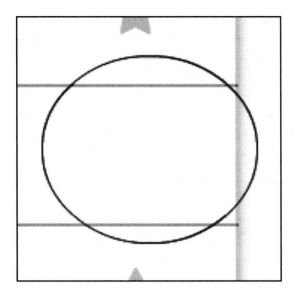

Figure 4.2 [appFavoriteIcon] set to false, with
a white star displayed but invisible

If you roll over a row where [appFavoriteIcon] is set to false, you'll be able to see
the white star because the background color changes to gray, as in figure 4.3.

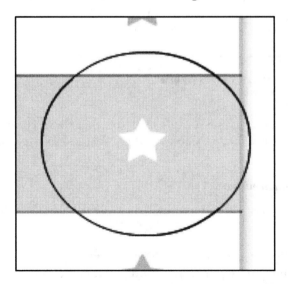

Figure 4.3 [appFavoriteIcon] set to false, with
white star displayed and visible while row is hovered over

ADDING COLOR AS A SECOND PARAMETER

`FavoriteIconDirective` defaults to the color gold, but you can pass in a second parameter that changes the color of the star.

Setting the `[color]` parameter of `[appFavoriteIcon]` looks like this:

```
<element [appFavoriteIcon]="expression" [color]="'color name'"></element>
```

In figure 4.4, you display a blue star when the `[appFavoriteIcon]` expression evaluates to `true` and you set the `[color]` parameter to blue using the following code:

```
<i [appFavoriteIcon]="contact.favorite" [color]="'blue'"></i>
```

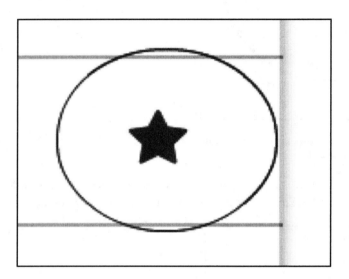

Figure 4.4 `[appFavoriteIcon]` set to `true`, with solid blue
star displayed when the `[color]` parameter is set

The rest of the cases are the same as the default star. Now that we've covered the functionality of `FavoriteIconDirective`, let's go over the test cases, so you can start writing tests!

4.2.2   *Creating tests for FavoriteIconDirective*

Let's separate the test cases into three different parts:

1 When `FavoriteIconDirective` is set to `true` (table 4.1)

2 When `FavoriteIconDirective` is set to `false` (table 4.2)

3 When a `[color]` parameter is passed in as a second parameter and you need to make sure it works as expected (table 4.3)

The first two sets of cases will be the most common use of the directive, and you'll have a third set of tests for when the color of the star is changed to blue. Tables 4.1, 4.2, and 4.3 summarize cases for the three parts.

Table 4.1   Test cases for when `FavoriteIconDirective` is set to `true`

Test Case	Event	Displays
The element should include a gold star after the page loads.	After page loads	Gold star
The element should still display a gold star if the user rolls over the star.	Roll over	Gold star
The element should still display the black outline of a star after the user clicks on the star.	On click	Black outline star
The element should still display a gold star if the user rolls off the star.	Roll off	Gold star

Table 4.2   Test cases for when `FavoriteIconDirective` is set to `false`

Test Case	Event	Displays
The element should include a white star after the page loads.	After page loads	White star
The element should display the black outline of a star if the user rolls over the star.	Roll over	Black outline star
The element should display a gold star after the user clicks on the star.	On click	Gold star
The element should display a white star after the user rolls off the star.	Roll off	White star

Table 4.3   Test cases for when the `[color]` parameter is set to a color

Test Case	Event	Displays
The element should display a star of the color that's specified in the second parameter after the page loads.	After page loads	Specified color star
If a color is unrecognized, the color of the star should be set to black by default.	After page loads	Black star

4.2.3   *Setting up the FavoriteIconDirective test suite*

Now that we've planned out the test cases, you can create your test suite. Create a file named favorite-icon.directive.spec.ts in the /website/src/app/contacts/shared/favorite-icon directory. First, you import the dependencies that you'll be using to execute your tests. Add the following statements at the top of your file to import the Angular dependencies:

```
import { Component } from '@angular/core';
import { ComponentFixture, TestBed, TestModuleMetadata } from
  '@angular/core/testing';
```

Now that you've imported the Angular dependencies, you can import the dependencies that we created for the Contacts app by adding the following code:

```
import { constants } from './favorite-icon.constants';
import { FavoriteIconDirective } from './favorite-icon.directive';
import { getStarElement, doClassesMatch } from '../../testing';
```

To test a directive, you need to create a host component that uses it. Your host component has a different <i> element for each test case. Add the following code after the import statements:

```
@Component({
  template: `
      <i [appFavoriteIcon]="true"></i>
      <i [appFavoriteIcon]="false"></i>
      <i [appFavoriteIcon]="true" [color]="'blue'"></i>
      <i [appFavoriteIcon]="true" [color]="'cat'"></i>
  `
})
class TestComponent { }
```

You may notice that tick marks wrap the HTML, appearing at the start and end of the `template` section. The tick marks are used for multiline strings. Now create a `describe` block that will house all your tests for `FavoriteIconDirective`. After the `TestComponent` class you just created, add the following lines of code:

```
describe('Directive: FavoriteIconDirective', () => {
});
```

Inside the `describe` block, you need to create some variables that you'll use in all the favorite icon tests by adding the following code:

```
let fixture: ComponentFixture<any>;
const expectedSolidStarList = constants.classes.SOLID_STAR_STYLE_LIST;
const expectedOutlineStarList = constants.classes.OUTLINE_STAR_STYLE_LIST;
```

You'll set the `fixture` variable in the `beforeEach` block, which will create a fresh fixture for each test. Add the `beforeEach` code in the following listing after the variables you just declared.

Listing 4.1 Creating a fresh `fixture` with `beforeEach`

Declares the testModuleMetadata to contain the information needed to configure TestBed

Configures TestBed using the testModuleMetadata variable

```
beforeEach(() => {
  const testModuleMetadata: TestModuleMetadata = {
    declarations: [FavoriteIconDirective, TestComponent]
  };
  fixture = TestBed.configureTestingModule(testModuleMetadata)
         .createComponent(TestComponent);
  fixture.detectChanges();
});
```

Uses TestBed.createComponent to create a component fixture to use with your tests

Uses detectChanges to initiate change detection

Let's take a minute to recap what's included in the `beforeEach` statement. If you read chapter 3, some of this may look familiar.

In the first line of the `beforeEach` method, you declare a variable called `testModuleMetadata`. This variable implements the `TestModuleMetadata` interface, which you use to provide test metadata to configure the `TestBed`. In the previous chapter, you used test metadata itself to configure `TestBed`. The difference this time is that you've created a separate variable to contain that data. In doing so, you've passed an object that conforms to the `TestModuleMetadata` interface to the `configureTestingModule` method that configures `TestBed`.

After you configure `TestBed`, you use the `createComponent` method from `TestBed` to return an instance of a `ComponentFixture`. Finally, you call `fixture.detectChanges()` to invoke change detection and render updated data whenever an event occurs, such as `click` or `mouseenter`.

Now you should add an `afterEach` block after the `beforeEach` block to make sure the `fixture` object is destroyed by setting it to `null`, as follows:

```
afterEach(() => { fixture = null; });
```

You've finished setting up the tests, and now you can move on to writing them. Almost all your tests will follow a similar pattern. You'll create a new instance of a component, run some kind of event, and then check that the element changed as expected.

4.2.4 *Creating the FavoriteIconDirective tests*

First off, create a `describe` block directly after the `afterEach` code you just added. This will allow you to group together all the tests that cover when `[appFavoriteIcon]` is set to `true`. It should look like this:

```
describe('when favorite icon is set to true', () => {
});
```

Create a variable named `starElement` to reference the star element and set it to `null`. You initialize the variable to `null` because you'll set it later in the `beforeEach` block that will execute before each test. Add this line after the `describe` block:

```
let starElement = null;
```

Now you'll create another `beforeEach` method that's scoped only to this suite. Add the following code after the variable you just declared:

```
beforeEach(() => {
  const defaultTrueElementIndex = 0;
  starElement = getStarElement(fixture, defaultTrueElementIndex);
});
```

Notice that in the line after `beforeEach` you declare a constant named `default-TrueElementIndex` and set it to 0. You may recall that earlier, when you created `Test-Component`, the template contained four different sets of HTML tags for the different test cases. The different elements are stored in an array. You're testing the first element in `fixture` for this set of tests, so you use the 0 index to retrieve it from the array. Recall that using `TestComponent` creates the class `fixture`.

To get `starElement` from `fixture`, you use a helper method called `getStarElement`. All the `getStarElement` method does is extract a child element from `fixture`. If you're curious about the implementation, you can read the source code at /website/src/app/contacts/testing/get-star-element.ts.

Finally, you can create the `afterEach` method that will set `starElement` to `null`:

```
afterEach(() => { starElement = null; });
```

Next you'll check to see if the favorite icon appears after the page loads.

ELEMENT INCLUDES A SOLID GOLD STAR AFTER THE PAGE LOADS

To start, create an `it` block and place it after the `beforeEach` block you just added:

```
it('should display a solid gold star after the page loads', () => {
});
```

Your first test case will check that the element's color is gold, as expected. Inside the `it` block, add the following code:

```
expect(starElement.style.color).toBe('gold');
```

For your second test, you'll check that the colors list matches the colors in your elements list. To do this, you can use another helper method called `doClassesMatch`. As with the `getStarElement` method, you can find this method at /website/src/app/contacts/testing/. All this method does is take an element and a list of styles and make sure they match by looping through the styles in the lists. The result of the comparison is `true` if the element has all the expected styles.

The style classes for a solid star are stored as a list called `expectedSolidStarList`. If you looked at the contents of this list, you'd find three classes: `['fa', 'fa-star', 'fa-lg']`. These are all the classes that you can expect for a solid star. You would expect your `starElement` to include these classes to be correctly styled.

To ensure that `starElement` has the correct styles, add the following code to your test:

```
expect(doClassesMatch(starElement.classList,
  expectedSolidStarList)).toBeTruthy();
```

Your completed test should look like this:

```
it('should display a solid gold star after the page loads', () => {
  expect(starElement.style.color).toBe('gold');
  expect(doClassesMatch(starElement.classList,
    expectedSolidStarList)).toBeTruthy();
});
```

Now, in your terminal, run the `ng test` command. You should see something similar to figure 4.5.

```
21 10 2016 09:09:06.123:INFO [karma]: Karma v1.2.0 server started at http://localhost:9876/
21 10 2016 09:09:06.124:INFO [launcher]: Launching browser Chrome with unlimited concurrency
21 10 2016 09:09:06.129:INFO [launcher]: Starting browser Chrome
21 10 2016 09:09:06.898:INFO [Chrome 53.0.2785 (Mac OS X 10.11.6)]: Connected on socket /#L_sISeVv8TCyMBUdAAAA with id 78894617
Chrome 53.0.2785 (Mac OS X 10.11.6): Executed 1 of 1 SUCCESS (0.132 secs / 0.109 secs)
```

Figure 4.5   First test of displaying a gold star after page loading successfully executed

ELEMENT STILL DISPLAYS A SOLID GOLD STAR IF THE USER ROLLS OVER THE STAR

Your second test is a bit more complicated than the first test because you need to simulate a rollover effect. You can use the `Event` class to create a `mouseenter` event to simulate the user moving the pointer over the star. You manually dispatch the event by using the `dispatchEvent` method that's part of every DOM element. Add the following code after your first test:

```
it('should display a solid gold star if the user rolls over the star',
  () => {
  const event = new Event('mouseenter');
  starElement.dispatchEvent(event);
});
```

Your two test cases are the same as the first test case because you still expect the gold star to display when the user hovers over it. Add the following code after the event code that you just added:

```
expect(starElement.style.color).toBe('gold');
expect(doClassesMatch(starElement.classList,
  expectedSolidStarList)).toBeTruthy();
```

Run `ng test`. You now should have two completed tests.

ELEMENT STILL DISPLAYS THE OUTLINE OF A BLACK STAR IF THE USER CLICKS ON THE STAR

This test is similar to the previous one. The only difference is that because this is a `click` event, you use a different argument when you create an instance of the `Event` class. You also change the expected color to be `black` and the class list to `expectedOutlineStarList`, because you expect the star to be only an outline instead of a solid star.

Because you only need to make small changes, the following code presents the full test with the changes in bold. You can add this test after the previous one:

```
it('should display a black outline of a star after the user clicks on the
  star', () => {
  const event = new Event('click');
  starElement.dispatchEvent(event);

  expect(starElement.style.color).toBe('black');
  expect(doClassesMatch(starElement.classList,
    expectedOutlineStarList)).toBeTruthy();
});
```

Execute the tests again in your terminal by running `ng test`, and you now should have three successful tests. We've covered all the tests for your attribute directive. The completed test is at /chapter04/favorite-icon.directive.spec.ts for your reference. Next up, we'll look at how to test structural directives.

4.3   *Testing structural directives*

Testing structural directives is similar to testing attribute directives. You're checking that the DOM is rendered as you expect when you use the directive. Before you start writing tests, let's look at the directive you'll be testing, `ShowContactsDirective`.

4.3.1   *Introducing ShowContactsDirective*

The structural directive you'll be testing is `ShowContactsDirective`. You can use `ShowContactsDirective` to add elements to or remove them from the DOM. It mimics the implementation of `ngIf`; we're using it only to demonstrate how to test structural directives.

USAGE

Here's an example of using `ShowContactsDirective`:

```
<div *appShowContacts="contacts.length"></div>
```

In this example, you can see that you set `*appShowContacts` to the `contacts.length` expression, which in JavaScript resolves to `true` if the length is greater than 1 and `false` if the length is 0. We've taken this example directly from the application, and you can find the code at /website/src/app/contacts/contact-list.component.html on the first line if you would like to see it for yourself.

> **NOTE**   What's the deal with the asterisk? The asterisk transforms the element the directive is attached to into a template. The directive then controls how that template is rendered to the DOM, which is how it can alter the structure of the page. To learn more about the asterisk prefix, check out https://angular.io/guide/structural-directives#asterisk.

To see how the directive works, start the application using `ng s` and then open your browser to http://localhost:4200/. You should see something like figure 4.6.

Figure 4.6   The Contacts app with contacts

Now click the Delete All Contacts button. The result should look like figure 4.7.

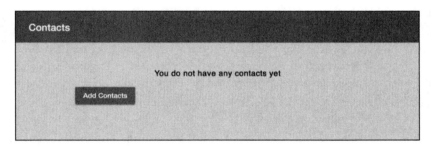

Figure 4.7   The Contacts app with no contacts

Notice that the table completely disappeared, and now there's a message stating, "You do not have any contacts yet." That's because ShowContactsDirective is hiding and showing elements based on whether there are any contacts. The Delete All Contacts button text has also changed to Add Contacts. Two different buttons are shown or hidden using ShowContactsDirective. Go ahead and click Add Contacts, and you'll see the same screen that you saw in figure 4.6.

If you'd like to see the ShowContactsDirective source code, navigate to /website/ src/app/contacts/shared/show-contacts/ and view the show-contacts.directive.ts file. Now that you understand the basic functionality of ShowContactsDirective, let's go over all the test cases you'll be writing tests for.

4.3.2   *Creating your tests for ShowContactsDirective*

When you test ShowContactsDirective, you only care about two test cases: one when the input evaluates to true and one when the input evaluates to false (table 4.4).

Table 4.4   When `ShowContactsDirective` **is set to** `true` **or** `false`

Test Case	Input	Displays
The element should be hidden when the input evaluates to `true`.	`true`	Element
The element should be hidden when the input evaluates to `false`.	`false`	Nothing

Now that you've seen the two test cases, you can create the test suite.

4.3.3   *Setting up the ShowContactsDirective test suite*

To start, navigate to /website/src/app/contacts/shared/show-contacts and create a file called show-contacts.directive.spec.ts. The first thing you include is the dependencies that the tests need. Add the following statements at the top of your file to import the Angular dependencies:

```
import { Component } from '@angular/core';
import { ComponentFixture, TestBed } from '@angular/core/testing';
```

These are the same classes that you imported for your `FavoriteIconDirective` tests. Because we already covered these classes, we won't cover them again. Now you need to import two custom dependencies we created for the Contacts app.

```
import { ShowContactsDirective } from './show-contacts.directive';
import { getElement } from '../../testing';
```

`ShowContactsDirective` is the code that you'll be testing. The `getElement` function is similar to the `getStarElement` function that you used earlier—it's a small helper function that takes in a `fixture` and returns the element that you want to test. If you'd like to see how it's implemented, check out /website/src/app/contacts/testing/get-element.ts.

Now that you have your imports, you need to create a `TestComponent`, as you did for your attribute test. Add the following code under the `import` statements:

```
@Component({
  template: `
      <div *appShowContacts="true">
        <p>This is shown</p>
      </div>
      <div *appShowContacts="false">
        <p>This is hidden</p>
      </div>
    `
})
class TestComponent { }
```

You'll notice that the first `<div>` contains `*appShowContacts="true"`. `appShowContacts` is the name used in the template for `ShowContactsDirective`. You can think of `appShowContacts` as an alias for `ShowContactsDirective`.

You'll check this element first, and it should contain the child <p> element, because appShowContacts is set to true. The second <div> contains *appShowContacts="-false". For this test, you want to check to see that this <div> doesn't contain the child <p> element, because appShowContacts is set to false.

Now create a describe function to house all of your tests. Also, go ahead and add the fixture and beforeEach method. In the line below the import statements, add the following code:

```
describe('Directive: ShowContactsDirective', () => {
  let fixture: ComponentFixture<any>;

  beforeEach(() => {
    fixture = TestBed.configureTestingModule({
      declarations: [ShowContactsDirective, TestComponent]
    }).createComponent(TestComponent);
    fixture.detectChanges();
  });

  afterEach(() => { fixture = null; });
});
```

You may notice that this is almost exactly the same as the attribute directive tests. The only difference is that you replaced FavoriteIconDirective with ShowContactsDirective because you're testing a different directive.

4.3.4 *Creating the ShowContactsDirective tests*

The two tests will follow the same format as before. You get the element you want to test from the fixture and then check the DOM to see if it renders as it should. For your first test, you check if an element is rendered if the input is set to true. Add the following code before the afterEach:

```
it('should be displayed when the input evaluates to true.', () => {
  const element = getElement(fixture);
  expect(element.innerText).toContain('This is shown');
});
```

This test case will pass because the child element with the text "This is shown" uses appShowContacts=true in your TestComponent. For your second test, you check that the content from the second div with the appShowContacts set to false doesn't show in the rendered HTML. Add the following code after the previous code:

```
it('should be hidden when the input evaluates to false.', () => {
  const element = getElement(fixture);
  expect(element.innerText).not.toContain('This is hidden');
});
```

Go ahead and fire up your terminal if you don't have it open and run ng test. Both tests should pass. You can check out the completed tests at /chapter04/show-contacts. directive.spec.ts for your reference. That's it for testing directives! In the next chapter, we'll look at testing another important concept in Angular, pipes.

Summary

- Angular allows three types of directives: components, attribute directives, and structural directives. They're all similar in that they encapsulate reusable functionality. The difference between components and attribute and structural directives is that components have a view.
- You can use attribute directives to change the appearance of an element, whereas you use structural directives to add elements to and remove them from the DOM.
- Testing attribute and structural directives is similar in that you set the initial state of an element, perform the desired action, and then test to confirm that the expected change occurs.
- The `configureTestingModule` method takes in an object that has to use the `TestModuleMetadata` interface. You can either create a variable that sets the type to `TestModuleMetadata` and then pass the variable into the `configureTestingModule` method, or create an object with the relevant configuration data and then pass that into the `configureTestingModule` method.

Testing pipes

SW 198 6854

This chapter covers

- Testing pipes
- Understanding pure functions versus functions with side effects
- Using the `transform` method

Often, you'll want to modify data that's displayed in a template. For example, you may want to format a number as currency, transform a date into a format that's easier to understand, or make some text uppercase. In situations like these, Angular provides a way to transform data using something known as a *pipe*.

Pipes take input, transform it, and then return some transformed value. Because the way pipes operate is straightforward, writing tests for them is too. Pipes depend only on their input. A function whose output depends on only the input passed to it is known as a *pure function*.

When a function can do something other than return a value, it's said to have a *side effect*. A side effect could be changing a global variable or making an HTTP call. Pure functions like pipes don't have side effects, which is why they're easy to test.

In this chapter, we'll cover everything you need to know to test pipes.

5.1   *Introducing PhoneNumberPipe*

In this chapter, you'll be testing a custom pipe called PhoneNumberPipe. This pipe takes in a phone number as a number or string in valid format and puts it into a format that the user specifies. You need to write tests for the pipe so you can confirm that it transforms data into the right format.

Each pipe in Angular has a method named transform. This method is responsible for formatting the pipe's input. The signature for the transform function for PhoneNumberPipe looks like this:

```
transform(value: string, format?: string, countryCode?: string): string
```

value is passed into the function from the left of the pipe and represents a phone number. format is an optional string parameter that determines how the phone number is formatted. Different valid values for format are listed in table 5.1.

Table 5.1   Recognized format values

Number separator format	Phone number format
default	(XXX) XXX-XXXX
dots	XXX.XXX.XXXX
hyphens	XXX-XXX-XXXX

countryCode is another optional string parameter that adds a prefix to the phone number as an international country code. For example, if you pass in a countryCode of 'us' (for the United States) and a format 'default', the resulting phone number would be +1 (XXX) XXX-XXXX.

To keep it simple, PhoneNumberPipe only works with phone numbers that follow the North American Numbering Plan (NANP), so the country codes you can use are limited to the countries in the NANP. If you're curious about the acceptable country codes, look at the country-dialing-codes.ts file. An object there contains the two-character country abbreviation as a key and the international country code as the value.

Now that you know a bit about PhoneNumberPipe, you can test it like so:

1 Set up the test dependencies.
2 Test the default behavior.
3 Test the format parameter.
4 Finally, test the countryCode parameter.

You'll continue with testing the Contacts app, as you've done in previous chapters. If you need to set it up, follow the instructions in appendix A.

5.2 *Testing PhoneNumberPipe*

Open website/src/app/contacts/shared/phone-number, and you should see the files described in table 5.2.

Table 5.2 Description of files

File	Description

`index.ts`	You use the index.ts file so that you can import `PhoneNumberPipe` without using the complete file name. That way, when you're trying to import `PhoneNumberPipe`, you can use
	
	`import { PhoneNumberPipe } from './`
	`    phone-number.pipe';`
	
	instead of the more verbose
	
	`import { PhoneNumberPipe } from './`
	`    phone-number.pipe/`**`phone-number.`**
	`pipe``';`
	
	Notice the addition to the file name in bold. Using an index.ts file like this is a common practice to shorten file paths.

`country-dialing-codes.ts`	This file contains the country dialing codes that your `PhoneNumber` model uses.
`phone-number-error-messages.ts`	This file contains all the error messages that `PhoneNumberPipe` and the `PhoneNumber` model use.
`phone-number.model.ts`	This is the model that you'll use to store data. The `PhoneNumber` model also contains the utility methods to transform the data.
`phone-number.pipe.ts`	This is the file that contains `PhoneNumberPipe`.

Feel free to open these files to get a feel for the source code you'll be testing. When you're ready to move on, create a file named phone-number.pipe.spec.ts in the phone-number directory to store your tests.

5.2.1 *Testing the default usage for a pipe*

Start by testing the default behavior of `PhoneNumberPipe`. Here's an example of the default usage of `PhoneNumberPipe`:

`{{ 7035550123 | phoneNumber }}`

You need to test two different cases of the default usage of `PhoneNumberPipe`, as listed in table 5.3.

Table 5.3   Default test cases

Test case	Number	Displays
A phone number that's a 10-character string or 10-digit number should transform to the (XXX) XXX-XXXX format.	7035550123	(703) 555-0123
Nothing will be displayed when a phone number isn't a 10-character string or 10-digit number.	703555012	

TESTING FOR A VALID PHONE NUMBER

Start by testing the default usage to see if the phone number is valid. Copy the code for the first default test in the following listing into the phone-number.pipe.spec.ts file that you just created.

Listing 5.1   First default test case

Test suite for all of your tests

Imports PhoneNumberPipe

```
import { PhoneNumberPipe } from './phone-number.pipe';

describe('PhoneNumberPipe Tests', () => {
  let phoneNumber: PhoneNumberPipe = null;

  beforeEach(() => {
    phoneNumber = new PhoneNumberPipe();
  });

  describe('default behavior', () => {
    it('should transform the string or number into the default phone
      format', () => {
      const testInputPhoneNumber = '7035550123';
      const transformedPhoneNumber =
        phoneNumber.transform(testInputPhoneNumber);
      const expectedResult = '(703) 555-0123';

      expect(transformedPhoneNumber).toBe(expectedResult);
    });
  });

  afterEach(() => {
    phoneNumber = null;
  });
});
```

The setup part of your tests using beforeEach to set a new instance of PhoneNumberPipe to the phoneNumber variable before each test

A nested, second test suite only for default behavior

The assertion where you expect a correct phone number to be formatted correctly

The teardown part of your test where you set the phoneNumber variable to null to destroy the reference

Let's break this down by section:

```
import { PhoneNumberPipe } from './phone-number.pipe';
```

First, you import all of the dependencies that your test needs. Because the pipe is a pure function, you don't need any of the Angular testing dependencies:

```
describe('PhoneNumberPipe Tests', () => {

});
```

You then add a `describe` function to house all your tests for `PhoneNumberPipe`:

```
let phoneNumber: PhoneNumberPipe = null;

beforeEach(() => {
  phoneNumber = new PhoneNumberPipe();
});
```

Inside your test suite, you need to create a global variable named `phoneNumber` that has a type of `PhoneNumberPipe` and is set to null. You use a `beforeEach` function to create a new instance of `PhoneNumberPipe` before each test is executed:

```
describe('default behavior', () => {
  it('should transform the string or number into the default phone format',
    () => {
    const testInputPhoneNumber = '7035550123';
    const transformedPhoneNumber =
      phoneNumber.transform(testInputPhoneNumber);
    const expectedResult = '(703) 555-0123';

    expect(transformedPhoneNumber).toBe(expectedResult);
  }));
});
```

This `describe` block defines the nested test suite that contains your tests for default behavior. You declare your test input in the `testInputPhoneNumber` variable, save the transformed result in `transformedPhoneNumber`, and set your expected result in `expectedResult`. The assertion at the bottom of the test checks that the transformed phone number matches your expected result:

```
afterEach(() => {
    phoneNumber = null;
});
```

Finally, the `afterEach` function makes sure the `phoneNumber` variable doesn't contain a reference to an instance of `PhoneNumberPipe`. Run `npm test`, and you should see output like figure 5.1.

```
13 06 2016 08:52:13.990:INFO [Chrome 51.0.2704 (Mac OS X 10.11.5)]: Connected on
 socket /#g0Euu8Bk3eZbin35AAAA with id 49045452
Chrome 51.0.2704 (Mac OS X 10.11.5): Executed 1 of 1 SUCCESS (0 secs / 0.007 sec
Chrome 51.0.2704 (Mac OS X 10.11.5): Executed 1 of 1 SUCCESS (0.009 secs / 0.007
 secs)
```

Figure 5.1 First successfully executed pipe test

That's it for your first test. The tests in the rest of the chapter follow the same format as the first one:

```
describe(describe a suite of tests, () => {
  it(describe the specific test case, () => {
    declare your test variables
    transform the data
    expect(the transformed data).toBe(what you expect);
  });
});
```

Tests for pipes all follow this structure because, as mentioned before, pipes are pure functions. There's no need to mock or set anything up—you pass the function some input and confirm the result is what you'd expect.

TESTING THE PIPE WITH AN INVALID PHONE NUMBER

For the second test, you'll verify that if the input number doesn't have 10 digits, nothing will be shown. Copy the code in the `it` block that you created previously and paste it directly after your first test.

Change the descriptive text in the `it` block to `'should not display anything if the length is not 10 digits'`. Then change `testInputPhoneNumber` to `'703555012'`. Notice that the new phone number is only nine digits long. Now, set `expectedResult` to `''`. You expect the result to be an empty string because that's what should be returned if the phone number is invalid.

The completed test should look like the following listing.

Listing 5.2   Test for invalid phone number

Updates the title of the test   Updates test input to an invalid phone number

```
it('should not display anything if the length is not 10 digits',
  () => {
  const testInputPhoneNumber = '703555012';
  const transformedPhoneNumber =
    phoneNumber.transform(testInputPhoneNumber);
  const expectedResult = '';

  expect(transformedPhoneNumber).toBe(expectedResult);
});
```

Updates expected result to an empty string

If you run `ng test`, you'll see something like figure 5.2.

```
Chrome 51.0.2704 (Mac OS X 10.11.5): Executed 1 of 2 SUCCESS (0 secs / 0.007 sec
ERROR: 'The phone number you have entered is not
    the proper length. It should be 10 characters long.'
Chrome 51.0.2704 (Mac OS X 10.11.5): Executed 1 of 2 SUCCESS (0 secs / 0.007 sec
Chrome 51.0.2704 (Mac OS X 10.11.5): Executed 2 of 2 SUCCESS (0 secs / 0.009 sec
Chrome 51.0.2704 (Mac OS X 10.11.5): Executed 2 of 2 SUCCESS (0.013 secs / 0.009
 secs)
```

Figure 5.2 Two passing default behavior tests with an error message

Notice that the error message 'The phone number you have entered is not the proper length. It should be 10 characters long.' is printed out to the console along with the successful test execution messages. This is expected because `PhoneNumberPipe` throws an error message if the phone number is not 10 characters long. When you add console logging statements to testing using the Angular CLI default setting, they will be printed out to the terminal when tests run, as shown in figure 5.2.

Now that you've tested the default behavior, let's look at testing a pipe with a single parameter.

5.2.2 Testing a pipe with a single parameter

Sometimes, you'll need to change the behavior of a pipe by passing it a parameter. For example, you can change the format of the output of `PhoneNumberPipe` by passing 'dots', 'hyphens', or 'default' as a parameter.

Table 5.4 shows the different options for the `format` parameter.

Table 5.4   Test cases for the `format` parameter

Test case	Format	Number	Displays
If 'default' is used or no parameter is specified, then the number will be in the default (XXX) XXX-XXXX format.	default	7035550123	(703) 555-0123
If 'dots' is passed in as a parameter, then the number should be in XXX.XXX.XXXX format.	dots	7035550123	703.555.0123
If 'hyphens' is passed in as a parameter, then the number should be in XXX-XXX-XXXX format.	hyphens	7035550123	703-555-0123
If an unrecognized format is passed in as a parameter, then the default (XXX) XXX-XXXX format should be used.	gibberish	7145550111	(714) 555-0111

Here's an example usage of `PhoneNumberPipe` with a single parameter:

```
{{ 7035550123 | phoneNumber | 'dots' }}
```

In this example, you pass 'dots' as a parameter.

Let's look at some tests for when you use a single parameter for a pipe. Add the code in the following listing directly after the `describe` block that you created in listing 5.1.

> **Listing 5.3** `'dots'` format test

Test suite   **The format type**

```
describe('phone number format tests', () => {   #A
  it('should format the phone number using the dots format', () => {
    const testInputPhoneNumber = '7035550123';
    const format = 'dots';
    const transformedPhoneNumber =
      phoneNumber.transform(testInputPhoneNumber, format);
    const expectedResult = '703.555.0123';

    expect(transformedPhoneNumber).toBe(expectedResult);
  });
});
```

Passing the format to your transform function

First off, notice that you've put this test inside a test suite using a `describe` block. On the fourth line of the code, you have a constant named `format` that you've set to `'dots'`. On the fifth line of the code, you pass that `format` variable in as a second parameter in your `transform` method. You test for the first parameter that a pipe uses by sending the *first* parameter into your `transform` method as the *second* parameter.

Run `ng test`, and your output should look like figure 5.3.

```
Chrome 51.0.2704 (Mac OS X 10.11.5): Executed 1 of 3 SUCCESS (0 secs / 0.007 sec
ERROR: 'The phone number you have entered is not
       the proper length. It should be 10 characters long.'
Chrome 51.0.2704 (Mac OS X 10.11.5): Executed 1 of 3 SUCCESS (0 secs / 0.007 sec
Chrome 51.0.2704 (Mac OS X 10.11.5): Executed 2 of 3 SUCCESS (0 secs / 0.01 secs
Chrome 51.0.2704 (Mac OS X 10.11.5): Executed 3 of 3 SUCCESS (0 secs / 0.011 sec
Chrome 51.0.2704 (Mac OS X 10.11.5): Executed 3 of 3 SUCCESS (0.016 secs / 0.011
 secs)
```

Figure 5.3   Three passing tests with an error message

Now that you understand how to test the first parameter, it's time for a little exercise.

EXERCISE

After the first parameter test that you added in listing 5.3, create the three tests for the `'default'`, `'hyphens'`, and `'gibberish'` formats using the information provided in table 5.4.

SOLUTION

All your tests should be similar. The only difference should be the new `format` type and the expected result based on that `format` type. Your three new tests should look like the following listing.

Listing 5.4   Remaining format tests

```
it('should format the phone number using the default format', () => {
  const testInputPhoneNumber = '7035550123';
  const format = 'default';                              Format types
  const transformedPhoneNumber =
    phoneNumber.transform(testInputPhoneNumber, format);        The expected formatted
  const expectedResult = '(703) 555-0123';                      phone number

  expect(transformedPhoneNumber).toBe(expectedResult);
});


it('should format the phone number using the hyphens format', () => {
  const testInputPhoneNumber = '7035550123';
  const format = 'hyphens';                              Format types
  const transformedPhoneNumber =
    phoneNumber.transform(testInputPhoneNumber, format);        The expected formatted
  const expectedResult = '703-555-0123';                        phone number

  expect(transformedPhoneNumber).toBe(expectedResult);
});

it('should format the phone number using the default format if unrecognized
  format is entered',() => {
  const testInputPhoneNumber = '7035550123';
  const format = 'gibberish';                            Format types
  const transformedPhoneNumber =
    phoneNumber.transform(testInputPhoneNumber, format);        The expected formatted
  const expectedResult = '(703) 555-0123';                      phone number

  expect(transformedPhoneNumber).toBe(expectedResult);
});
```

Run ng test, and now you should see six passing tests. Now that you have one-parameter tests under control, let's take a look at how to test multiple parameters.

5.2.3   *Pipes with multiple parameters*

Pipes can take multiple parameters if needed. PhoneNumberPipe can handle two parameters. So far, we've covered the first parameter and how it's responsible for formatting the phone number. The second parameter is the country code. Table 5.5 shows the test cases for the country code parameter.

Table 5.5   Test cases for country code parameter

Test case	Number	Country code	Displays
If 'dots' is passed in as a parameter and the country code is correct, then the number should be in XXX.XXX.XXXX format with a plus sign and the country code before it.	7035550123	us	+ 1 703.555.0123
If 'dots' is passed in as a parameter and an unrecognized country code is passed in, then the number should be in XXX.XXX.XXXX format with no country code applied.	7035550123	zz	703.555.0123

For simplicity, PhoneNumberPipe only supports countries in the NANP. You need to test to make sure that each parameter is accepted and works as expected. Add the code in the following listing directly after the describe block that you created earlier that contains the phone number format tests.

Listing 5.5   Country code test

```
describe('country code parameter tests', () => {
  it('should add respective country code', () => {
    const testInputPhoneNumber = '7035550123';
    const format = 'default';
    const countryCode = 'us';                          ← New variable that stores
    const transformedPhoneNumber =                        the country code
      phoneNumber.transform(testInputPhoneNumber, format, countryCode);
    const expectedResult = '+1 (703) 555-0123';       ←

    expect(transformedPhoneNumber).toBe(expectedResult);
  });
});                                                    Expected result with country code
```

The countryCode variable is passed into the
transform method as a third parameter.

This test is similar to the earlier tests for passing the first parameter to the pipe. The only difference is that earlier you were testing the *second* parameter, whereas now you're passing a *third* parameter to your transform method. You may be picking up on a pattern. If you want to test a *fourth* pipe parameter, then you'd pass a value into the *fifth* parameter in your transform method. This pattern will continue for as many pipe parameters as you want to test.

EXERCISE

Write a test case such that when the country code is not recognized, PhoneNumberPipe only transforms the phone number format and doesn't add a telephone country code. Make sure you run ng test to see if your test works as expected:

- *First hint*—You can copy the listing 5.5 test and make modifications as necessary.
- *Second hint*—The country code should be for a country code not listed in the NANP (http://mng.bz/R55f).

SOLUTION

You need to change only two variables. Change countryCode to something that's unrecognized, and then change expectedResult to the default format with no country code prefixed to the phone number. Your test should look something like the following listing, which shows the changes in bold.

Listing 5.6   Test for invalid country code

```
it('should not add anything if the country code is unrecognized', () => {
  const testInputPhoneNumber = '7035550123';
  const format = 'default';
  const countryCode = 'zz';              ← Unrecognized country code
  const transformedPhoneNumber =
    phoneNumber.transform(testInputPhoneNumber, format, countryCode);
  const expectedResult = '(703) 555-0123';    ← The expected result
                                                 without a country code
  expect(transformedPhoneNumber).toBe(expectedResult);
});
```

Run ng test, and you now should see eight passing tests. If you have any issues, check out the complete test at and look for any discrepancies. In the next chapter, we'll start looking at testing services.

Summary

- Because pipes only take in a value as input, transform that value, and then return transformed input, testing them is straightforward. That's because they're *pure functions*, which means they have no side effects.
- *Side effects* are changes that occur outside a function after that function is executed. A common side effect is the changing of a global variable.
- When you're testing pipes, you're mainly testing the transform method that's included in every pipe. The transform method is what takes in the different parameters you want to manipulate, performs the manipulation, and then returns the changed values.

Testing services

This chapter covers

- Understanding what services do in Angular applications

- Using dependency injection with service unit tests

- Creating isolated unit tests by using spies as test doubles

- Testing services that return results asynchronously using promises and RxJS observables

- Testing web services with Angular's HTTP utilities

In this chapter, you'll create and test the services you need for setting preferences in the Contacts app, and for loading and saving contacts from a server. Preferences-Service will save application settings to the user's browser using either cookies or localStorage. The example we'll look at will show you how to test with both synchronous services and asynchronous services (services that return promises or observables). You'll learn how to isolate your code under test from its related dependencies by using Jasmine spies. ContactService uses Angular's HttpClient to fetch and store data from a REST service using observables, which are like promises but return continuous streams of values. You'll learn how to configure service tests, set up mocks and dependencies, and exercise service interfaces through test-driven development.

By the end of this chapter, you'll know how to write and test services that use HttpClient and how to move the code associated with manipulating data (the business logic) into tested services to help organize your application's architecture.

6.1   *What are services?*

Generally, Angular services are the parts of your application that don't interact directly with the UI. Picture this: you're looking for pictures using an image service like Imgur. You type a search term, a spinner pops up briefly, and then images matching your search appear onscreen. What's happening while the spinner's running? Services in the application are doing invisible, behind-the-scenes work. What type of work? Often, it's saving or getting data. Or it might be changing or creating data for the UI to use. Services also can work as communication channels between application components.

Services allow you to write non-UI code in a way that's modular, reusable, and testable. As you'll see, code located in services is easier to understand and maintain than the same kind of functionality inside a UI component.

Angular services usually don't change the DOM or directly interact with the UI, but otherwise there's no limit to what functionality an Angular service can provide. Well-designed applications have most of the application logic and I/O inside a service. Any code creating UI elements or handling user input should be in a component.

Let's start with an overview of how the Contacts app uses services. The application loads with a list of contacts. How do they get there? As shown in figure 6.1, when ContactListComponent initializes, it asks ContactService for a list of contacts. ContactService looks to see if it has any contacts, and if it doesn't, it prepares a request to the server to retrieve them. But instead of contacting the server directly, ContactService relies on yet another service (HttpClient) that knows the ins and outs of handling HTTP requests, which responds with a list of contacts. HttpClient has no knowledge of the payload, and ContactService doesn't know how to communicate with the server, but by working together, these services can ask for and supply contacts to the ContactListComponent. Organizing the application's architecture this way follows a software development principle called *separation of concerns*, where each element of the application only knows how to fulfill its own responsibility.

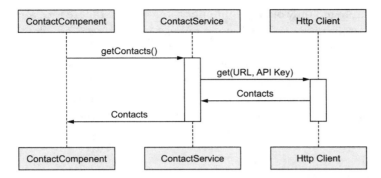

Figure 6.1 `ContactListComponent` **uses** `ContactService`, **which uses a built-in Angular service (**`HttpClient`**).**

Do I need services for my app?

You could, but probably shouldn't, write a complete Angular application without using any services. When you're prototyping an application or trying to get a feature to work, it can be easier to put all of a feature's code in the component that uses it. But over time, it gets harder to maintain that code and even harder to share the work between components. That's when you need a service.

Let's look at an example using the Contacts app. While a list of contacts is showing, the user should be able to sort the list by first name, last name, or email address. To remember the sort order for the user's next visit, you save a value to the browser's local storage. The first time you write this code, it's easy to add to the `ContactList` component. But what happens when you need to save other user preferences? And what if you need more flexibility for saving the preferences to a web service?

As your needs get more complex, it makes sense to move this logic into a service. In fact, you may want to create two services: one to handle organizing application preferences and another for interacting with whatever storage medium you're using. Moving this logic into a service makes it easier for you to add preference functionality in other areas of the application.

6.2 How do services work in Angular?

At the most basic level, Angular services are JavaScript classes. They're singletons—you create them once and can use them anywhere in the application.

Angular services often implement the `@Injectable` class decorator. This decorator adds metadata that Angular uses for resolving dependencies. Angular uses the class itself to create a provider token that other components will use for defining provider dependencies.

A service is instantiated only once. Components that define that service as a dependency will share that instance. This technique reduces memory use and allows services to act as brokers for sharing data between components.

By now, it should be clear that services and Angular's dependency injection are closely related concepts. In fact, Angular offers many built-in services, including Http-Client and FormBuilder. Many third-party libraries designed to work with Angular are also services. Before you start testing your services, you need to have a clearer understanding of what Angular's dependency injection does, because you can't write services without it.

6.2.1   *Dependency injection*

The key to understanding testing Angular services is to understand Angular's dependency injection system. Why do you need dependency injection in the first place? Isn't it good enough to use import to pull other JavaScript libraries into your source code?

When you create new instances of your classes, you may not know the details about the dependencies your classes need. For example, suppose you create a dependency on a Storage service. If your service imports a specific storage mechanism, you're locked into using that one implementation and no others, even though you don't care about the specific implementation, only that it supports the methods you'll invoke when persisting data.

Dependency injection is a system that supplies instances of a dependency at the time your own class is instantiated. You don't need your service to do the work of importing and instantiating a dependency; the dependency injection system will do it for you. When the constructor of your service executes, it will receive an instance of a dependency that the dependency injection system already created, and the service will use the injected code instead of the imported class, as shown in the following listing.

Listing 6.1   A service using Angular dependency injection

Imports the class so that you can use the
token to define the dependency

Angular dependency injection uses the service
constructor to look up and supply dependencies.

```
import { Injectable } from '@angular/core';
import { BrowserStorage } from './browser-storage.service';

@Injectable()
export class PreferencesService {

  constructor(private browserStorage: BrowserStorage ) { }
```

```
public saveProperty(preference: IContactPreference) {
  this.browserStorage.setItem(preference.key, preference.value);
}

public getProperty(key: string) : any {
  return this.browserStorage.getItem(key);
  }
}
```

PreferencesService uses injected services, not BrowserStorage directly.

In listing 6.1, the constructor method of PreferencesService defines a parameter with type BrowserStorage. Angular uses this information to supply an instance of BrowserStorage when PreferencesService is first created via dependency injection. Dependency injection makes software a little bit more abstract and complex, but it gives you a lot more flexibility in extending its functionality. As long as an added service implements the same interface as an existing service, it's possible to take advantage of it without having to change any other code. For example, in listing 6.1, PreferencesService only needs to use the methods setItem and getItem without having to understand the underlying storage mechanism. This feature is useful when unit testing because it helps you test in small, separate units while controlling the side effects of your software.

The bottom line is that dependency injection allows you to write code that's not tightly coupled to other code—that's against an *interface* instead of an *implementation*. Angular's dependency injection helps you develop better code, and it's one of the features that makes Angular a great framework for organizing large applications.

Dependency-injection tokens

As you set up your unit tests for services, you'll notice that each file imports the classes that are dependencies for the services you're testing only to replace the implementation of those dependencies with your own mock objects. Why are you doing this? Because Angular's dependency injection uses the class type as the *token*, which becomes the key for its internal *token-provider* map.

When you define a service with dependencies, it provides a copy of the token to Angular's injection system. Angular uses that token to look up the corresponding provider and returns it to the service.

What about cases where you want to provide a string or object instead of a service function? It's possible to use a string as a token instead by using the InjectionToken function from @angular/core. See the Angular documentation for further details (https://angular.io/guide/dependency-injection).

6.2.2   *The @Injectable class decorator*

As mentioned in chapter 4, a decorator is a TypeScript feature that adds some properties or behavior to a class or method. Angular includes a decorator for services, @Injectable, that's a convenient way to mark your service as a class that can serve as a provider for Angular's dependency injection system. The decorator tells Angular that the service itself has its own dependencies that need to be resolved. Although it's possible to manually define your service as a provider, you'd rarely want to do so (unless you're using straight JavaScript ES5, in which case it's unavoidable).

A service, like a component, is able to define its own dependencies. A common example is any service that uses HttpModule for communicating with external services. As applications get more complex, it's more likely you'll have several layers of services. Separating code into modular units helps promote reuse and makes it easier to maintain the code. In Angular, services are designed to support reusability.

Is the @Injectable decorator required for Angular services? No. If your service has no dependencies of its own, you can get by without marking the service as @Injectable. You can unit test a service without dependencies without needing the Angular TestBed or any Angular testing utilities. That's right; you can use simple unit tests! Before you head down that road, keep this in mind: if you think you might add dependencies in the future, you may as well unit test your code with Angular so you don't have to refactor your unit tests so much.

Now that you have some background on Angular services and dependency injection, it's time to create your first service. Although it's a straightforward matter to create services by hand, you'll use Angular CLI because it also sets up basic unit tests for you.

6.3   *Creating services with Angular CLI*

We recommend using Angular CLI whenever you extend your application with a new component or service. The advantage of using Angular CLI to create services is that it automatically generates a basic service and a corresponding test file that provides the boilerplate code for the Angular TestBed.

To create a service using Angular CLI, run the following command from your project directory in your terminal:

```
$ ng generate service my.service.name
```

This command creates these two files: my.service.name.ts and my.service.name.spec.ts. After these services are created, Angular CLI produces this message:

```
Warning: Service is generated but not provided, it must be provided to be
    used
```

Never fear, this is Angular CLI reminding you that you need to add services to the provider metadata property of a component or module to use them. Where you include a service depends on whether it's local to a component or used throughout the module.

The unit test file that Angular CLI generates (which ends with spec.ts and is shown in listing 6.2) is a basic test that does nothing more than make sure your service exists. This is all you need to get started. Even better, Angular CLI also prepares the boilerplate code that configures `TestBed`, which (as previous chapters explain) sets up Angular for use with unit testing.

Listing 6.2 Basic service test spec generated by Angular CLI

```
import { TestBed, inject } from '@angular/core/testing';
import { ContactService } from './contact.service';

describe('ContactService', () => {
  beforeEach(() => {
    TestBed.configureTestingModule({
      providers: [ContactService]
    });
  });

  it('should ...', inject(
    [ContactService], (service: ContactService) => {
      expect(service).toBeTruthy();
  }));
});
```

> **TestBed is configured with the ContactService before every test.**

> **Angular CLI creates the first test, which only asserts the existence of the service.**

You can run the test in listing 6.2 with Angular CLI as follows:

```
$ ng test
```

You should see output that shows that the test passed:

```
Executed 1 of 1 SUCCESS (0.263 secs / 0.254 secs)
```

You've learned the basics of using Angular CLI to set up your services and tests. Before you jump into writing service tests, let's make sure you understand why you're writing this service in the first place.

6.4 Testing PreferencesService

The first service you'll create and test is `PreferencesService`, which you'll use to store the user's last sort order for the `ContactsList` table. This service will take a value and save it to the browser's built-in storage system. When the app starts, it will use this value to set the sort state for the `ContactsList` table to be in the order that the user last used, even if they've refreshed the page or restarted the browser. This improves the user experience of your app and keeps the user from having to reset the sort order each time they open it.

Before you start, you might ask if you even need to create a service. You could instead write the logic for persisting user preferences in the `ContactsList` component. After all, it seems easy to write settings directly to the user's browser. That's true, and it might even be the right choice if your task is to create a rapid prototype rather than build a production application. But you have good reasons for splitting this functionality out of the component and into a service. Let's look at some of them.

Whenever you start using a browser feature like `localStorage`, it isn't long before you start discovering requirements that weren't obvious at first, such as

- Validating key names and values
- Preventing naming conflicts with other preference keys
- Making sure the app has a fallback mechanism, such as using browser cookies
- Limiting the size of the storage used by your app
- Checking that storage is available

These requirements may not all seem obvious when your only goal is to use a browser's built-in storage, but they're important for a production application. Say you write the logic in your component. How do you use it when you need to save more information to the browser's storage? If you copy and paste your code, you'll have a hard time remembering to change it everywhere whenever you need to fix a bug or add a feature. The way to solve this challenge is to write your code once in a service and use that service wherever you need it.

Now that you know why you need a service, you can start creating one.

WRITING PREFERENCESSERVICE

Start by using Angular CLI to create the preference service. Run the following command in your terminal:

```
$ ng generate service PreferencesService
```

This command creates the files preferences.service.ts and preferences.service.spec.ts, and, as before, Angular CLI reminds you that the service must be provided to be used. Before writing tests, add the `PreferencesService` provider to the application's `AppModule`, as shown in the following listing.

Listing 6.3   Adding the newly created service to app.module.ts

```
@NgModule({
  {…}
  providers: [
    BrowserStorage,           Declaration and imports are hidden.
    ContactService,
    PreferencesService,
    PreferencesAsyncService
    ],
  })
export class AppModule { }
```

Now that you've created the service, you can start setting up the unit test framework. Angular CLI has already done the basic work, so you can proceed with setting up the parts you need to test `PreferencesService`. Add the code in the following listing to preferences.service.spec.ts.

Listing 6.4 Setting up the unit tests for `PreferencesService`

```
import { TestBed, inject } from '@angular/core/testing';
import {
  IContactPreference,
  PreferencesService } from './preferences.service';

describe('PreferencesService', () => {

  beforeEach(() => {
    TestBed.configureTestingModule({
      providers: [PreferencesService]
    });
  });

  it('should create the Preferences Service', inject(
    [PreferencesService], (service: PreferencesService) => {
    expect(service).toBeTruthy();
  }));
});
```

The TestBed module is configured before every test.

The first test only checks that the service test setup is right.

In this listing, you have the bare minimum for unit testing a service. You may remember configuring `TestBed` from earlier chapters—it tells Angular what modules it needs to load and how they need to be configured for testing this file. Later in this chapter, you'll see how to customize `TestBed` for testing services that have their own dependencies. Angular CLI also created the first test, which is only a check to verify that the service exists. Although it doesn't look like much, it's helpful to know that the basic setup for testing is in place.

Now that your basic unit test is working, you need to think about how your service will persist the data. Are you going to use `localStorage`, cookies, or some other browser API? You don't know right now, so pretend you have the information by creating a fake service called `BrowserStorage` to let you avoid relying on any specific kind of storage. That way, you can keep writing `PreferencesService` without having to solve the storage problem.

To use this technique, you'll create a simple service that doesn't implement any logic—the service only exists to provide a token and a simple storage interface. Later on, when you're ready to use a real service implementation, you can expand `BrowserStorage` to connect to the real persistence service. For now, you'll put the code shown in the following listing in browser-storage.service.ts. It only has two methods, `getItem` and `setItem`, and they don't need to do anything other than define their input and output types.

Listing 6.5 The `BrowserStorage` stubbed class

```
@Injectable()
export class BrowserStorage {
  getItem: (property: string) => string | object;
  setItem: (property: string, value: string | object) => void;
}
```

Stubbed class prior to implementing storage

In this listing, you'll create a *stub*, which is a barebones class that defines its properties and methods but doesn't contain any logic. Hang on, why is this a class instead of a TypeScript interface? As mentioned earlier in this chapter, Angular uses tokens for resolving dependencies. TypeScript interfaces don't get translated into JavaScript, so there's no way for Angular to resolve the token. To tell Angular what to inject, you'll need to create a class that fills in like it's an interface. For more on this issue, see the Angular documentation (http://mng.bz/35U7).

You can use this stub to create a `BrowserStorageMock` for your test. A *mock* is an object that substitutes for a real service. To clarify, the stub represents the storage service that you haven't written yet, even though you know what methods you want to call. The mock is an object you use only within the unit test that provides canned responses within the test. With your mock, you'll define the `getItem` and `setItem` methods. Later, you'll use the mock in the unit test as a substitute for the real service.

Within individual unit tests, you'll use spies. A *spy* is a function that invisibly wraps a method and lets you control what values it returns or monitor how it was called. A test uses a spy to measure if a method was called, how many times it was called, and with what arguments.

By using the token from `BrowserStorage` and supplying the same methods, you can use your mock for unit testing instead of relying on the real implementation. You only need to configure `TestBed` to use `BrowserStorageMock` whenever a service calls for `BrowserStorage` as a dependency.

Now let's look at the `PreferencesService` class, which has only two methods: `save-Property()` and `getProperty()`. The `saveProperty()` method takes a `ContactPreference` object and saves it for later retrieval. The `getProperty()` method takes the property name and returns the saved value. In this chapter, you'll only look at the unit test for saving the property, but you can see all of the unit tests in this book's project repository (https://github.com/testing-angular-applications).

As shown in listing 6.6, the `saveProperty` method takes one argument, an object that represents the name and value of the preference item you're saving. For consistency, you'll create a TypeScript interface (`IContactPreferences`) to describe that object. The method uses the object and writes that value to the injected instance of the `BrowserStorage` service, which is called `browserStorage`. (Remember that `Brows-erStorage` helps you separate the read and write operations from the persistence implementation.)

Listing 6.6   The `saveProperty` method

```
interface IContactPreference {
  key: string;
  value: string | object;
}

public saveProperty(preference: IContactPreference) {
```

```
if (!(preferences.key && preference.key.length)) {
  throw new Error('saveProperty requires a non-blank property name');
}
this.browserStorage.setItem(preference.key, preference.value);
}
```

The first test in listing 6.7 ensures that saveProperty works correctly. This function receives a ContactPreference object and stores it. To test it, you need to make sure the method receives a valid argument and tries to persist it with BrowserStorage. To write this test, you'll spy on the BrowserStorage service, invoke saveProperty with a valid argument, and confirm that your expectations are met.

Listing 6.7 Testing the saveProperty method

```
import { TestBed, inject } from '@angular/core/testing';
import { PreferencesService } from './preferences.service';
import { BrowserStorage } from "./browser-storage.service";

import { logging } from "selenium-webdriver";
import Preferences = logging.Preferences;          ◄——— Creates BrowserStorageMock

class BrowserStorageMock {
  getItem = (property: string) => ({ key: 'testProp', value: 'testValue '});
  setItem = ({ key: key, value: value }) => {};
}

describe('PreferencesService', () => {
                                                    Configures the TestBed dependency
                                                    injection to use BrowserStorageMock
                                                    instead of the real service
  beforeEach(() => {
    TestBed.configureTestingModule({
      providers: [PreferencesService, {          ◄———
        provide: BrowserStorage, useClass: BrowserStorageMock
      }]
    });

  });
                                                         Uses inject to get the
                                                         BrowserStorageMock
  describe('save preferences', () => {

    it('should save a preference',
      inject([PreferencesService, BrowserStorage], (service:
        PreferencesService, browserStorage: BrowserStorageMock) => {    ◄———

        spyOn(browserStorage, 'setItem').and.callThrough();    ◄———
        service.saveProperty({ key: 'myProperty', value: 'myValue' });
        expect(browserStorage.setItem)
          .toHaveBeenCalledWith('myProperty', 'myValue');
      })
    );
  });
});
                                                    Adds a spy to browserStorage.setItem
```

Checks the spy to make sure it was called
from saveProperty()

Because you're using a spy on the `BrowserStorage` service, from now on you can check to see how many times the method was invoked and with what parameters. In this test, you're checking to make sure the `setItem` method was called with the expected parameters.

Spies are not unique to Jasmine—most testing frameworks support them. You can learn more about Jasmine spies in the Jasmine documentation at http://jasmine. github.io.

TESTING THE HAPPY PATH

Let's review your work so far. You've done the following:

1 Started by using Angular CLI to generate a service and its associated unit test file
2 Added the service to the `AppModule`
3 Wrote a basic unit that verifies that the service and test file are set up correctly
4 Expanded the unit test setup by creating a mock for the `BrowserStorage` service
5 Created a unit test that checks for the existence of `saveProperty`
6 Created a unit test that verifies the behavior of `saveProperty` when called with a valid parameter

What's left to do? You might have noticed you only tested the *happy path*, the condition where you used the method correctly. To make sure your code can handle bad input, you'll need to create more tests.

6.4.1   *Testing for failures*

What if something goes wrong? The input to your function could be bad. Maybe some parameters will be missing or have the wrong type—for example, you expect an array but receive a number. Or maybe the input looks good, but the values don't pass the validation checks. Multiple things could go wrong, and it's good to have a plan to deal with the misuse of your code.

Testing for failures works much the same way as testing the happy path. You'll set up the tests the same way and invoke the method the same way, but you'll provide incorrect inputs to make sure your code responds correctly.

In the following example, you'll call `saveProperty()` using the incorrect parameter of not having a value for the key name. What you expect to happen is that the service will throw an error. Not having a key might not break your code, but it could cause problems with the persistence solution you end up using. To catch the problem early, your code should throw an error if the key is empty or not defined.

Normally, if a function in a test is executed and throws an error, it causes the whole test to fail. Because this test is meant to ensure that the function throws an exception, Jasmine needs more setup. To solve this puzzle, the test needs to define a function that itself calls the function that will throw the error. In listing 6.8, this test function for setting up the assertion is called `shouldThrow`. When you provide this function to Jasmine in the expect block, and then use the `toThrowError()` matcher, Jasmine will execute the function and anticipate that an error will be thrown as a result. When Jasmine executes `shouldThrow`, the function will throw an error, and you can verify that the error value has the correct type and error message. For the purposes of this test, you just need to check that an error was thrown.

Listing 6.8 Unit test for checking that a bad input throws an error

```
it('saveProperty should require a non-zero length key',
  inject([PreferencesService], (service: PreferencesService) => {

  const shouldThrow = () => {
    service.saveProperty({ key: '', value: 'foo' });
  };

  expect(shouldThrow).toThrowError();
  })
);
```

Creates a wrapper for any function that's supposed to throw an error

Expects the function to throw an error

Remember that the Jasmine methods for testing if errors are thrown require that the `expect` parameter be a function. This differs from typical tests that assert the value passed to expect, so make sure you aren't calling your test function inside the `expect` method!

What you've learned so far in this chapter works well for services that operate synchronously. We looked at the example of synchronous persistence, and this pattern works well whenever you want two services to work together without directly coupling them. But you often need to handle asynchronous events such as remote service calls or user interactions. Testing asynchronous services is a bit more complex.

6.5 Testing services with promises

As you've been reading this chapter, you may have wondered, "What if I want to use some type of web service to save my preferences?" That's a great question, because the way you've designed the `ContactPreferences` service so far depends on having a synchronous persistence media. In this section, you'll create an alternate preferences service with asynchronous methods that return promises. You'll also see an alternative asynchronous pattern using RxJS observables in conjunction with `HttpClient` later in section 6.6.

> **NOTE** If you haven't worked with promises before, all you need to know for now is that a promise provides a way to write asynchronous JavaScript without nesting multiple levels of callbacks. Promises became a standard JavaScript feature in ES2015. You can learn more about promises at the Mozilla Developer Network (http://mng.bz/8tEi).

There's an important difference between testing synchronous and asynchronous services when it comes to setting up tests. You need to test services that asynchronously respond to method calls differently because Jasmine needs to know when to end an individual test. Jasmine will automatically complete a test if you don't explicitly tell it to wait, and it will report inaccurate results. The second parameter to a Jasmine it block is a function that takes an optional callback parameter, usually called done. If a test supplies this parameter, Jasmine will wait for done to be called before ending the test.

> **WARNING**   If you write a test with an expect inside an async block without letting Jasmine know that it's an async test, Jasmine will report the test as passing! Watch out for this behavior and remember that the practice of red-green-refactor helps keep you aware of these types of oversights. If your test skipped red and went straight to green, then you might have an error in your code!

If you've ever spent a lot of time in Jasmine trying to figure out why your async test was passing when it obviously should be failing, you're not alone. If this is your first time using Jasmine, you'll be glad to know about this issue right from the start. The correct way to write an async unit test in Jasmine is to pass the done callback to the unit test and invoke it when you want the test to end.

Listing 6.9 illustrates a common mistake in an async test—forgetting to supply and invoke the done callback argument from the it method. Later, you'll see that Angular supplies some helpers so you don't need the done method, but for basic async tests in Jasmine, follow this example.

Listing 6.9   Incorrect and correct way to write asynchronous Jasmine tests

```
it('is an asynchronous test', () => {
  setTimeout(() => {
    expect(true).toBe(false);
  });
});
```
← Unit test unexpectedly passes because done callback isn't defined or called

```
it('is an asynchronous test', (done) => {
  setTimeout(() => {
    expect(true).toBe(false);
    done();
  });
});
```
← Unit test fails as expected because it doesn't complete until the done callback is invoked

This method of writing async tests will always work with Angular unit tests. But when you're writing tests that need to inject dependencies into the test block, this syntax isn't easy to use. You need to access the dependencies by exposing them with a beforeEach block, and that can make it less clear which tests require which injected services. Fortunately, Angular gives you more options for easily writing tests with asynchronous logic.

The evolving Angular asynchronous testing story

Angular has a system for detecting changes that happen when asynchronous JavaScript is called. This system, called a *zone*, changes the way asynchronous browser APIs like `setTimeout` work. When Angular was publicly released, developers needed to understand how zones worked to write unit tests, so those who were new to Angular had a hard time doing so.

The Angular team responded by adding support to `Zone.js` to make it easier to write async tests. The first API they made available to developers was `async`. Running a test in an `async` zone made it much easier to write tests for code that changed the DOM. After changing the application state, a developer could wait for the `fixture` to say when it was safe to continue a test. Tests with `async` use the helper method `whenStable`, which returns a promise, making it fairly easy to write tests that work correctly with asynchronous changes. The drawback of `async` is that it requires additional test boilerplate.

Later, they made another API available, `fakeAsync`, which makes it easier to write tests in a more synchronous style. If you write tests inside a `fakeAsync` block, they can pretend to fast-forward asynchronous events by calling `tick()`. (See chapter 3, section 3.2.1.) The drawback of `fakeAsync` is that you can't test some scenarios with this helper.

When writing async tests, should you use `done`, `async`, or `fakeAsync`? It's your choice, but in this chapter, you'll use `fakeAsync` because it's newer and the Angular team seems to prefer it.

Although you can invoke asynchronous JavaScript in several ways, including timeouts, DOM events, generator functions, and so on, your async re-implementation of `PreferencesService`, `PreferencesAsyncService`, will use promises. In the previous section, we looked at `setProperty`, so in this example we'll look at the asynchronous version of `getProperty`, or `getPropertyAsync`.

In the async version of the preferences service, you'll use an async data storage service for saving and retrieving the preferences. Unlike synchronous code, which always has to finish executing before any of your other code can run, the asynchronous use of storage allows you to read and write data without pausing your other code.

Listing 6.10 is the async version of the preferences service. It needs to be async now because its underlying storage system handles its read and write operations asynchronously. When reading the preferences, `BrowserStorageAsync` returns a promise already, so you'll return that promise with no modification. If `getPropertyAsync` is called with an invalid parameter, you'll return a rejected promise with an appropriate error message, as shown in the following listing. Keep in mind that the `BrowserStorage` service itself might encounter an error, in which case it would also return a rejected promise.

Listing 6.10 `PreferencesAsyncService`

```
import { Injectable } from '@angular/core';
import { BrowserStorageAsync } from './browser-storage.service';
import { IContactPreference } from './preferences.service';

@Injectable()
export class PreferencesAsyncService {

  constructor(private browserStorage: BrowserStorageAsync) { }

  getPropertyAsync(key: string) : Promise<IContactPreference> {
    if (!key.length) {
      return
        Promise.reject('getPropertyAsync requires a property name');
    } else {
      return this.browserStorage.getItem(key);
    }
  }
}
```

Rejects with an error message if no key is passed

Otherwise returns the promise from BrowserStorageAsync

6.5.1   *How asynchronous changes testing*

Before continuing on to the test for the async preferences service, let's consider the differences between synchronous and asynchronous code, and how the differences affect how you write tests.

When you write synchronous code, you're telling the computer to *do this thing and wait until it's finished before continuing*. Almost all code is synchronous—each line is evaluated, and the next line waits to run until the prior line completes. Writing (and testing) this style of code is relatively easy, because it flows like a story. You can think about the program running in sequence. As useful as synchronous code is, at times using it would make the software unusable. For example, when you fetch data from a web API, it could take several seconds before the server responds to the request. If you handled this fetching with synchronous code, the whole user interface would be unresponsive until the request finished. Users hate that!

In contrast, with asynchronous code, you're telling the computer to *do this thing, and later do more work when it's finished*. Writing asynchronous code is hard because it no longer reads like a story. You write the code out of sequence. It becomes even harder when one asynchronous action causes other asynchronous actions to fire. Though it's harder to write and think about, asynchronous code makes it possible to create programs that are more responsive to user input.

As for testing asynchronous code, you need to understand a couple of differences in both setting up the test and writing the test. First, any of the mocks you create need to reflect asynchronous inputs and outputs (usually by returning promises or observables).

Second, each individual test needs to indicate to Jasmine that it's testing asynchronous code. Let's take these one at a time.

To test the async preferences service, you'll need to create a mock for the async version of the browser storage service. Why do you need this? It could be that the storage is using a browser technology like IndexedDB (http://mng.bz/w1Eu), which defines an asynchronous interface for storing and retrieving data. Or it's possible that the storage could be implemented as a web service with the data being stored remotely. In either case, the preferences service needs to be able to handle getting and saving a user's data without pausing the application.

When you write the tests themselves, you need to make sure each individual test indicates to Jasmine that it's testing asynchronous code. Angular includes several testing utilities to make this task easier and to reduce the amount of boilerplate code needed to write the test.

The following listing shows the setup changes for the async testing and a test that incorporates the async test utilities.

Listing 6.11 Importing `inject` **and** `fakeAsync` **from** `@angular/core/testing`

```
import {
  TestBed,
  fakeAsync,                              Imports asynchronous
  flushMicrotasks,                        testing methods
  inject } from '@angular/core/testing';

import { BrowserStorageAsync } from "./browser-storage.service";
import { PreferencesAsyncService } from './preferences-async.service';

class BrowserStorageAsyncMock {          Mocks the asynchronous service response
  getItem = (property: string) => {
    return Promise.resolve({ key: 'testProp', value: 'testValue '});
  };
  setItem = ({ key: key, value: value }) => Promise.resolve(true);
}
describe('PreferencesAsyncService', () => {
  beforeEach(() => {
    TestBed.configureTestingModule({
      providers: [PreferencesAsyncService, {
        provide: BrowserStorageAsync, useClass: BrowserStorageAsyncMock
      }]
    });
  });

  it('should get a value', fakeAsync(inject(
      [PreferencesAsyncService, BrowserStorageAsync],
    (service: PreferencesAsyncService, browserStorage:
    BrowserStorageAsyncMock) => {
      spyOn(browserStorage, 'getItem').and.callThrough();

      let results, error;                      Invokes the promise and
                                               assigns the results
      service.getPropertyAsync('testProp')
```

```
          .then(val => results = val)
          .catch(err => error = err);                Processes the promise microtasks

      flushMicrotasks();

      expect(results.key).toEqual('testProp');        Ensures the error value
      expect(results.value).toEqual('testValue');     wasn't assigned
      expect(error).toBeUndefined();
      expect(browserStorage.getItem).toHaveBeenCalledWith('testProp');
    }))
  );
});
```

In the imports section of listing 6.11, you include two new methods from the Angular testing package, fakeAsync and flushMicrotasks. You'll use these methods to test the async preferences service.

As mentioned before, when testing async services, the mocks for these services should also be asynchronous. BrowserStorageAsyncMock sets up the input and output methods getItem and setItem to each return a promise. In the real implementation of the browser storage service, these promises would be resolved after completing an asynchronous operation. In this test, they'll resolve immediately with predefined data.

When you write the test for getPropertyAsync, you'll see that the whole test is wrapped within a function called fakeAsync. The fakeAsync test helper aids you in two ways. First, it reduces the amount of boilerplate code you need to write an async test. Second, it makes it easy to use inject to provide instances of dependencies at the point of writing a test.

The main part of the test, the part that exercises PreferencesAsyncService, calls the getPropertyAsync method on your system under test and then saves the results to locally defined variables of results and error. You'll use those values to verify the expected results. After the main test block, you invoke flushMicrotasks (which you imported at the beginning of the test). You need to call flushMicrotasks to let Angular know that it's time to process the promises in the test.

Remember that your Angular services don't need to call flushMicrotasks—this is a testing-only helper that makes it easier to test asynchronous services. You use it here to make sure the promises resolve before checking your expected values. Note that by using fakeAsync, you don't need to call Jasmine's done to end your asynchronous test.

The last part of this test is to confirm that the results are as expected. The getPropertyAsync method should correctly return values from the async browser storage service, and there should be no errors. The test also verifies via the test spy that the browser storage mock was called with the right arguments.

In the next section, we'll cover asynchronous unit testing for expected failures.

6.5.2   *Testing for failures with asynchronous services*

Testing for failures in services that use promises is like what we covered in section 6.4.1 for testing synchronous errors. One major difference is that promises have a different way of resolving errors.

In the following listing, you'll see how testing for failures with promises differs from testing for failures in synchronous code.

Listing 6.12   Testing for rejected promises

**Calls getPropertyAsync
with an invalid value**

```
it('should throw an error if the key is missing',
  fakeAsync(inject([PreferencesAsyncService],
    (service: PreferencesAsyncService) => {
      let result, error;
      service.getPropertyAsync('')
        .then(value => result = value)
        .catch((err) => error = err);

      flushMicrotasks();
      expect(result).toBeUndefined();
      expect(error)
        .toEqual('getPropertyAsync requires a property name');

  }))
);
```

**Uses the BrowserStorageAsyncMock
default return value**

**Catches the expected
error and assigns it locally**

**You should get an error
with this error message.**

**You shouldn't get a
preference value back.**

When you tested for failures with synchronous code, you had to have special handling to make sure Jasmine could anticipate that an error would be thrown. But when something goes wrong when calling a promise, the `reject` callback of the promise will be called with any error information, and then the `catch` method that resolves the promise can handle any error processing. Therefore, Jasmine doesn't need to have any special test setup when testing for error conditions with promises.

Remember to write tests that cover all of your expected paths into and out of your functions. Promises make writing asynchronous code easier than ever, but you still need to write robust code that checks for correct input values and raises errors when problems arise.

So far, you've used promises in the asynchronous examples, but in the next section, you'll write unit tests that handle RxJS-based observables. Angular relies heavily on RxJS in its design, especially in `HttpClient`. This type of code requires special setup, so we'll cover an example in depth.

6.6   *Testing HTTP services with observables*

In this section, we'll cover one of the most common uses of Angular services: connecting an application to a remote API using `HttpClient`. We'll also cover unit testing services that return an RxJS observable, because it's the default response type for `Http-Client`. As of Angular 4.3, testing services that interact with `HttpClient` is a painless process. Previously it required dozens of lines of boilerplate, but, fortunately for you, the process is now streamlined and easy.

Tests for HTTP services require special setup so they avoid accessing web services. Making a network call from your unit tests would break their isolation. If your unit tests aren't isolated, it's much harder to pinpoint a failure in the system under test.

You also shouldn't call web services directly from your tests because

- The computer running the unit tests may need to make calls over a network, making your test configuration more complex.
- There's no way to guarantee the same result for each run of the test.
- You might not have control over the service, so you may get back different results if the service specification changes.
- The service itself may be discontinued or moved to a different address.
- You can't control the response times of servers, leading you to set long timeouts as you try to guess how quickly your calls will return.

You may feel like you're in a difficult position. You need to test that your service is making the correct calls to HttpClient, and that your service correctly responds to both successes and failures. How can you do so without running into the difficulties we listed? Fortunately, Angular has anticipated this problem and gives you support for HttpClient that makes unit testing much easier.

When you were testing PreferencesService, you created a fake storage service to isolate your test from the browser's real storage system. This is a common pattern in unit testing, and it's so predictably similar to HttpClient that Angular includes Http-ClientTestingModule to facilitate the process. Because of HttpClientTestingModule, there's no need to manually create stubs or manually configure Angular for testing, as was the case in previous versions of Angular. This test helper includes a bonus feature of simplifying testing observables returned from HttpClient.

ContactService makes different calls to the web service for working with Contacts data. Each of these calls is based on an HTTP verb (such as GET, POST, or DELETE). For each of these operations, you'll need to set up your tests to respond appropriately. Because the setup for this test is so simple, the following listing includes both the setup and a test that gets a list of contacts from the server.

> Listing 6.13   **Testing services that use** `HttpClient`

```
import { TestBed } from '@angular/core/testing';
import {
  HttpClientTestingModule,
  HttpTestingController } from '@angular/common/http/testing';
import { ContactService } from './contact.service';

describe('ContactsService', () => {
  beforeEach(() => {
    TestBed.configureTestingModule({
      imports: [ HttpClientTestingModule ],
```
◄─── **Configures the TestBed to use HttpClientTestingModule**

```
      providers: [ ContactService ]
    });
  });

  describe('getContacts', () => {

    let contactService: ContactService;
    let httpTestingController: HttpTestingController;
    let mockContact: any;

    beforeEach(() => {
      contactService = TestBed.get(ContactService);
      httpTestingController = TestBed.get(HttpTestingController);
      mockContact = {
        id: 100,
        name: 'Erin Dee',
        email: 'edee@example.com'
      };
    });

    it('should GET a list of contacts', () => {
      contactService.getContacts().subscribe((contacts) => {
        expect(contacts[0]).toEqual(mockContact);
      });

      const request = httpTestingController.expectOne('app/contacts');
      request.flush([mockContact]);
      httpTestingController.verify();
    });
  });
});
```

Assigns a reference to the HttpTestingController for interacting with the HttpClientTestingModule

Exercises the contactService method that makes a call to the server, which emits an observable later, so is not evaluated on this line

Causes the observable in #C to run

Verifies there are no outstanding requests

The new concept in this test is the HttpClientTestingModule and its related test helper HttpTestingController. The HttpClientTestingModule removes the need for manually blocking calls from HttpClient trying to reach a server. The HttpTestingController lets you interact with its testing module to verify that calls are being attempted and to supply canned responses.

Unlike the other asynchronous tests in this section, for tests involving HttpClient, you don't need to wrap the test function with fakeAsync or use a done callback. For these tests, the asynchronous observable behavior is simulated without you having to add anything to your tests.

In the test itself, you call getContacts on contactService, which defines an observable of contacts as its return value. This syntax looks similar to how promises are tested, but instead of using then, you use subscribe. One important difference between promises and observables is that observable callbacks are called whenever new values are emitted from an observable, whereas promises are only resolved once.

Since contactService interacts with the server, you'll verify the service makes a call to the api/contacts endpoint, and you'll use the returned request object to send a response by calling flush with a predefined object, the mockContact. Each method in your service (for example, getContacts, setContacts) needs to set up the unit test differently for different types of server responses. The response from a GET request will be different from that of a POST, for example.

NOTE Although you're creating a fake server response, this technique exposes one of the difficulties of writing these types of tests: you still have a hidden dependency on the server itself. You're trusting that the server response will match what your code does. One way to deal with this thorny situation is to write a contract for the service using a specification language, such as OpenAPI, and use those specifications as an input for your unit tests. That goes beyond the scope of this chapter, but it's worth looking into if you're writing code to access web services.

After each test, you'll also check the instance of HttpTestingController to verify no connections to the backend are pending or unresolved. If any are, the test will show an error. As you can see, testing HttpClient using Angular's test helpers saves you a lot of work.

Summary

- Angular services are a way to separate user interface code like buttons and forms from code that handles business logic and data persistence. Using services promotes writing testable code and reusability.
- Angular components and services define their dependencies, which Angular then injects when they're needed. Dependency injection lets you decouple the implementation of your code from the type of work the service is supposed to perform; for example, your component can load and save user preferences without having to know the storage mechanism itself.
- Mocks and spies are test doubles that are nonfunctional or low-functional substitutes for the real dependencies that your application will use. Mocks allow you to provide predefined responses in your tests so your tests will always generate the same results, whereas spies allow you to measure how your code is executing so you can guarantee that methods are called with the correct parameters.
- With asynchronous code, the value produced isn't known until sometime after the function is called, so testing it takes special setup in Jasmine. Angular includes test helpers for making testing asynchronous code easier.
- Common ways of dealing with asynchronous code include promises and observables. Exception handling with promises requires its own type of setup and testing.
- Angular's HttpClient uses RxJS observables as its output for code that makes calls to remote servers. Angular has a special test module to make it easy to test components and services that interact with HttpClient.

Testing the router

7

This chapter covers

- An overview of the router and what it does in single-page applications
- Configuring the router for an Angular application
- Testing components that use the router
- Testing advanced router configuration options

Almost every Angular application needs a way to convert the web address in the location bar to some destination in the web application, and that's where the router comes in.

In simple applications, such as the Contacts app you use throughout this book, the router configuration may only involve associating a URL path with a component, but you can do much more with the router. For example, your application may have sections that a user can only access if they have permission to see the data. A router can verify the user's credentials before even loading that part of the application.

In this chapter, you'll learn more about the router, including how to configure it, and go through some examples of testing both the router code and components that need to use it. Understanding how to test the router in your application builds on skills you've already learned for testing components and services, so make sure you understand the chapters on those topics before continuing with the material in this chapter.

7.1   *What is the Angular router?*

The Angular router is a part of the Angular framework that converts a web address to a specific view of the Angular application; it's integral to the Angular application architecture. In practice, all Angular applications need to define a router, so the router a key part of Angular development. When a user goes to a URL for an Angular application, the router parses the URL to determine which component and data to load. Whenever a URL changes, whether someone enters it directly or clicks a link, the router sets up the appropriate application state. Each segment of the path encodes information about that state. The Angular router examines the path and breaks it into a series of tokens that you can use for loading components and making data available to them.

Suppose the Contacts app is available at www.example.com, and a user wants to edit the contact for the person with ID 5. The page for doing so is http://www.example.com/app/contacts/5/edit. Figure 7.1 shows how the website URL corresponds to the router configuration. First, notice that the base path, which you configure in the HTML of your application using the `<base href>` tag, isn't included as part of the router configuration. Angular uses the base path as the starting point (or default view) of the application. All the other URLs in the application will be under the base path. Second, notice that the dynamic portion of the URL, the `contactId`, has a colon in front of it. The router will use the name of this label to send this parameter along to any components that need to use it.

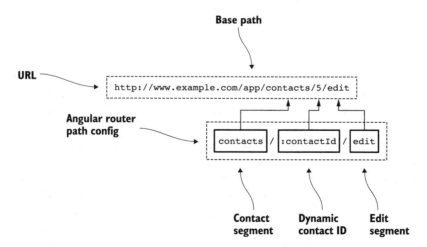

7.1 How the application URL corresponds to the router configuration

The router configuration could be simple for an application that has only a handful of routes, such as the Contacts app, or it could be long and spread among many different files, say for a large enterprise application. As we explain the details, *route configuration* refers to the configuration of a single URL, and the collection of all the route configurations is called the *router configuration*. A router configuration will contain one or more route configurations.

The process of starting and completing a route change is called its *lifecycle*. Over the course of the route change lifecycle, multiple opportunities are available for checking whether the route change can continue. Generically, these are called *lifecycle hooks*, but they're known in Angular as *route guards*. Whenever the router loads a new route, components configured for that route have access to the route's parameters. These parameters have no prescribed use, but they're often used for retaining information about something the component is displaying (for example, pagination or table sorting information).

The router configuration affects how components will function throughout an application, so it's useful to add tests to validate the ones that interact with it, or to test the route guards that the router itself fires.

You can test code related to the router in two different ways. The first is by testing how components receive values from the router or call actions on it. The second is by testing the application code invoked by the route guards

Imagine the router from a component's point of view. A component may need route information passed into it, or it may need to tell the router to perform navigation actions. When writing tests from this approach, you'll use a fake router configuration (the components won't care that it's fake) and write tests to make sure the components work together correctly.

Now think of testing from the router's point of view. Suppose an unauthorized user is trying to access the app's administration panel. You'll want to use a router configuration that checks to see if the user is logged in and has permission to view the content before allowing them to continue. In this case, the router configuration itself should be the subject of the test because it drives which route guards the router calls.

You test router and component interactions by following the same pattern of testing you'd use for any other parts of Angular, so what you've already learned about testing components and services applies. The only difference is that in these tests, you'll use the Angular `RouterTestingModule`, a built-in testing utility that was created for such scenarios.

In either case, you'll need to have a router configuration to test your code. The next section will help you create one.

7.1.1 Configuring the router

You need to have a router configuration to use the router. During testing, you can use your application's router configuration, but usually you'll create a configuration meant for testing so you'll have more control over your tests.

The most basic router configuration associates a URL path with a component. Listing 7.1 shows the router configuration for the Contacts app, which includes the default home page, pages for adding and modifying contact entries, and a default for an unknown route. In some of the path entries, you'll see part of the path with a colon in front of it (for example, `'edit/:id'`). The colon prefix tells the router that the value in that part of the path is dynamic and the router should make that data available to all the components. Testing a configuration this simple has little worth because there's no behavior to test. The only reason why it might be worth it to write a test is to provide an extra layer of control when changing any of the path information. We recommend writing tests only when a particular route configuration is more complex, such as when using route guards. It's valuable to test a route if the route behaves differently under various conditions.

Listing 7.1   Router configuration for the Contacts application

Default application route, which is the home page of the application

Routes with dynamic path sections

```
export const routes: Routes = [
    { path: '', component: ContactsComponent },
    { path: 'add', component: NewContactComponent },
    { path: 'contacts', component: ContactsComponent },
    { path: 'contact/:id', component: ContactDetailComponent },
    { path: 'edit/:id', component: ContactEditComponent },
    { path: '**', component: PageNotFoundComponent }
];
```

Default component for when the path doesn't match any routes in the router configuration

Typically, testable code related to the router concerns some type of state change, such as attempting to navigate to a route or loading a component after a transition (including initial load). In a test, you only need to configure the router properties that the test requires. Because of this, it's unusual to use your application's live router configuration for unit testing. Your unit tests usually will contain as much route information as needed to execute a single group of tests.

7.1.2   *Route guards: the router's lifecycle hooks*

You may want to add some application before, during, or after the route change. To help you do this, the router has a defined set of methods it looks for on a route configuration. When the route change happens, the router looks at the route configuration to see if the method exists. If it does, it executes the method and uses its return value to determine whether the route change can proceed.

Route guards make it easy to coordinate application behavior as the user moves from place to place in the application. When a route guard is defined, the router will pass the route guard method some parameters (which vary by route guard) and will wait for a return value that tells the router whether it can continue to the next step in loading the route or whether it should abort the route change attempt.

The order of execution for route guards is as follows:

- `CanDeactivate`—Runs before a user can leave the current route. This is useful for prompting the user if they have any unsaved forms or other unfinished activities.
- `CanActivateChild`—For any route that has child routes defined, this hook runs first. This is useful if a feature has some sections that are restricted to users based on permissions.
- `CanActivate`—This hook must return `true` for the route to continue loading. Like with `CanActivateChild`, this hook is useful for keeping unauthorized users from loading application features.
- `Resolve`—If a user is allowed to activate the attempted route, the `resolve` method is used to load data prior to activating the route itself. The data is then available from the `ActivatedRoute` service in the routed components.

In addition to these route guards, the `CanLoad` guard is useful for dynamically loading only the parts of an application relevant to a user's needs (also known as *lazy loading*).

This wraps up the introduction to the Angular router, router configuration, and route guards. The next section covers testing your application code related to the router.

7.2 Testing routed components

In this section, you'll see two different examples of tests related to interactions between components and the router. The first example is a component that makes dynamic calls to the router service. The test will check the calls to the router to make sure the component is creating the dynamic paths correctly. The second example is a component that receives parameters passed from the `ActivatedRoute` service.

Because the Contacts app doesn't use advanced routing features, the examples we look at in this chapter will be standalone code, but you'll still be able to run them on your computer.

7.2.1 Testing router navigation with RouterTestingModule

Suppose you have a component that dynamically generates a navigation menu. Your test finds the menu element and clicks it. You expect the next route to load with the right parameters, but clicking the link changes the URL and causes the tests to fail in the Karma test runner. How do you work around this problem?

When you're testing a component that could cause a navigation event (as you are here by clicking a link), use `RouterTestingModule` to keep Angular from loading the navigation target component. This module intercepts navigation attempts and allows you to check their parameters. Could you do so manually by providing your own mock router service? Yes, but it's easier to use the helper that Angular provides. In this section, the component you're testing generates links dynamically based on a menu configuration, and the test uses `RouterTestingModule` to confirm that the link is working and the target is correct.

> **TIP** It can help to ask what's being tested here. It's important to separate the ideas of testing a component and testing a router configuration. Yes, you can test a component together with your application's router configuration, but you have to import into the test every component that the routes define. In practice, this leads to fragile tests, because they will break whenever you change or update the route configuration. Using your production route configuration for testing will test your entire app! We recommend not coupling your component tests to your application's route configuration. Instead, write your components so that they pass the router configuration to the component as a dependency. (See chapter 6, section 6.2.) That way, you can provide the route value as a mock value in testing.

GENERATE LINKS

The `NagivationMenu` component in the following example shows how to test components that interact with the router. If you were writing this component for production, it would have other behaviors, like animation or nested menus. Remember, in this example, you're testing how the component behaves with respect to the router, not the router configuration itself.

In listing 7.2, notice when the `NavigationMenu` component initializes (`ngOnInit`), it receives its configuration from `NavConfigService` containing route information, which it uses to generate a list of links using the `RouterLink` directive. The test for this component makes sure that `NavConfigService` generates the links correctly and they link to the expected targets.

Listing 7.2   The `NavigationMenu` component

```
@Component({
  selector: 'navigation-menu',
  template: '<div><a *ngFor="let item of menu" [id]="item.label"
    [routerLink]="item.path">{{ item.label }}</a></div>'
})
class NavigationMenu implements OnInit {
  menu: any;
  constructor(private navConfig: NavConfigService) { }
  ngOnInit() {
    this.menu = this.navConfig.menu;
  }
}
```

CONFIGURE ROUTES AND CREATE TEST COMPONENTS

Although the `NavigationMenu` component is simple, tests using `RouterTestingModule` require some setup. You need to configure at least two routes for the route configuration: the initial route and a second route to be the target of the navigation attempt. The initial route loads the component under test, and although the target doesn't affect the outcome of the test, it should be a valid target for whatever link the component constructs.

It's helpful to create a simple component for the test that only exists to be its target. You could import another component in your application for this setup, but defining a simple target component in your test, as shown in the following listing, reduces the complexity and the number of things that could go wrong.

> **Listing 7.3 Creating test components for `NavigationMenu` test**

AppComponent test fixture tests the component

```
@Component({
  selector: 'app-root',
  template: '<router-outlet></router-outlet>',
})
class AppComponent { }

@Component({
  selector: 'simple-component',
  template: 'simple'
})
class SimpleComponent { }
```

SimpleComponent stands in as the target component in the test route configuration.

SET UP ROUTES

The last step in the setup is to import `RouterTestingModule`, which will spy on navigation calls and make their results available for checking in the tests. `RouterTestingModule` takes an optional router configuration.

Instead of using the application's router configuration, it's better to create a fake router configuration so you don't need to import all of the components into your test and configure them. You should make the test as simple as possible by avoiding pulling in dependencies you don't need. For this test, you'll need two routes: the default route, which loads the component under test, and the target route.

Before each test, you configure `TestBed` with modules and mocks needed for the tests themselves. You run this prior to each test to make sure the values the tests create are reset between each instance, so the tests won't interact with one another. To avoid repetition in each test, the router will load the initial page and then advance the Angular application to settle any asynchronous events.

When a navigation event occurs, it resolves asynchronously, and you have to account for this in the test. The example in listing 7.4 uses the Angular `fakeAsync` helper to handle settling asynchronous calls. When using `fakeAsync`, you have to resolve outstanding asynchronous calls manually with the `flush` method, and then update the fixture with `detectChanges`. When writing a full suite of unit tests, you can avoid repetition by creating a helper method to call `flush` and `detectChanges` together. This test defines a helper function called `advance` that makes the test code a bit easier to read.

Listing 7.4   Setup code to run before each test

```
let router: Router;
let location: Location;

let fixture;
let router: Router;
let location: Location;

beforeEach(() => {
  TestBed.configureTestingModule({
    imports: [RouterTestingModule.withRoutes([
      { path: '', component: NavigationMenu },
        { path: 'target/:id', component: SimpleComponent }
      ])],
    providers: [{
      provide: NavConfigService,
      useValue: { menu: [{ label: 'Home', path: '/target/fakeId' }] }
    }],
    declarations: [NavigationMenu, SimpleComponent, AppComponent],
  });
});

beforeEach(fakeAsync(() => {
  router = TestBed.get(Router);
  location = TestBed.get(Location);
  fixture = TestBed.createComponent(AppComponent);
  router.navigateByUrl('/');
  advance();
}));

function advance(): void {
  flush(); //
  fixture.detectChanges();
}
```

Configures RouterTestingModule with fake testing routes

Starts each test by navigating to the default route

A test helper for fakeAsync that resolves and detects asynchronous side effects

This component involves a lot of setup for testing, so let's do a quick review:

- The component under test generates navigation links.
- The setup creates two mock components to facilitate the test, one for the app fixture and one for the target.
- The `TestBed` configuration uses `RouterTestingModule` with fake route information. Before each test, the `RouterTestingModule` loads the default route and updates the test fixture.

Now you can write the first test, which is pretty simple. After you've set up the fixture, `NavigationMenu` should generate links based on its input. The test in the following listing gets a copy to a link, clicks it, and then checks with the `Location` service to see if the path updated to the expected target.

Listing 7.5 Testing generated `NavigationMenu` links

Gets reference to a generated link element   Sends the link a click event

```
it('Tries to route to a page', fakeAsync(() => {
  const menu = fixture.debugElement.query(By.css('a'));
  menu.triggerEventHandler('click', { button: 0 });
  advance();
  expect(location.path()).toEqual('/target/fakeId');
}));
```

Processes the navigation attempt   Tests that the router location
and updates the fixture   updated to the expected target

Why did it take so much setup for such a small test? Remember that the router is tightly integrated into the backbone of an Angular application. Because of that, it takes extra work to isolate it from its configuration and from any side effects caused by navigating to different routes.

> **NOTE** Although this test uses DOM elements and click events to activate it, you can use this same technique to test components that call `Router.navigate()`. The setup is the same, but in the test, you'd trigger whatever event would cause the navigation method to fire.

In the next section, we'll cover another case of testing interactions between a component and the router, but this time the component receives values from the router.

7.2.2 Testing router parameters

Deep linking is the ability to link to a view of specific content in a website or a web application. A URL for a deep link embeds information about the content (usually through an identifier), sorting and filtering parameters, and sometimes pagination parameters. For example, a car sales web app makes it possible to deeply link into a specific model and year range sorted by price. You can save and share that link, and although the content is generated dynamically, the parameters are always the same.

TESTING ACTIVATEDROUTE COMPONENTS

In an Angular application, you implement deep linking through route parameters. The router captures these parameters and makes them available to any component that needs them through the `ActivatedRoute` service. Whenever a user navigates to a different route, the `ActivatedRoute` service makes information about the route change available to components that use the service.

One of the most basic uses of ActivatedRoute is to pass along a unique identifier for further content lookup. For example, in the Contacts app, the ContactEdit component uses ActivatedRoute to get the identifier for a contact. When the user navigates to http://localhost/edit/1, the router compares the path to the router configuration and extracts the last part of the path to be used as the value of id. After that, the router publishes this value to ActivatedRoute, which sends the update to all subscribing components.

The test in this section will use a simplified example of how to test a component that depends on ActivatedRoute. Components can subscribe to the values that ActivatedRoute publishes either as an observable or as a *snapshot,* an object holding the last updated values for all parameters. Subscribing to an observable is a good choice for a long-lived component that needs to update regularly based on route changes. (See chapter 6, section 6.6.) Using the snapshot is simpler and is a good choice for when a component only needs to use route parameters when it's constructed. The testing setup for either is similar, but this example will use a snapshot.

The example in listing 7.6 is simplified for illustration purposes. Normally, a component for editing data would have a form and controls for modifying and saving the data, but here you're focusing on loading the Contact ID from the ActivatedRoute service and using it in the template.

> **Listing 7.6   Simplified ContactEdit component using ActivatedRoute**

Shortened template for illustration purposes

```
@Component({
    selector: 'contact-edit',
    template: '<div class="contact-id">{{ contactId }}</div>',
})
class ContactEditComponent implements OnInit {
private contactId: number;
constructor(private activatedRoute: ActivatedRoute) { }
ngOnInit () {
    this.contactId = this.activatedRoute.snapshot.params['id'];
}
}
```

Injects the ActivatedRoute service during construction

Assigns the Contact ID on initialization

SETTING UP THE TEST

Compared with testing components that cause navigation events to occur, setting up the test for ActivatedRoute is much simpler. This component only listens for data and then renders its template.

The only mock this test requires is a mock for `ActivatedRoute`. `TestBed` will provide the mock value to the component. Notice that in the following listing, the test, unlike the `NavigationMenu` component test, doesn't use `RouterTestingModule`. It isn't necessary for this test because no navigation is occurring.

> **Listing 7.7 Setting up the `ActivatedRoute` mock for component testing**

The mock is the snapshot that ActivatedRoute would generate as part of a route event.

```
let fixture;
const mockActivatedRoute = {
  snapshot: {
    params: {
      id: 'aMockId'
    }
  }
};

  beforeEach(() => {
    TestBed.configureTestingModule({
    providers: [
      { provide: ActivatedRoute, useValue: mockActivatedRoute}
    ],
    declarations: [ContactEditComponent],
  });
});

beforeEach(async(() => {
  fixture = TestBed.createComponent(ContactEditComponent);
  fixture.detectChanges();

}));
```

Injects the mock ActivatedRoute as the value for ActivatedRoute

TestBed asynchronously initializes the TestBed fixture with the component under test.

TESTING THE COMPONENT

When the router resolves a navigation event, `ActivatedRoute` produces a snapshot of the route data associated with the component when the component is instantiated. You can avoid incorporating the `RouterTestingModule` into this type of test by mocking the router snapshot that `ActivatedRoute` normally supplies. Providing your own test snapshot avoids the extra setup work that would be required to have the router generate the snapshot automatically. As long as you know what the snapshot looks like, you can use a mock instead, which simplifies the test.

As shown in listing 7.8, the test involves initializing the component and checking the result. This is another asynchronous test. When the component's ngOnInit method is activated, the `TestBed` returns the mock snapshot for `ActivatedRoute`. This process happens asynchronously, and this test is easier to read using the Angular `async` test helper instead of the `fakeAsync` helper. The test checks the value of the Contact ID after it's rendered in the form to ensure that it's the value coming from the `ActivatedRoute` service.

Listing 7.8   Testing the `ContactEdit` component loading route parameters

The test is wrapped in the async helper because the
test is waiting for the component to initialize.

A reference to the DOM node where the
Contact ID should be rendered

```
it('Tries to route to a page', async(() => {
  let testEl = fixture.debugElement.query(By.css('div'));
  expect(testEl.nativeElement.textContent).toEqual('aMockId');
}));
```

Verifies the template is rendered with
the Contact ID from ActivatedRoute

Because this component uses the `ActivatedRoute` snapshot, setting up the test is easy. If your component uses properties of `ActivatedRoute` that emit observables, then your mock would be an observable emitting the mocked properties, as shown in the following listing.

Listing 7.9   Using a mock observable for `ActivatedRoute`

Creates an observable that will be used
for testing ActivatedRoute params

```
const paramsMock = Observable.create((observer) => {
  observer.next({
    id: 'aMockId'
  });
  observer.complete();
});

beforeEach(() => {                                    Uses the observable as the params
  TestBed.configureTestingModule({                    method for the injected mock service
    providers: [
      { provide: ActivatedRoute, useValue: { params: paramsMock }}
    ],
    declarations: [ContactEditComponent],
  });
});
```

USING A MOCK OBSERVABLE

Whether you use a route snapshot or create an observable for your mock `Activated-Route`, testing a component that reads values from `ActivatedRoute` is straightforward.

We've covered all you need to know about testing routes from the point of view of a component. The rest of this chapter will look at testing special features of routes that are especially useful in an enterprise single-page application—route guards and resolved data services.

7.3 *Testing advanced routes*

The router can perform functions that enable Angular applications to implement enterprise application-level features. With the router, it's easy to route unauthenticated users to a login page, pre-fetch data before loading components, and lazy-load other modules to help reduce application start time. As discussed earlier, the router configuration can define route guards that the router calls before navigation events. Another feature of the router is pre-loading, or *resolving*, data before activating components.

7.3.1 *Route guards*

Enterprise web applications, unlike other web applications, have user authentication, user roles, privileges, and other means of allowing users to access features, or keeping them from doing so. The Angular router makes it easy to add application logic to make sure users can only access the features they're allowed to access. The mechanism for this system is called a route guard. Route guards are specialized services that the router runs prior to a router navigation event. Route guards are simple in design—if a route guard method returns `true`, the navigation attempt can continue. Otherwise, the navigation attempt fails.

Why would you want to use a route guard instead of adding these functions directly to a component? Because route guards exist outside of your component, they let you separate the access or permissions functions from the core functionality of the component. Also, if you define route-guard services separately from components, you can reuse the validation logic by configuring your route configuration rather than having to add component logic.

You can divide route guards into two main categories: those that check before a user tries to leave a current route, and those that check before a user can load a new route. We'll cover a third type of route guard, called a `resolver` guard, in the next section.

In listing 7.10, you'll see a `CanActivate` route guard. To use this route guard, a route configuration entry specifies a new property called `canActivate`, which takes an array of route guards. The system under test in this example is `AuthenticationGuard`, a route guard that depends on the `UserAuthentication` service to see if a theoretical user is allowed to access the route. If not, the navigation attempt fails.

Listing 7.10   `AuthenticationGuard` service

The route guard implementing the CanActivate
interface, which is the focus of the test

```
@Injectable()
class AuthenticationGuard implements CanActivate {
  constructor(private userAuth: UserAuthentication) {}
  canActivate(): Promise<boolean> {
    return new Promise((resolve) =>
      resolve(this.userAuth.getAuthenticated())
    );
  }
}

@Injectable()
class UserAuthentication {
  private isUserAuthenticated: boolean = false;
  authenticateUser() {
    this.isUserAuthenticated = true;
  }
  getAuthenticated() {
    return this.isUserAuthenticated;
  }
}
```

A fake service used to demonstrate separating
the responsibility of the route guard from the
user authentication service

We've chosen to show `UserAuthentication` as a separate service. This makes the example a little more complicated, but it's good to reinforce the idea that you should separate a service that handles user authentication—which in real life would make network calls and have other complexities—from the route guard service itself. Smaller services are easier to test, and with this level of separation, it's easy to mock the dependencies for the system under test.

Setting up the test is similar to the setup for the `NavigationMenu` test. This test requires a component for initializing the application fixture and a simple component to act as the target for the navigation attempt. (Refer to listing 7.3 for an example of this type of test component.) What's new in the test setup in listing 7.11? First, notice that this test again uses `RouterTestingModule` with a configuration specific to testing `AuthenticationGuard`. As mentioned before, it's better to create a test router configuration, because it's less complicated and more reliable than trying to use the application's router configuration. The test configuration specifies the `canActivate` property, which activates the code that's the focus of this test.

Listing 7.11   Setting up the `AuthenticationGuard` test

```
beforeEach(() => {
  TestBed.configureTestingModule({
    imports: [RouterTestingModule.withRoutes([
      { path: '', component: AppComponent },
      {
        path: 'protected',
```

Uses RouterTestingModule

```
        component: TargetComponent,
        canActivate: [AuthenticationGuard],
      }
    ])],
  providers: [AuthenticationGuard, UserAuthentication],
  declarations: [TargetComponent, AppComponent],
});

router = TestBed.get(Router);
location = TestBed.get(Location);
userAuthService = TestBed.get(UserAuthentication);
});

beforeEach(fakeAsync(() => {
  fixture = TestBed.createComponent(AppComponent);
  router.initialNavigation();
}));
```

Specifies the route guard for the test

Allows the authentication check to pass

AuthenticationGuard will check the UserAuthentication service when the route navigation attempt occurs, so you capture a reference to the service to control it during the test. The testing setup is finished, so what remains are two tests, shown in listing 7.12. Both will try to navigate to the protected route. The first will try without authenticating, and in the second you'll manually authenticate the user. After the navigation attempt, the tests check the Location service for the expected result.

> **Listing 7.12** AuthenticationGuard **tests**

```
it('tries to route to a page without authentication', fakeAsync(() => {
  router.navigate(['protected']);
  flush();
  expect(location.path()).toEqual('/');
}));
```

Tries to navigate to the protected route before authentication

```
it('tries to route to a page after authentication', fakeAsync(() => {
  userAuthService.authenticateUser();
  router.navigate(['protected']);
  flush();
  expect(location.path()).toEqual('/protected');
}));
```

Authenticates first and tries again. This time it works.

These tests make sure the route guards behave correctly under different application scenarios. You could use other approaches for testing route guards. For example, you could spy on the canActivate method to make sure it's called as expected and is returning the correct response. Both methods work, so use whichever you prefer.

7.3.2 *Resolving data before loading a route*

Sometimes you'll want to load data before activating a component. The resolver route guard specifies an object of key-value pairs, where the keys are the names of data properties and the values are route guard services that fetch the data. Once all services have resolved, the router makes the data available to components through the

ActivatedRoute service on the data property. In the following listing, you can see an example where user preferences and contacts data is loaded prior to the route change via UserPreferencesResolver and ContactsResolver respectively.

Listing 7.13   Configured `resolver` route guard

```
{
  path: 'contacts',
  component: TargetComponent,
  resolve: {
    userPreferences: UserPreferencesResolver,
    contacts: ContactsResolver
  }
}
```

Testing a resolver route guard uses the techniques we already covered in section 7.3, so we won't be providing a separate example. To test these resolvers, follow the same process as the canActivate route guard. The resolvers themselves usually interact with some other data service, for which you'll want to provide mock services. Then in the unit test, you'll inject the ActivatedRoute service and check that the values available on ActivatedRoute.snapshot.data match your expected values.

Summary

- The Angular router is like the backbone of your application. It takes a URL and figures out which components to load based on the URL segments.
- Angular components can navigate to other parts of an application by including the RouterLink directive. When testing navigation components, you use the Location service to verify the navigation path is correct.
- Angular components also can receive route information from the ActivatedRoute service. You saw an example of the test configuration required to test a component that depends on ActivatedRoute values.
- Whenever any route change occurs, the router can check if the route change is allowed to happen. Route guards are methods that either let the route change continue or stop it from happening.
- The RouterTestingModule helps you to write tests for your components that interact with the router by providing test router configurations and inspecting the calls to the router itself.

part 2

End-to-end testing

Unit tests are great: they run quickly and let you exercise the functionality of your components. But at the end of the day, you still need to be sure that your entire application works as expected. In this part of the book, we cover writing tests that control a browser using Protractor, Angular's end-to-end (E2E) testing framework. These tests can be hard to write and debug, but having a few E2E tests is a good way to catch issues that might not show up in unit tests.

Chapter 8 is an introduction to Protractor. It covers how Protractor works, writing a basic test, and making your tests easier to maintain with page objects.

Because Protractor tests can interact with your application only through a browser, these tests fail, usually with a *timeout error*, in which the test times out while waiting for some particular HTML to show up in the page. Chapter 9 explores in depth what these errors mean. In the process, it explains how Angular's change-detection system works and how Protractor interacts with it.

Finally, chapter 10 is a grab bag of advanced Protractor testing techniques that can make your life easier. This includes customizing Protractor with plugins, different ways to debug failing tests, and writing tests that compare pages using screenshots.

Getting started with Protractor

This chapter covers

- Understanding how Protractor works
- Writing your first Protractor test
- Interacting with elements
- Interacting with a list of elements
- Organizing tests with page objects

In the first part of the book, you saw how to create unit tests that verify your application's features work as expected in isolation. Having a good suite of unit tests isn't enough to make sure your application will do what it's supposed to. Because unit tests validate the Contacts app in isolation, they can't confirm that external services or dependencies work together with the application.

You could test both the workflow and external dependencies with a set of tests that interact with the Contacts app like a real-world user. You could manually test the application, but it's better to have automated tests. Tests that interact with the application like a real-world user are *end-to-end tests*. These tests launch a browser, navigate to the Contacts app and interact with. This kind of test would be expensive to run, so instead of exhaustively testing every possible real-world user scenario, we'll pick a set of tests that cover the most important scenarios.

The testing pyramid we talked about toward the end of chapter 1 (figure 1.2) showed that 70% of tests should be unit tests, 20% integration tests, and 10% end-to-end tests. With such a high percentage, your unit tests shoulder a lot of the testing burden. You should look at which scenarios your unit tests have already covered before picking which tests you need to perform here.

Because integration tests involve validating external dependencies, we group them together with end-to-end tests. Integration tests use mock versions of external dependencies (an in-memory database, for example), and end-to-end tests use the real version, but they're equivalent for our purposes.

You can write end-to-end tests two ways: with the Selenium WebDriver library or Angular's Protractor test framework. If you've previously written a Selenium WebDriver test, you might have found that your tests became a nested chain of promises to synchronize browser commands. In contrast, Protractor wraps the Selenium WebDriver APIs to make asynchronous commands appear synchronous. Because of this wrapping, Protractor exposes the same set of APIs as Selenium WebDriver, making it interchangeable. When writing end-to-end tests for Angular, it's better to use Protractor than Selenium WebDriver.

Before you can create a Protractor test suite, we'll need to cover the basics. This chapter will demonstrate how Protractor works and how to write your first Protractor test. You'll create a simple test that interacts with web elements on the screen. We'll also show you how to organize test code with page objects. When refactoring your test suite, using page objects helps reduce code duplication and creates maintainable code.

If you're already familiar with Protractor, feel free to skip to chapter 9, where we talk about timeouts, and chapter 10, where we'll cover advanced Protractor topics.

8.1   How Protractor works

Let's look at the big picture of how Protractor helps you write your browser tests. Protractor tests run on Node.js and send commands to a Selenium Server. The Selenium Server controls the browser via WebDriver commands and JavaScript functions (figure 8.1).

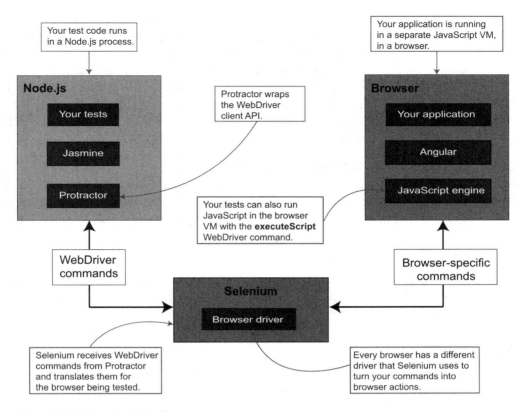

Figure 8.1   Protractor block diagram

Protractor is a Node.js program. After Protractor launches, it hands the execution of your tests over to Jasmine (or Mocha, or whichever test framework you prefer). Protractor wraps the Selenium WebDriver client and adds features for testing Angular applications. It then communicates to the browser via a Selenium Server. The Selenium Server controls the browser using vendor-specific browser drivers—for Firefox, Chrome, and so on. After the browser driver creates a session, Protractor loads the Angular application under test.

NOTE Selenium is an open source project (https://github.com/seleniumHQ) that automates browser testing. The Selenium Standalone Server handles launching browsers and sending commands to the browser drivers using the WebDriver protocol. The WebDriver protocol is a W3C specification defined at https://www.w3.org/TR/webdriver. Browser vendors maintain the driver for their browser.

The important thing to take away from all of this is that browser tests run in a browser that's independent of your test. Your tests are running in a Node.js process, and the Angular application is running in a browser. Because these are two separate processes, you need to provide some sort of synchronization between the Angular application running in the browser and the Protractor test. Protractor does this by inserting a JavaScript function that runs in the browser and waits for Angular to be stable. In this case, stable means that an event or background task isn't pending that might cause a change to your application's DOM.

8.2   *Writing your first Protractor test*

In this section, you'll create the files you need to run a simple Protractor test in Type-Script. For your first Protractor test, we'll guide you through some of the features in the Contacts app. When you run your test, a Chrome browser will launch, navigate to the application's default page, and verify the URL address. You can find the code for this chapter at http://mng.bz/Fp9u.

> **TIP** You can find Protractor documentation at http://protractortest.org. Another good resource is the Protractor cookbook at https://github.com/angular/protractor-cookbook.

8.2.1   *File structure*

Let's take a look at the files and folder structure from the chapter 8 GitHub repository. These are the bare minimum files you need to run a Protractor test with TypeScript:

```
.
├── e2e/
│   ├── first-test.e2e-spec.ts
│   └── tsconfig.json
├── package.json
└── protractor-first-test.conf.js
```

> **NOTE** If you're using the Angular CLI to create a new Angular project, it generates the scaffold files you need to create your first Protractor test. The chapter 8 GitHub repository folder structure mimics these files.

PACKAGE.JSON

The first file you need to create is package.json, shown in listing 8.1. devDependencies specifies that your project uses type definitions that the @types node modules specify. These are TypeScript typings for node modules written in JavaScript. In addition to type definitions, you also depend on typescript, protractor, and ts-node.

> **INFO** Protractor is written in TypeScript as of Protractor version 4+, and no additional type definitions are required. Prior to Protractor version 4, you would find the type definitions at @types/angular-protractor.

The scripts portion of package.json defines a pree2e and an e2e script, as shown in the following listing. The pree2e script launches the webdriver-manager node module to download binaries required to control a web browser. When running the e2e script to launch Protractor, the pree2e script automatically runs first.

Listing 8.1 Node package configuration—package.json

```
{
  "name": "protractor-tests",
  "scripts": {
    "pree2e": "webdriver-manager update --gecko false
    --standalone false",
    "e2e": "protractor"
  },
  "devDependencies": {
    "@types/jasmine": "^2.53.43",
    "@types/jasminewd2": "^2.0.1",
    "@types/selenium-webdriver": "^3.0.0",
    "typescript": "^2.2.1",
    "protractor": "^5.1.1",
    "ts-node": "^2.1.0"
  }
}
```

> Automatically downloads support files when running the "e2e" script

> Runs the Protractor node module when provided with a Protractor configuration file

TYPESCRIPT CONFIGURATION FILE

The next file you need is the TypeScript configuration file, tsconfig.json, in the e2e folder. The configuration file shown in listing 8.2 tells the TypeScript compiler (tsc command) which TypeScript files to transpile and which type definitions to use. Also, this file tells the transpiler to emit ES6 (ECMA2015) JavaScript, and that the JavaScript output files should be written to dist/out-tsc-e2e.

Listing 8.2 TypeScript compiler configuration—e2e/tsconfig.json

```
{
  "compileOnSave": false,
  "compilerOptions": {
    "declarations": false,
    "emitDecoratorMetadata": true,
    "experimentalDecorators"
    "lib": [ "es2016" ],
    "module": "commonjs",
    "moduleResolution": "node",
    "outDir": "../dist/out-tsc-e2e",
    "sourceMap": true,
    "target": "es6",
    "typeRoots": [
      "../node_modules/@types"
    ]
  }
}
```

> When transpiling TypeScript to JavaScript, write the files to a folder that git will ignore.

> Includes all type definitions from @types

PROTRACTOR CONFIGURATION FILE

Now that you have the package dependencies and TypeScript support files, you need to create the Protractor configuration, protractor-first-test.conf.js, shown in listing 8.3. The Protractor configuration file tells Protractor how to launch your test. You can break it down into several parts: how to launch the browser, the path of the test files, the test framework, and plugins.

Listing 8.3   Protractor configuration file—protractor-first-test.conf.js

```
exports.config = {
  capabilities: {                          Specifies to launch the Chrome browser
    browserName: 'chrome'                   directly with ChromeDriver
  },
  directConnect: true,
  baseUrl: 'https://testing-angular-applications.github.io',
  framework: 'jasmine',
  specs: [
    './e2e/first-test.e2e-spec.ts'          Specifies the TypeScript test files
  ],                                         Protractor will launch via ts-node
  onPrepare: () => {
    require('ts-node').register({
      project: 'e2e'
    });
  }
}
```

In this listing, `directConnect` and `capabilities` define how to launch and interact with the browser. In `capabilities`, you specify that you want a Chrome browser. If you don't include any capabilities, Protractor launches Chrome by default. You'll launch the Chrome browser with `directConnect` using the `chromedriver` binary that web-driver-manager downloads.

A few lines further down in protractor-first-test.conf.js are `framework` and `specs`. You specify that you'd like to use Jasmine as the test framework. If you didn't specify the `framework`, Protractor would run the test with Jasmine by default. Because you've used the Jasmine test runner to write unit tests in previous chapters, we also recommend you use Jasmine for Protractor tests. The test runner will run e2e/first-test.e2e-spec.ts listed in the `specs` array.

> **NOTE** Protractor allows other test frameworks, including Mocha and Cucumber. It provides limited support for these frameworks, and they're beyond the scope of this book. If you'd like to try out other frameworks, see the framework documentation at http://mng.bz/d64d.

The last section of test-8-1.conf.js is an `onPrepare` function. The `onPrepare` function uses the `ts-node` node module, which lets the Protractor test run the TypeScript files without compilation. You register the e2e directory, which has your tests, with `ts-node`.

PROTRACTOR TEST FILE

The last file you need is the test specification, e2e/first-test.e2e-spec.ts, shown in listing 8.4. Because you use the Jasmine framework, the spec file looks similar to the unit tests you've seen in previous chapters. The first line imports the `browser` from Protractor and uses it to navigate to the Contacts app and validate that the current URL is the `browser.baseUrl`, which is https://testing-angular-applications.github.io.

Listing 8.4 Test specification—e2e/first-test.e2e-spec.ts

```
import { browser } from 'protractor';

describe('your first protractor test', () => {
  it('should load a page and verify the url', () => {
    browser.get('/#/');
    expect(browser.getCurrentUrl())
        .toEqual(browser.baseUrl + '/#/');
  });
});
```

Now that you have the bare minimum files, you can install the node module dependencies and run your first Protractor test.

8.3 *Installing and running*

You start by installing the node modules defined in package.json with `npm install`. After the node modules are downloaded, you can launch Protractor using the scripts defined in package.json. You can launch the Protractor test with the command `npm run e2e protractor-first-test.conf.js`. At the beginning of the test, the `pree2e` script downloads the `chromedriver` binary using `webdriver-manager`. After the files are downloaded, Protractor launches the test using the Protractor configuration file protractor-first-test.conf.js.

Protractor starts the new WebDriver instance according to the configuration file. The new WebDriver instance launches a Chrome browser window using the `chromedriver` binary. The console output should look similar to the following listing.

Listing 8.5 Running Protractor with the e2e script

Before launching the e2e test, automatically launches the pree2e task

Downloads the chromedriver binary to the node module webdriver-manager/selenium folder

```
npm run e2e protractor-first-test.conf.js

> chapter-8-code@0.0.0 pree2e /path/to/protractor-first-test
> webdriver-manager update --gecko false --standalone false

[11:48:53] I/file_manager - creating folder /path/to/selenium
[11:48:54] I/downloader - curl -o /path/to/selenium/chromedriver_2.28.zip
      https://chromedriver.storage.googleapis.com/2.28/chromedriver_mac64.zip
[11:48:54] I/update - chromedriver: unzipping chromedriver_2.28.zip /path/to/
      selenium/chromedriver_2.28.zip
```

```
[11:29:38] I/update - chromedriver: unzipping chromedriver_2.28.zip
[11:29:38] I/update - chromedriver: setting permissions to 0755 for /path/to/
    selenium/chromedriver_2.28
[11:29:38] I/update - chromedriver: chromedriver_2.28 up to date

> chapter-8-starter@0.0.0 e2e /path/to/protractor-first-test
> protractor "protractor-first-test.conf.js"

[11:29:39] I/launcher - Running 1 instances of WebDriver
[11:29:39] I/direct - Using ChromeDriver directly...
Started
.

1 spec, 0 failures
Finished in 2.484 seconds
```

The period shows that the first test passes.

The e2e task that you specified in package.json

Launches the Protractor test with directConnect to run Chrome

> **NOTE** You can launch Protractor in a couple of ways. In the first method, if you installed Protractor as a global install, you can run `protractor test-8-1.conf.js`. The second method is to launch Protractor by referencing the node_module folder. From the root directory of chapter 8's sample code, you could run `./node_modules/.bin/protractor protractor-first-test.conf.js`, or, for Windows machines, `node node_modules/.bin/protractor protractor-first-test.conf.js`. The second method isn't recommended and is the equivalent to running the e2e script, which we covered in the package.json file.

During the test, you'll see the Chrome browser launch and close quickly. In this short time, Protractor runs the Jasmine test, launches the Chrome browser, navigates to the Contacts app, validates the URL, and closes the browser window.

Now that you've run your first Protractor test, you'll write some new tests to expand your test suite. To add these tests, you'll first need to learn some additional Protractor APIs to handle HTML web element interaction.

8.4   *Interacting with elements*

In the last section, you learned about the bare minimum files you needed to write your first Protractor test. In this section, we'll introduce two new Protractor APIs: `element` and `by`. These APIs help you interact with the Contacts app. By the end of this section, you'll create several test scenarios around creating a new contact.

The related files from the GitHub repository for the next section are e2e/add-contact .e2e-spec.ts, e2e/add-second-contact.e2e-spec.ts, and protractor-add-contact.conf.js.

In protractor-add-contact.conf.js, you need to copy over most of the test configurations from protractor-first-test.conf.js. You also need to change the Protractor configuration `specs` array from including a single file to using file globbing, as shown in listing 8.6. Globbing match selects a set of files based on a file path pattern and wildcard characters. This will allow you to test both e2e/add-contact.e2e-spec.ts and e2e/add-second -contact.e2e-spec.ts without having to specify the exact files you're using.

Listing 8.6   Protractor configuration file with file globbing

```
exports.config = {
  capabilities: {
    browserName: 'chrome'
  },
  directConnect: true,
  baseUrl: 'https://testing-angular-applications.github.io',
  framework: 'jasmine',
  specs: [
    './e2e/add-*contact.e2e-spec.ts'
  ],
  onPrepare: () => {
    require('ts-node').register({
      project: 'e2e'
    });
  }
}
```

Adds specs by file globbing

Because you're using the file globbing option, your Protractor test will run all tests that are in the e2e directory starting with "add-" and match the file suffix of "contact.e2e-spec.ts".

8.4.1   *Test scenario: creating a new contact*

Usually it's easy to figure out the happy path when coming up with end-to-end tests. To expand on the definition we provided in chapter 6, you also can look at the happy path as being the workflow a user follows to successfully complete a set of tasks. In this case, figure 8.2 shows the happy path—the user interacts with the Contacts app to create a new contact. The user clicks the + button, fills out the required fields, and clicks the Create button.

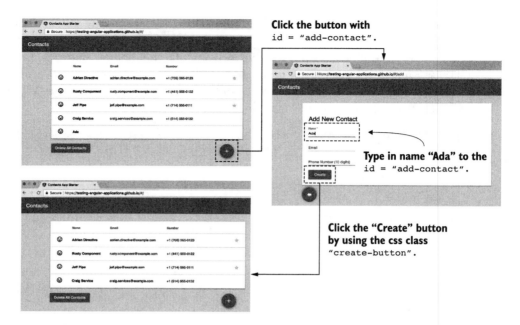

Figure 8.2   Create new contact workflow

To test this workflow, it's helpful to look at the HTML to identify the elements you need to interact with. The test case will first click the + symbol. In the HTML snippet below, you see the + symbol is generated by the `mat-icon class "add-fab-icon"`. You could try to click the icon, or you could find the web element by either the button or the `<a>` tag. For this example, you'll use the `<a>` tag. Because the web page could have several `<a>` tags, you also need to use the `id="add-contact"` to find the link, as shown in the following snippet:

```
<a *ngIf="!isLoading && !deletingContact" id="add-contact" routerLink="/add"
      mat-fab class="add-fab">
  <button mat-fab class="add-fab">
    <mat-icon class="add-fab-icon"
              mdTooltip="Add new contact">
      add
    </mat-icon>
  </button>
</a>
```

TIP   When writing Protractor tests, you can use Chrome's developer console to see the HTML for the application. You access the Chrome developer console using the keyboard shortcut Cmd+Opt+I on a Mac and Ctrl+Shift+I in Windows or Linux.

You can find and click on the `<a>` tag web element using two Protractor APIs: `by` and `element`. The `by` API has methods to find web elements using an identifier. The `element` API consumes the object generated by the `by` API and returns a Protractor `ElementFinder` object that represents the web element. After you call the click method on the web element, the Contacts app will navigate to a new page that contains the new contact.

In listing 8.7, your test will fill out the form using the `id` attribute of the input tag. Similar to the previous step, you can find the HTML input tag using the `id` attribute equal to `contact-name`. After finding the element, the test fills out the form with the name Ada using the `sendKeys` method. Because this is the first time you're finding a web element, you should verify that its text matches the expected value. You'll need to get the value attribute from the input field and compare it to the text that the test just entered. After you assert that the text is Ada, you'll find the Create button by using the css class `create-button` so you can add a new contact. After your test has clicked the Create button, it will check that the route navigated back to the `browser.baseUrl`.

Listing 8.7 Test specification to create a new contact—e2e/add-contact.e2e-spec.ts

```
import { browser, by, element } from 'protractor';

describe(adding a new contact with only a name', () => {
  beforeAll(() => {
    browser.get('/#/');
  });

  it('should find the add contact button', () => {
    element(by.id('add-contact')).click();
    expect(browser.getCurrentUrl())
        .toEqual(browser.baseUrl + '/#/add');
  });

  it('should write a name', () => {
    let contactName = element(by.id('contact-name'));
    contactName.sendKeys('Ada');
    expect(contactName.getAttribute('value'))
        .toEqual('Ada');
  });

  it('should click the create button', () => {
    element(by.css('.create-button')).click();
    expect(browser.getCurrentUrl())
        .toEqual(browser.baseUrl + '/#/');
  });
});
```

> Finds the name input field with the 'contact-name' id attribute

> Finds the Create button with the 'create-button' css class

When you filled out the name input field on the contact form, you might have noticed that the form also populated an email and phone number fields. Another useful test scenario would be to fill out the form completely. In the e2e/add-second-contact.e2e-spec.ts file shown in the following listing, you move some of these interactions into the `beforeAll` step because the previous test has already tested loading up the main page and filling out the name field.

Listing 8.8   Test to create another contact—e2e/add-second-contact.e2e-spec.ts

```
import { browser, by, element } from 'protractor';

describe('adding a new contact with name, email,' +
    'and phone number', () => {
  beforeAll(() => {
    browser.get('/#/');
    element(by.id('add-contact')).click();
    element(by.id('contact-name')).sendKeys('Grace');
  });

  it('should type in an email address', () => {
    let email = element(by.id('contact-email'));
    email.sendKeys('grace@hopper.com');
    expect(email.getAttribute('value'))
        .toEqual('grace@hopper.com');
  });

  it('should type in a phone number', () => {
    let tel = element(by.css('input[type="tel"]'));
    tel.sendKeys('1234567890');
    expect(tel.getAttribute('value'))
        .toEqual('1234567890');
  });

  it('should click the create button', () => {
    element(by.css('.create-button')).click();
    expect(browser.getCurrentUrl())
        .toEqual(browser.baseUrl + '/#/');
  });
});
```

When an action is called, Protractor locates the web element on the screen and sends the string to the input field.

Locates the web element by using the css class

When declaring the element, WebDriver doesn't search the browser for the web element.

Why use Protractor APIs?

You might ask yourself, if Protractor wraps the Selenium WebDriver APIs, shouldn't I just use the underlying library? You might have noticed that the returned `element` object is of type `ElementFinder`. The `ElementFinder` object is a Protractor defined object. With the Protractor API, you'll see the following:

```
import {by, element, ElementFinder} from 'protractor';
let email: ElementFinder = element(by.id('contact-email'));
```

Protractor exposes some of the Selenium WebDriver APIs via `browser.driver`. You could access the WebElement by the following code snippet:

```
import {By, WebElement} from 'selenium-webdriver';
let email: WebElement;
email = browser.driver.findElement(By.id('contact-email'));
```

> **(continued)**
>
> If you can find web elements with both Protractor and Selenium WebDriver, why should you use the Protractor APIs to find them? When you use the Selenium WebDriver APIs, Selenium will try to locate that object on the browser session when declared. Protractor, on the other hand, will let you define your locators as reusable variables. When you finally decide to interact with a Protractor `element`, Protractor will use the Selenium WebDriver `findElement` method to locate the web element and then interact with it.

Finally, you can run the Protractor test using the command `npm run e2e protractor-add-contact.conf.js`. When running the `npm` command, you can see Protractor launching browsers and creating the contacts you specified in this section.

8.4.2 Test scenario: workflows that don't create a new contact

In the not-so-happy path, a user could enter incorrect data. For example, they might forget to enter a required field, enter a malformed telephone number, or enter an invalid email address.

We'll guide you through test scenarios using the Contacts app that fail because of invalid data. For example, if you try to create a new contact with an invalid email, the result is a modal alert window (figure 8.3).

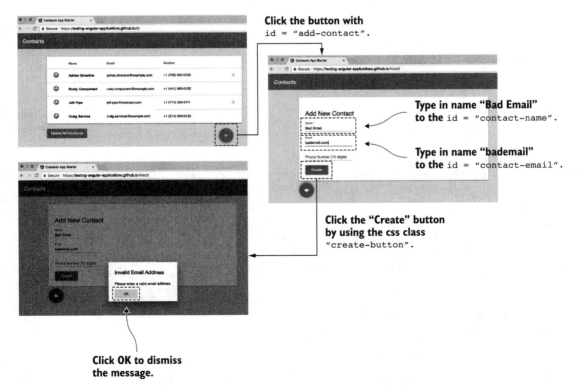

Figure 8.3   Workflow that doesn't create a new user

How do you translate this scenario into a test case? In the GitHub repository, e2e/invalid-contact.e2e-spec.ts and protractor-invalid-contact.conf.js cover this test scenario to create a new contact with invalid information.

In listing 8.9, the test enters a valid name and an invalid email address, baduser.com. After the test clicks the Create button, it should check if the modal alert window is visible and dismiss the message. After dismissing the modal alert message, it's a good idea to verify that the modal alert did disappear. To test this, you can use another Protractor API called ExpectedConditions. The ExpectedConditions API combined with the browser.wait method allows the test to wait for some condition to occur on the web application within a set period of time. In this example, you're waiting for the web element to not be present within five seconds. Finally, because the test should fail to create a new contact, the test also should check to see if the Contacts app route URL is still on the /#/add route.

> **Listing 8.9   Test that doesn't create a new contact—e2e/invalid-contact.e2e-spec.ts**

```
import { browser, by, element, ExpectedConditions as EC } from 'protractor';

describe('adding a new contact with an invalid email', () => {
  beforeEach(() => {
    browser.get('/#/add');
    element(by.id('contact-name')).sendKeys('Bad Email');
  });

  it('shouldn't create a new contact with baduser.com', () => {
    let email = element(by.id('contact-email'));
    email.sendKeys('baduser.com');
    element(by.buttonText('Create')).click();

    let invalidEmailModal = element(by.tagName(
        'app-invalid-email-modal'));
    expect(invalidEmailModal.isPresent()).toBe(true);          Checks to see that
                                                               the modal is present

    let modalButton = invalidEmailModal.element(
        by.tagName('button'));
    modalButton.click();                                       Finds the button from
                                                               the modal web element

    browser.wait(EC.not(
        EC.presenceOf(invalidEmailModal)), 5000);
    expect(invalidEmailModal.isPresent()).toBe(false);
    expect(browser.getCurrentUrl()).toEqual(
        browser.baseUrl + '/#/add');
  });                                                          Checks to see that the
});                                                            modal is no longer present
```

Waits five seconds for the invalid email
modal to disappear

If you try other email inputs, you might also find that you can still create an account if the email field is @bademail.com. This is obviously incorrect, so you might want to add a new feature to your web app to not accept an email with this specific malformed email address.

Now that you have one not-so-happy test scenario, you could try other test scenarios. You could implement more combinations of text inputs, but this defeats the purpose of having a strong suite of unit tests. You should have covered this email validation feature with a set of text input unit tests.

So far, you've written several Protractor tests that have found web elements by `buttonText`, `id`, and `css`. Unfortunately, you can't find all web elements using these three locators. In the next section, we'll cover other ways to identify web elements.

8.5 *by and element methods*

In the previous section, we showed a subset of the different ways to use locators to identify web elements. Other locators are available. Table 8.1 lists the common locator methods and where to use them.

Table 8.1 Locating web elements with the `by` API

Locator	Usage
`by.css`	Finding a web element by css
	HTML:
	`<input class="contact-email"`
	`        id="contact-email" type="email">`
	Protractor:
	`let e1 = element(by.css('.contact-email'));`
	`let e2 = element(by.css('#contact-email'));`
	`let e3 = element(by.css('input[type="email"]'));`
`by.id`	Finding a web element by id
	HTML:
	`<input class="contact-email"`
	`        id="contact-email" type="email">`
	Protractor:
	`let email = element(by.id('contact-email'));`
`by.buttonText`	Finding a button with the matching text
`by.partialButtonText`	HTML:
	`<button>Submit Contact</button>`
	Protractor:
	`let fullMatch = element(by.buttonText(`
	`    'Submit Contact'));`
	`let partialMatch = element(by.`
	`    partialButtonText('Submit'));`

Table 8.1   Locating web elements with the by API *(continued)*

Locator	Usage

`by.linkText`
`by.partialLinkText`
	Finding a link by matching text
	
	HTML:
	
	`<a href="/add">Add contact</a>`
	
	Protractor:
	
	`let fullMatch = element(by.linkText(`
	`    'Add contact'));`
	
	`let partialMatch = element(by.`
	`    partialLinkText('contact'));`

`by.tagName`	Finding a web element by tag name
	
	HTML:
	
	`<app-contact-detail>...</app-contact-detail>`
	
	Protractor:
	
	`let tag = element(by.tagName(`
	`    'app-contact-detail'));`

`by.xpath`	Finding a web element by xpath. Using xpath as a locator strategy can create brittle tests requiring high maintenance. We recommend not using xpath as a locator strategy.
	
	HTML:
	
	`<ul><li><a>Foobar</a></li></ul>`
	
	Protractor:
	
	`let xpath = element(by.xpath('//ul/li/a'));`

`by.binding`	Finding a web element by binding for objects in AngularJS. Currently, this isn't implemented for Angular.
	
	HTML:
	
	`<span ng-bind="contact.name"></span>`
	
	Protractor:
	
	`let binding = element(by.binding(`
	`    'contact.name'));`

`by.model`	Finding a web element by model in AngularJS. Currently, this isn't implemented for Angular.
	
	HTML:
	
	`<input ng-model="contact.name">`
	
	Protractor:
	
	`let model = element(by.model(`
	`    'contact.name'));`

Protractor's by API isn't the same as Selenium WebDriver's by API

You should remember that Protractor's by and Selenium WebDriver's by are different. This difference is important because Protractor exposes some of the Selenium Web-Driver APIs, and remembering the difference hopefully will help you during debugging. The following code snippet shows how to use the Protractor by API:

```
import { browser, by, element } from 'protractor';
element(by.buttonText('Create'));
```

Because you're using the Protractor APIs here, you should use its by API. When you use Selenium WebDriver APIs that are exposed through Protractor to find a web element, you should consistently also use Selenium WebDriver's by locator. The following code snippet shows how to use the Selenium WebDriver by API:

```
import { browser } from 'protractor';
import { By as WebdriverBy } from 'selenium-webdriver';
browser.driver.findElement(WebdriverBy.css('.contact-email'));
```

The following code snippet is slightly different from previous examples. It doesn't work, because you're passing the Selenium WebDriver findElement method a Protractor by finder:

```
import { browser, by } from 'protractor';
browser.driver.findElement(by.buttonText('Create'));
```

So far, we've covered sendKeys, click, and getAttribute, but you can interact with web elements in other ways. Table 8.2 covers the commonly used element methods. All of these methods return a WebDriver promise. Protractor's test framework takes those WebDriver promises and makes the browser interactions appear synchronous. Synchronizing these asynchronous WebDriver calls cuts some of the complexity that such WebDriver promises introduce.

Table 8.2 Interacting with web elements with the element API

Element method	Usage

getWebElement	Occasionally, you'll need to access Selenium WebDriver WebElement's APIs, which aren't available from Protractor's element object. One example of this would be verifying a web element's x and y location via the getLocation method, which exists only on the WebElement object. After calling the getWebElement method, you'll need to wait for the WebDriver promise for the WebElement to resolve:
	
	`let button = element(by.css(`
	`    '.contact-email')).getWebElement();`
	`button.getLocation().then(point => {`
	`    console.log('x = ' + point.x + ', y = ' +`
	`    point.y);`
	`});`

Table 8.2   **Interacting with web elements with the element API**   *(continued)*

Element method	Usage

isPresent
 	
isElementPresent
	When testing Angular structural directives like `*ngIf`, you need to call `isPresent` to validate if a web element exists on the screen. In the Contacts app, after the test enters the name of the new contact, the email field appears, and you could test it like so:
	
	`browser.get('/#/add');`
	
	`expect(element(by.id('contact-email'))`
	
	    `.isPresent()).toBe(false);`
	
	`element(by.id('contact-name')).sendKeys('foo');`
	
	`expect(element(by.id('contact-email'))`
	
	    `.isPresent()).toBe(true);`

getTagName	When writing tests, you can use identifiers like css to find the web element. Use the `getTagName` method to validate the current tag that Protractor is returning:
	
	`browser.get('/#/add');`
	
	`let body = element(by.tagName('body'));`
	
	`let mdToolbar = body.element(`
	
	    `by.css('[color="primary"]'));`
	
	`expect(mdToolbar.getTagName()).toBe('mat-toolbar');`

getCssValue	Use `getCssValue` to get the value of a given css property:
	
	`browser.get('/#/add');`
	
	`let toolbar = element(by.tagName('mat-toolbar'));`
	
	`expect(toolbar.getCssValue('background-color'))`
	
	  `toBe('rgba(33, 150, 243, 1)');`

getAttribute	When typing values into input fields, you can validate you entered them properly using the `getAttribute` method. To get the contents of an input field, you'll need to get the `'value'` attribute. A common mistake is to try to use the `getText` method to get the text from an input field:
	
	`browser.get('/#/add');`
	
	`let email = element(by.id('contact-email'));`
	
	`email.sendKeys('foobar');`
	
	`expect(email.getAttribute('value')).toBe('foobar');`

Table 8.2 Interacting with web elements with the element API *(continued)*

Element method	Usage
getText	When you use the `getText` method, Protractor will return a promise for the text that appears on the web element. Note that to get the text for an input field, you'll need to use `getAttribute('value')`: ```\nbrowser.get('/#/');\n\nelement(by.tagName('tbody')).getText()\n\n .then(text => {\n\n console.log(text);\n\n expect(text.match(/craig.service@example.com/)\n\n .index > 0).toBe(true);\n\n expect(text.match(/something that doesn't match/))\n\n .toBe(null);\n\n});\n```
sendKeys	Use `sendKeys` to simulate typing in text—for example, to fill out an input field: ```\nbrowser.get('/#/add');\n\nelement(by.id('contact-name')).sendKeys('foobar');\n\nexpect(element(by.id('contact-name'))\n\n .getAttribute('value')).toBe('foobar');\n```
clear	Use `clear` to remove the text from an input field: ```\nbrowser.get('/#/add');\n\nlet name = element(by.id('contact-name'));\n\nname.sendKeys('foo bar');\n\nname.clear();\n\nexpect(name.getAttribute('value')).toBe('');\n```
isDisplayed	You can check if an element is present but hidden from view with `isDisplayed`. If a web element is hidden but still part of the DOM, Protractor will return that it's present but not displayed: ```\nbrowser.get('/#/add');\n\nlet contactName = element(by.id('contact-name'));\n\nexpect(contactName.isDisplayed()).toBe(true);\n\n// Change the input to not be visible by style.\n\nbrowser.executeScript("arguments[0].setAt-\ntribute('style', 'display:none;')", contactName.\ngetWebElement());\n\nexpect(contactName.isPresent()).toBe(true);\n\nexpect(contactName.isDisplayed()).toBe(false);\n```

In this section, we reviewed commonly used methods of interacting with web elements. In the next section, we'll examine how to work with a collection of web elements.

8.6   Interacting with a list of elements

Interacting with a list of elements is similar to interacting with a single element. Finding web elements is asynchronous, whether it's a single element or a collection, so the result is a promise. A common gotcha is to try to iterate over the collection of web elements with a `for` loop. You can't loop through a promise, so instead you'll use the Protractor API methods for `element.all`. For the Contacts app, you can call `element(by.tagName('tbody')).all(by.tagName('tr'))` to get the array of table row web elements. In the following sections, we'll cover several methods that will help you.

8.6.1   Filtering web elements

Let's consider creating a new contact in the Contacts app. How do you validate that the new contact exists in the list of contacts? You could find the `tbody` web element, get all the text from the table body, and create a phone number regular expression to match the new contact. But what if two contacts have the same phone number? How can you get the information for a single contact? You use the `filter` function, which will find a subset of contacts from the contact list. Figure 8.4 shows how to find a contact that matches the name that's equal to Craig Service.

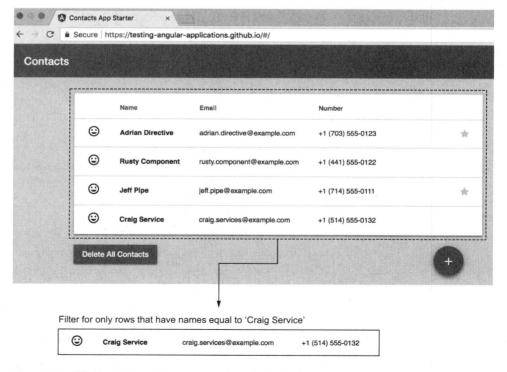

Figure 8.4   Filtering strategy for names equal to 'Craig Service'

When you call the `filter` function shown in figure 8.5, the returned object is an array of web elements that satisfy the callback function. In this example, the filter callback function, `filterFn`, returns `true` when the name matches Craig Service. See the lower part of the diagram for the function signature.

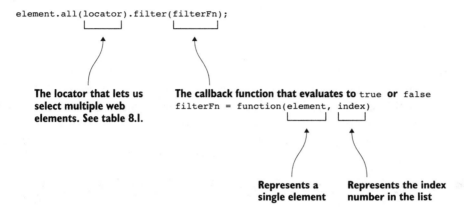

```
element.all(locator).filter(filterFn);
```

The locator that lets us select multiple web elements. See table 8.I.

The callback function that evaluates to `true` or `false`
```
filterFn = function(element, index)
```

Represents a single element

Represents the index number in the list

Figure 8.5 `filter` function

For this example, look at the contact component template shown in listing 8.10. Notice that you can't call `element.all(by.tagName('tr'))` because that would also include the table headers. You might wonder if you could use `*ngFor` to identify only the rows of the contacts. That doesn't work, because `*ngFor` tells Angular how to modify the DOM's structure, and that attribute isn't included in the rendered output.

Listing 8.10   HTML template of the contact list

```html
<table class="mdl-data-table mdl-js-data-table mdl-shadow--2dp">
  <thead>
    <tr>
      <th class="mdl-data-table__cell--non-numeric"></th>
      <th class="mdl-data-table__cell--non-numeric">Name</th>
      <th class="mdl-data-table__cell--non-numeric">Email</th>
      <th class="mdl-data-table__cell--non-numeric">Number</th>
      <th class="mdl-data-table__cell--non-numeric"></th>
      <th class="mdl-data-table__cell--non-numeric"></th>
      <th class="mdl-data-table__cell--non-numeric"></th>
    </tr>
  </thead>
  <tbody>
    <tr *ngFor="let contact of contacts"          ← Finds the table rows that
        (click)="onSelect(contact)">                represent contacts
      <td class="mdl-data-table__cell--non-numeric"
          (click)="onClick(contact)">
        <mat-icon>mood</mat-icon>
      </td>
      <td class="mdl-data-table__cell--non-numeric"  ← Uses the table column
          (click)="onClick(contact)">                 to check the name
        <strong>{{ contact.name }}</strong>
```

```
      </td>
      <td class="mdl-data-table__cell--non-numeric"
          (click)="onClick(contact)">{{ contact.email }}</td>
      <td class="mdl-data-table__cell--non-numeric"
          (click)="onClick(contact)">
{{ contact.number | phoneNumber : "default" : contact.country : true }}
      </td>
    </tr>
  </tbody>
</table>
```

Listing 8.11 shows a Protractor test against the rendered HTML from listing 8.10 that uses the filter method. First, you find the tbody web element using the by.tagName locator. Within that tbody, you then get all the table rows and assign them to trs. Next, you filter the table rows in trs to find the one you want. You pass filter() a callback function that evaluates to true if the text in the row matches 'Craig Service'. The resulting list only includes web elements that the callback function returned true for.

Listing 8.11   Filter for a contact—e2e/contact-list.e2e-spec.ts

Finds the array of table rows that represent contacts within the table body

Uses the second table column to compare the contact name

```
import { browser, by, element } from 'protractor';

describe('the contact list', () => {
  it('with filter: should find existing ' +
      'contact "Craig Service"', () => {
    let tbody = element(by.tagName('tbody'));
    let trs = tbody.all(by.tagName('tr'));
    let craigService = trs.filter(elem => {
      return elem.all(by.tagName('td')).get(1).getText()
        .then(text => {
          return text === 'Craig Service';
        });
    });
    expect(craigService.count()).toBeGreaterThan(0);
    expect(craigService.all(by.tagName('td'))
      .get(2).getText())
      .toBe('craig.services@example.com');
  });
});
```

Checks to see if craigService exists

As an additional check, verifies that the third column is the correct email address

getText returns a promise of the Boolean evaluation where text === 'Craig Service'.

To verify that you found the correct row for 'Craig Service', you could also check that you found only one element and that the email matches 'craig.services@ example.com'.

8.6.2 *Mapping the contact list to an array*

Let's consider a different scenario where you need to test all the contacts on the contact list. Instead of writing a filter function for each contact, you could use the map function. The map function converts the web elements returned from the element.all to an array shown in figure 8.6.

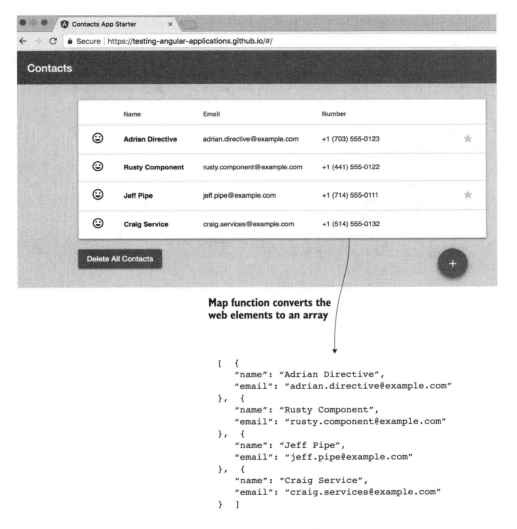

Figure 8.6   Convert the web elements to an array using the map function

Before you use the map function (in figure 8.6), you should review the map function for element.all shown in the figure 8.7 diagram.

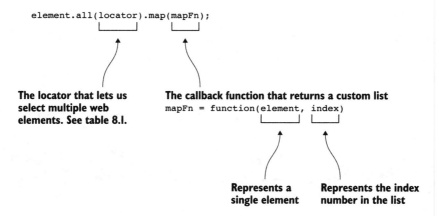

Figure 8.7   `map` **function**

In listing 8.12, you use `map` to transform the contact list into an array of objects that implement the `Contact` interface. To validate that the contact list appears as expected, you create an expected list of contacts using the same `Contact` interface and compare them at the end of the test.

Listing 8.12   Checking that all the contacts appear as expected with `map`

```typescript
import { browser, by, element } from 'protractor';
import { promise as wdpromise } from 'selenium-webdriver';

export interface Contact {
  name?: string;
  email?: string;
  tel?: string;
}

describe('the contact list', () => {
  let expectedContactList: Contact[] = [{
      name: 'Adrian Directive',
      email: 'adrian.directive@example.com',
      tel: '+1 (703) 555-0123'
    }, {
      name: 'Rusty Component',
      email: 'rusty.component@example.com',
      tel: '+1 (441) 555-0122'
    }, {
      name: 'Jeff Pipe',
      email: 'jeff.pipe@example.com',
      tel: '+1 (714) 555-0111'
    }, {
      name: 'Craig Service',
      email: 'craig.services@example.com',
      tel: '+1 (514) 555-0132'
    }];
```

```
beforeAll(() => {
  browser.get('/#/');
});

it('with map: should create a map object', () => {
  let tbody = element(by.tagName('tbody'));
  let trs = tbody.all(by.tagName('tr'));
  let contactList = trs.map(elem => {
    let contact: Contact = {};
    let promises: any[] = [];
    let tds = element.all(by.tagName('td'));
    promises.push(tds.get(0).getText().then(text => {
      contact.name = text;
    }));
    promises.push(tds.get(1).getText().then(text => {
      contact.email = text;
    }));
    promises.push(tds.get(2).getText().then(text => {
      contact.tel = text;
    }));

    return Promise.all(promises).then(() => {
      return contact;
    });
  });
  expect(contactList).toBeDefined();
  contactList.then((contacts: Contact[]) => {
    expect(contacts.length).toEqual(4);
    expect(contacts).toEqual(expectedContactList);
  });
});
});
```

For each contact, runs the mapFn callback for each tr element

Gets the table row columns

Gets the text and sets the value to the corresponding contact property, then pushes the promise to the promises array

Resolves the promises to set the properties to a single contact and returns the contact

Checks that the contact list isn't undefined

Checks that the contact list is equal to the expected contact list

Casts the resolved contact list to a Contact array

In listing 8.12, you use a promise array to keep track of promises to set the name, email, and telephone number to the contact when calling getText. After you've created the promises and added them to the promise array, you call Promise.all. Calling then on the Promise.all, resolves all the promises in the array. In this case, the contact properties are set. Finally, you return the contact for that row.

The map function iterates through all the web elements and returns a promise that resolves to the contact list. Next, the test calls then to get the contact list array. Having the contact list array, the test can verify if the expected contact list matches the one from the web application.

8.6.3 Reduce

Another possible test scenario might be testing that only the names match. As before, you could use map to create an array of names. An alternative solution would be to use the reduce function, which can turn a collection of contact web elements into a single string of names (figure 8.8).

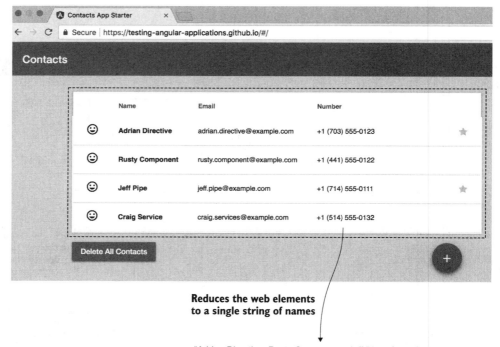

"Adrian Directive, Rusty Component, Jeff Pipe, Craig Service"

Figure 8.8   Reduces the contact list to a single string of names

The reduce function applies a callback to each element of the array and accumulates the result in a single value. The method signature is shown in figure 8.9.

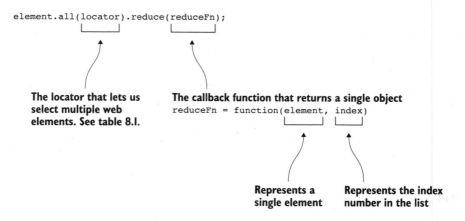

Figure 8.9   reduce function

In your Contacts app, you gather the contact names into a single string to check the default values. The reduce function returns a comma-delimited list of names, as shown in the following listing.

Listing 8.13   Reduce the list of elements to a single string

Gets each table row from the table body

```
describe('the contact list', () => {
  beforeAll(() => {
    browser.get('/#/');
  });

  it('with reduce: get a list of contact names', () => {
    let tbody = element(by.tagName('tbody'));
    let trs = tbody.all(by.tagName('tr'));
    let contacts = trs.reduce((acc, curr) => {
      let name = curr.all(by.tagName('td')).get(0);
      return name.getText().then(text => {
        return acc + ', ' + text;
      });
    });
    expect(contactList).toEqual(
        'Adrian Directive, Rusty Component, Jeff Pipe, ' +
        'Craig Service');
  });
});
```

Calls reduce to get a string of contacts

Gets the name column

Accumulates the names as a comma-delimited string

The curr parameter in the callback represents the table row web element. The callback gets the text from the first column. Then you take the text and concatenate it into the accumulator. Finally, the test checks whether the accumulated string matches the expected list of names.

8.7   Page objects

Let's say the developer (whether you or someone else) changes the ID from add -contact to create-contact. After the changes are published, if you don't update your tests, they'll fail because the ID is no longer add-contact. Having hardcoded strings like IDs or class names makes tests harder to maintain—you may have to manually update all your tests after one simple code change.

One way to make tests more maintainable is to use a common design pattern called *page objects*. Page objects organize your test code around logical interactions with your web app, instead of with raw elements. Instead of finding the Create button and then calling the click method, a page object would wrap this functionality with a method called createClickButton. If you needed to change the locator for the Create button, you could fix it in one location.

Previously you wrote a create contact test that typed in the new contact name and clicked the Create button. The examples so far have had IDs and class names that have provided helpful hints as to their function. In real-world applications, these identifiers aren't always so helpful and can be arbitrary.

Listings 8.14 and 8.15 bring together all the interactions for creating a new contact in a `NewContactPageObject` and a `ContactListPageObject`, respectively. The page objects group the WebDriver commands into typical interactions. Each constructor sets the element finders for the page view, but Protractor doesn't find the element until a call interacts with it, like a `click()` or `sendKeys()`.

Listing 8.14   Contact list page object—e2e/po/contact-list.po.ts

```typescript
import { browser, by, element, ElementFinder } from 'protractor';

export class ContactListPageObject {
  plusButton: ElementFinder;

  constructor() {
    this.plusButton = element(by.id('add-contact'));    ◀── Creates reusable element
  }                                                          finder objects

  clickPlusButton() {
    this.plusButton.click();
    return new NewContactPageObject();    ◀──
  }

  navigateTo() {
    browser.get('/#/');
  }
}
```

When clicking on the plus button, because the page navigates from the contact-list, calls the constructor to return a page object for creating a new contact

Listing 8.15   New contact page object—e2e/po/new-contact.po.ts

```typescript
import { browser, by, element, ElementFinder } from 'protractor';

export class NewContactPageObject {
  inputName: ElementFinder;
  inputEmail: ElementFinder;
  inputPhone: ElementFinder;

  constructor() {
    this.inputName = element(by.id('contact-name'));
    this.inputEmail = element(by.id('contact-email'));
    this.inputPhone = element(by.css('input[type="tel"]'));
  }

  setContactInfo(name: string, email: string,
      phoneNumber: string) {                      Finds the element finder object,
    this.inputName.sendKeys(name);    ◀──         then sends the keys
    if (email) {                      ◀──
      this.inputEmail.sendKeys(email);
    }
    if (phoneNumber) {                ◀──
```

Sends keys for optional fields

```
      this.inputPhone.sendKeys(phoneNumber);
    }
  }

  clickCreateButton() {
    this.element(by.buttonText('Create')).click();
    return new ContactListPageObject();
  }

  getName() {
    return this.inputName.getAttribute('value');
  }
}
  getPhone() {
    return this.inputPhone.getAttribute('value');
}
  getEmail() {
    return this.inputEmail.getAttribute('value');
}
```

> **Implicitly returns a WebDriver promise for a string** ← (pointing to `getName()`)

Now that you've seen how to make page objects, you can refactor your create contact test as shown in listing 8.16. First, the test creates the contactList object and navigates to the contact list page. The next it() block clicks the plus button and verifies that the current URL is the create contact page. On the create contact page, the test fills out the name input field and email input field. After the fields are filled, the test verifies that the input values match. Finally, the test clicks the Create button and returns to the contact list page.

Listing 8.16   Refactor creating a new contact—e2e/page-object.e2e-spec.ts

```
import { ContactListPageObject } from './po/contact-list.po.ts';
import { NewContactPageObject } from './po/new-contact.po.ts', , Contact }

describe('contact list', () => {
  let contactList: ContactListPageObject;
  let newContact: NewContactPageObject;

  beforeAll(() => {
    contactList = new ContactListPageObject();
  });

  describe('add a new contact', () => {
    beforeAll(() => {
      contactList.navigateTo();
    });

    it('should click the + button', () => {
      newContact = contactList.clickPlusButton();
      expect(browser.getCurrentUrl())
          .toBe(browser.baseUrl + '/#/add');
    });

    it('should fill out form for a new contact', () => {
      newContact.setContactInfo(
          'Mr. Newton', 'mr.newton@example.com', null);
```

```
      expect(newContact.getName()).toBe('Mr. Newton');
      expect(newContact.getEmail())
          .toBe('mr.newton@example.com');
      expect(newContact.getPhone()).toBe('');
    });

    it('should click the create button', () => {
      contactList = newContact.clickCreateButton();
      expect(browser.getCurrentUrl())
          .toBe(browser.baseUrl + '/#/');
    });
  });
});
```

Instead of importing in Protractor's `browser`, `by`, and `element`, the test imports the page objects and uses only methods from the page objects for navigation and validation.

Summary

- The Angular CLI provides a scaffold of Protractor files that you can use as a good starting point. The setup allows you to use the built-in TypeScript support when writing your Protractor tests.
- Protractor has many ways to locate objects on the screen. If you're looking for more than one web element, Protractor can find an array of elements.
- When you're looking for many objects on the screen, you can use Protractor's built-in `filter`, `map`, and `reduce` functions to manipulate a list of web elements.
- Using page objects when writing Protractor tests allows you to initialize locators in one location and encapsulate actions into methods.

Understanding timeouts

This chapter covers

- Understanding and avoiding the causes of timeout errors in Protractor
- Waiting for specific changes in your application, rather than relying on `browser.sleep()`
- Understanding flakiness and eliminating it with Protractor

Now that you know how to make basic end-to-end tests for Angular apps, let's talk about one of the most frequent issues you might run into. Timeout errors are the most common problems people encounter when using Protractor for the first time. Understanding what causes them and how to fix them requires a clear understanding of how browser tests run. You'll also need to know what Protractor is doing behind the scenes to make tests more reliable by waiting for Angular to be stable while running a test.

In this chapter, we'll explore how to avoid the common timeout-related pitfalls that new Protractor users stumble into. On the way, you'll learn how Angular's change detection works and how Protractor integrates with it. You'll also learn some advanced techniques for making your own waiting logic. You can find the example code from this chapter at www.manning.com/books/testing-angular-applications and http://mng.bz/6k1S.

9.1   Kinds of timeouts

Protractor tests involve many different pieces working together, so different kinds of timeouts are possible. For example, Jasmine will mark your test as failed if it takes too long to complete, and WebDriver will throw an error if a browser command takes too long. For this chapter, we're only concerned about one kind of timeout: the timeout that occurs if Protractor waits too long for Angular to be stable.

What is flakiness?

According to Dictionary.com, *flaky* is slang for eccentric or crazy. When we say a test is flaky, what we mean is that it's nondeterministic—it might fail even though there's nothing wrong with your app. You want to avoid flakiness—if the tests can fail when nothing has changed in the app, then they become less useful.

One potential cause of flakiness is having a test read the DOM of a page while Angular is in the middle of updating it. You could avoid this issue by adding sleep commands after every step in your tests that might cause Angular to update the page, but that would slow down your test runs, and it's not guaranteed to work. Protractor takes a more efficient route and syncs your tests with Angular to help prevent flaky test failures.

Waiting for Angular to be stable prevents your test from interacting with the page while Angular is in the middle of an update, which makes your tests less flaky. But it can cause problems, particularly when you need to test a page that isn't part of an Angular app.

9.2   Testing pages without Angular

Remember from chapter 8 that Protractor intercepts the commands your test sends to WebDriver and automatically waits for Angular to be ready. Figure 9.1 shows this process in detail. This mechanism is one of the biggest advantages of using Protractor, but sometimes it gets in the way.

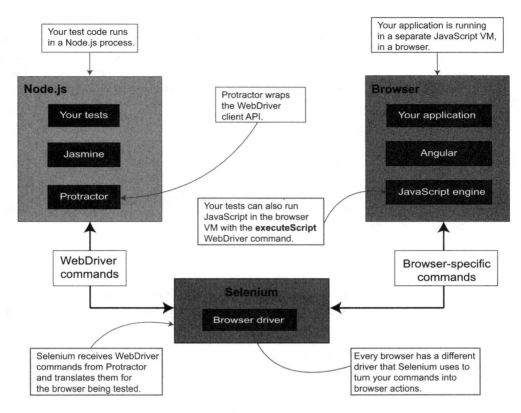

Figure 9.1 How Protractor interacts with WebDriver

One of the first problems new users of Protractor face is writing a test that logs in to their application. If the authentication page is static HTML and not part of the Angular app, then Protractor will throw an `Angular could not be found on the page` error. Protractor expects to see a page that's part of an Angular app and can't tell the difference between one that's not supposed to have Angular and one that's broken.

The example Contacts app doesn't have authentication, but pretend for a minute that it does and that you need to log in before you can run your tests. We've added a fake login page at /assets/login.html. This simple HTML file, which doesn't do anything, is bundled with the Contacts app.

9.2.1 *Disabling waitForAngular*

Make a test that navigates to the login page using `browser.get('/assets/login.html')`. Running the test produces this error:

```
1) the contact list should find the title
   - Failed: Angular could not be found on the page http://localhost:4200/
     assets/login.html. If this is not an Angular application, you may need
     to turn off waiting for Angular.
```

What does the error mean? As you saw earlier, Protractor automatically intercepts the commands your tests send to WebDriver and inserts commands that communicate with Angular and wait for your application to be ready for testing. When you navigate to a page that isn't an Angular app, Protractor throws an error, because it can't find Angular. To fix the error, you need to tell Protractor not to wait for Angular:

```
it('should be able to log in', () => {
  browser.waitForAngularEnabled(false);
  browser.get('/assets/login.html');
  element(by.css('input.user')).sendKeys('username');
  element(by.css('input.password')).sendKeys('password');
  element(by.id('login')).click();
);
```

Now, suppose you want to test whether clicking the login button redirects to the contact list page. You might add the following before the last line in your test:

```
  const list = element(by.css('app-contact-list tr'));
  expect(list.getText()).toContain('Jeff Pipe');
});
```

You're almost there, but now the test is failing for a different reason. You've turned off waiting for Angular, which means Protractor now has no way to know what the application is doing.

9.2.2 Automatically waiting for Angular

You'll see this error if you run the test from the previous section:

```
1) the contact list should find the title
   - Failed: No element found using locator: By(css selector, app-contact-list
     tr)
```

The problem is that when you're looking for the contact list, your app is still loading. Because you've told Protractor not to wait for Angular, it goes right ahead and looks for the contact list, then fails when it doesn't find it. The fix for this is simple—tell Protractor to start waiting for Angular again after you click the login button. The next listing shows the full, working test.

> **Listing 9.1   Testing a login page**

Disables automatically waiting for Angular

```
it('should be able to login', () => {                    Tests the login page
  browser.waitForAngularEnabled(false);
  browser.get('/assets/login.html');
  element(by.css('input.user')).sendKeys('username');
  element(by.css('input.password')).sendKeys('password');
  element(by.id('login')).click();
                                                         Re-enables waiting so you
                                                         can test the application
  browser.waitForAngularEnabled(true);
  const list = element(by.css('app-contact-list tr'));
  expect(list.getText()).toContain('Jeff Pipe');
});
```

Now your test won't wait for Angular on the login page but will go back to waiting for it when you return to the app. Why do you need to explicitly disable waiting? Why couldn't Protractor detect whether an Angular app was on the page and skip waiting if it didn't find one? Protractor has no way of telling the difference between a page that isn't an Angular app and an app that's loading slowly, so you need to let it know that you're intentionally sending it to a non-Angular page. Being explicit about your intentions prevents issues with tests that might be hard to debug, especially when you're relying on Protractor to automatically wait for Angular to finish updating the page. It's important that you know right away if that mechanism isn't working when you expect it to be.

9.2.3 When to use browser.waitForAngularEnabled()

Knowing how and when to enable and disable waiting for Angular, even on pages that are part of an Angular app, is an important part of writing tests using Protractor. But turning off waiting for Angular can have side effects. For example, your tests won't know when Angular is done updating the page, so you might have to use other synchronization methods. One such method is `ExpectedConditions`.

9.3 Waiting with ExpectedConditions

When you tell Protractor not to wait for Angular, you might start seeing test failures if Angular updates the page while your test is running. It's tempting to make the tests pass by sprinkling in `browser.sleep()` commands, but that is a bad idea for a couple of reasons. First, the right amount of time to sleep is arbitrary and hard to know ahead of time. It also slows down your tests, because you end up waiting a fixed amount of time, even if the condition you're waiting for has already occurred. Instead, you can use `browser.wait()` and `ExpectedConditions` to wait for specific conditions in your application to be true, like so:

```
let EC = browser.ExpectedConditions;
browser.wait(EC.visibilityOf($('.popup-title')), 2000,
  'Wait for popup title to be visible.');
```

This will pause your test and repeatedly check whether the given condition is true, up to some specified timeout (two seconds, in this case).

> **NOTE** You should always specify a timeout and an error message when using `browser.wait()`. If you don't specify a timeout, it will keep waiting until your per-test timeout is hit, and having an error message makes timeouts much easier to debug.

Table 9.1 lists all the expected conditions built in to Protractor. You also can combine any number of conditions with `and()`, `or()`, and `not()`, like this:

```
let EC = browser.ExpectedConditions;
let titleCondition =
EC.and(EC.titleContains('foo'),
    EC.not(EC.titleContains('bar'));
browser.wait(titleCondition, 5000,
  'Waiting for title to contain foo and not bar');
```

Table 9.1   Types of expected conditions

Name	When it's true
alertIsPresent	An alert dialog is open.
elementToBeClickable	The given element is visible and enabled.
textToBePresentInElement	The element contains the given string (case-sensitive).
textToBePresentInElementValue	The element's `value` attribute contains the given string (case sensitive).
titleContains	`document.title` contains the given string (case sensitive).
titleIs	`document.title` exactly matches the given string.
urlContains	The current URL contains the given string (case sensitive).
urlIs	The current URL exactly matches the given string.
presenceOf	The element is present in the current page (but may or may not be visible).
stalenessOf	The element is no longer part of the page's DOM (the opposite of `presenceOf`).
visibilityOf	The element is present in the page, is visible, and has a height and width greater than 0.
invisibilityOf	The element is either not present in the DOM or is not visible (opposite of `visibilityOf`).
elementToBeSelected	The element is currently selected (if the element is an `<option>` or an `<input>` with a `checkbox` or `radio` type).

Note that you can combine expected conditions and assign them to variables so you can reuse them.

> **WARNING**   The ExpectedConditions object holds a reference to the browser object. Be careful using it in tests that restart or create multiple browsers, and use `browser.ExpectedConditions` instead of `protractor.ExpectedConditions`. Get the reference to ExpectedConditions after you restart or fork the browser.

9.3.1   *Waiting for the contact list to load*

Now that you know the basics of expected conditions, you have another way to make the test from listing 9.1 pass, as shown in the next listing.

Listing 9.2   Using `ExpectedConditions` instead of `waitForAngular`

```
it('should be able to login', () => {
  let EC = browser.ExpectedConditions;
  browser.waitForAngularEnabled(false);
```

```
browser.get('/assets/login.html');
element(by.css('input.user')).sendKeys('username');
element(by.css('input.password')).sendKeys('password');
element(by.id('login')).click();

const list = element(by.css('app-contact-list'));
const listReady = EC.not(
  EC.textToBePresentInElement(list, 'Loading contacts'));
browser.wait(listReady, 5000, 'Wait for list to load');
expect(list.getText()).toContain('Jeff Pipe');
});
```

Builds the expected condition

**Waits up to five seconds for
'Loading contacts' to go away**

As shown, instead of turning on `waitForAngular`, you can wait for the `'Loading con-
tacts'` text to go away. There's no single right answer here—use whichever method is
more readable and maintainable for your tests. But expected conditions are a helpful
tool to have, especially when dealing with animations, as you'll see in the next section.

9.3.2 Testing a dialog

Another good time to use an expected condition is when you need to wait, like when
you're opening a dialog. Figure 9.2 shows a dialog from the Contacts app. On the
detail page for a contact, a button (circled in red) opens a dialog that shows a feed of
that contact's social media updates.

Contact feed button

Figure 9.2   The social media feed dialog of a contact

When you click the feed button, the dialog animates opening. When you click Close, it animates fading away briefly before closing. These animations can be problematic when you try to test the dialog, as the following listing shows.

Listing 9.3   Testing the feed dialog with `waitForAngular`

```
                                              Make sure that
                                      waitForAngular is turned on

describe('feed dialog', () => {
  beforeEach(() => {
    browser.get('/contact/4')
  });

  it('should open the dialog', () => {
    browser.waitForAngularEnabled(true);       ◄──────────┘
    let feedButton = element(by.css('button.feed-button'));
    feedButton.click();

    let dialogTitle = element(
      by.css('app-contact-feed h2.mat-dialog-title'));    │ You should see the title
    expect(dialogTitle.getText())                     ◄───│ of the feed dialog.
      .toContain('Latest posts from Craig Service');

    let closeButton = element(by.css('button[mat-dialog-close]'))
    closeButton.click();

    expect(dialogTitle.isDisplayed()).toBeFalsy();    ◄───│ The title should go away
  });                                                      │ when the dialog closes.
});
```

Closes the dialog

This is a simple test—it clicks the button to open the feed dialog, verifies that the expected title of the dialog is visible, and clicks the Close button. Unfortunately, when you run this test, you see this error:

```
1) contact detail feed dialog should open the dialog
  - Expected true to be falsy.
```

The last expectation fails, because after you click the Close button, you can still see the dialog title while the closing animation runs. Although Protractor is waiting for Angular to finish updating the page, it won't wait for the closing animation to end. This is the kind of situation where you might need to use expected conditions.

9.3.3   *Waiting for elements to become stale*

Let's fix this test by using expected conditions instead of relying on `waitForAngular`.

Listing 9.4   Testing the feed dialog with expected conditions

```
describe('feed dialog', () => {
  let EC;

  beforeEach(() => {
    browser.get('/contact/4');
    EC = browser.ExpectedConditions;
  });

  it('should open the dialog with expected conditions', () => {
    browser.waitForAngularEnabled(false);

    let feedButton = element(by.css('button.feed-button'));
    browser.wait(EC.elementToBeClickable(feedButton),
      3000, 'waiting for feed button to be clickable');
    feedButton.click();

    let dialogTitle = element(
      by.css('app-contact-feed h2.mat-dialog-title'))
    browser.wait(EC.visibilityOf(dialogTitle),
      1000, 'waiting for the dialog title to appear');
    expect(dialogTitle.getText())
      .toContain('Latest posts from Craig Service');

    let closeButton = element(by.css('button[mat-dialog-close]'))
    closeButton.click();
    browser.wait(EC.stalenessOf(dialogTitle),
      3000, 'wait for dialog to close');
    expect(dialogTitle.isPresent()).toBeFalsy();
  });
});
```

Waits for the feed button to be clickable

Waits for the dialog title to be visible

Waits for the dialog title to be removed from the page

This test passes because you wait for the dialog title to become stale before the last expectation. In WebDriver tests, a stale element is one that you may have a reference to, but that was removed from the page. In this case, the title of the dialog box becomes stale because the closing animation has finished and the dialog has been removed from the page. Elements that you remove from the page with *ngFor or *ngIf also would become stale.

This test disables waitForAngular and relies on expected conditions entirely, but you also can combine the two techniques. For example, you could have made the test from listing 9.3 pass by adding browser.wait(EC.stalenessOf(dialogTitle)) before the expectation and leaving waitForAngular enabled. Either way is fine—the important thing is that your tests reliably do the same thing each time they run.

9.4   *Creating custom conditions*

Expected conditions are powerful, but sometimes they aren't enough for your needs. Instead of waiting for an element to be present or text to be visible, you might want to wait for a more complicated condition to be true. For example, you might need to wait until a certain number of elements match a CSS selector. Or, perhaps a single selector can't describe the set of elements you're waiting for. In cases that are too hard to express with expected conditions, you can use browser.wait with a custom condition.

9.4.1   *Using browser.wait*

The feed dialog from figure 9.2 will update automatically with new posts from the contact. For testing purposes, it shows a new update after a random delay, on average every five seconds. Say you add a feature that the Follow button will be enabled only when the contact has made two or more posts. In the following listing, you can see a test that verifies that feature.

> **Listing 9.5   Using browser.wait with a custom condition**

```
describe('feed dialog', () => {
  beforeEach(() => {
    browser.get('/contact/4');
  });

  it('should enable the follow button with more than two posts', () => {
    let feedButton = element(by.css('button.feed-button'));
    feedButton.click();

    let followButton = element(by.css('button.follow'))
    expect(followButton.isEnabled()).toBeFalsy();          ◄─── Verifies that the Follow
    let moreThanOnePost = () => {                                button is initially disabled
      return element.all(by.css('app-contact-feed mat-list-item')).count()
        .then((count) => {
          return count >= 2;          ◄─── Counts the number of mat-list-items and
        })                                  returns true if there are two or more
    };
    browser.wait(moreThanOnePost, 20000, 'Waiting for two posts');

    expect(followButton.isEnabled()).toBeTruthy();          ◄───
  });                                                            Verifies that the Follow
});                                                              button is enabled
```

Waits until contact makes two or more posts

The first argument to browser.wait is a function that will run repeatedly until either it returns true or the timeout is elapsed. In the example, a function looks for all elements that match the 'app-contact-feed mat-list-item' selector, which will match each post in the feed. Because Protractor needs to send a request to the browser driver to inspect the page, the result of `element.all(...).count()` is a promise that's resolved with the number of elements that match the selector instead of a number. You then chain this promise with a `.then()` block that returns a Boolean, which is true if the count is greater than or equal to two.

This is similar to how expected conditions work. The expected conditions built in to Protractor (from table 9.1) are functions that inspect the page and return promises that are true when the condition is met. Listing 9.5 is an example of how you can create your own conditions if you need to.

9.4.2 Getting elements from the browser

WebDriver converts DOM elements returned from the browser via a `browser.executeScript` call into instances of WebElement classes that you can use in your tests. So, instead of using element finders, you can write custom JavaScript that will run in the browser and return the elements you're looking for. Here's the test from listing 9.5 but using a custom element finder.

> **Listing 9.6 Retrieving elements with a custom finder**

Function that runs in the browser and returns elements

```
it('should enable the follow button (custom finder)', () => {
    let feedButton = element(by.css('button.feed-button'));
    feedButton.click();

    let followButton = element(by.css('button.follow'))
    expect(followButton.isEnabled()).toBeFalsy();

    function findAllPosts() {
      return document.querySelectorAll('app-contact-feed mat-list-item')
    }

    browser.wait(() => {
      return browser.driver.executeScript(findAllPosts)
        .then((posts: WebElement[]) => {
          return posts.length >= 2;
        })
    }, 20000, 'Waiting for two posts');

    expect(followButton.isEnabled()).toBeTruthy();
});
```

Using the custom element finder in browser.wait

Waits at most 20 seconds before timing out

The test in listing 9.6 is the same as the one in 9.5. However, instead of using an element finder, it uses a JavaScript function that runs in the browser and returns an array of WebElements. Although this example may seem trivial, it shows how you can write custom JavaScript that extracts an arbitrary collection of DOM elements from the page. Remember that your tests are running in Node.js, but they can still execute JavaScript in the browser. The findAllPosts() function runs in the browser, but you can use the result it returns in your Node.js-based Protractor tests.

9.5   *Handling long-running tasks*

The feed dialog in the contact detail page (figure 9.3) continuously updates with new posts. For demonstration purposes, the example app does this with an observable that produces an infinite stream of random posts.

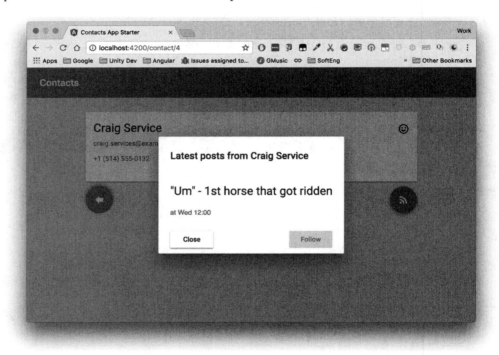

Figure 9.3   The social media feed dialog of a contact.

The following listing is the implementation of the service that the feed dialog uses. In a real application, you would make an HTTP call to get the posts. But the real service could easily have the same interface and return an observable stream of posts.

Listing 9.7   A service that creates a random stream of posts

```
import { Injectable } from '@angular/core';
import { Observable } from 'rxjs/Rx';
import { FEED_UPDATES } from './mock-updates';

@Injectable()
export class ContactFeedService {
  constructor() { }
```

```
public getFeed() {
  const updateId = Math.floor(Math.random() * FEED_UPDATES.length));
  return Observable.interval(500)
    .map((x) => Math.random() * 2 + 2)
    .concatMap((x) => Observable.of(x).delay(x * 1000))
    .map((x) => FEED_UPDATES[updateId]);
}
}
```

→ **Randomly picks a string from FEED_UPDATES and puts it in the stream**

→ **Transforms the observable stream into a stream of randomly delayed events**

FEED_UPDATES is an array of strings. The feed dialog component subscribes to this observable, as you can see in the following listing.

Listing 9.8 Testing the contact feed dialog

```
import {Component, OnInit, OnDestroy, Optional, Inject} from '@angular/core';
import {MdDialogRef, MD_DIALOG_DATA} from '@angular/material';
import {ContactFeedService} from '../shared/services/contact-feed.service';
import {Subscription} from 'rxjs/Subscription';

@Component({
  selector: 'app-contact-feed',
  templateUrl: './contact-feed.component.html',
  styleUrls: ['./contact-feed.component.css']
})
export class ContactFeedDialogComponent implements OnInit, OnDestroy {
  sub: Subscription;
  updates: string[] = [];
  name: string;
  closeDisabled = true;

  constructor(public dialogRef: MdDialogRef<ContactFeedDialogComponent>,
      private feed: ContactFeedService,
      @Optional() @Inject(MD_DIALOG_DATA) data: any) {
    this.name = data.name;
  }

  ngOnInit() {
    this.closeDisabled = false;

    this.sub = this.feed.getFeed().subscribe((x) => {
      this.updates.push(x);
      if (this.updates.length >= 4) {
        this.updates.shift();
      }
    });
  }

  ngOnDestroy() {
    this.sub.unsubscribe();
  }
}
```

Subscribes to feed updates and pushes them into the updates property

→ **Cleans up the subscription when the component is destroyed**

Unfortunately, the tests from listings 9.5 and 9.6 (which have waitForAngular enabled) will time out when trying to test this dialog:

```
1) feed dialog should enable the follow button with more than two posts using
      executeScript
   - Error: Timeout - Async callback was not invoked within timeout specified
     by jasmine.DEFAULT_TIMEOUT_INTERVAL.
```

Protractor's waitForAngular hooks into the same method that Angular uses to run change detection and update template bindings. That's how Protractor knows that Angular is done updating the page, but it means that by default, Protractor will wait until all asynchronous tasks that could update the page have finished. The contact feed dialog in the example polls forever, so Angular times out, because there's always a pending task that can update the page.

9.5.1   *Using expected conditions*

You could disable waiting for Angular. But if you want to avoid flaky tests, you'll need to use expected conditions to wait after every action that can cause the page to update. That's what the test from listing 9.4 did. Here it is again as a reminder.

Listing 9.9   Testing the feed dialog with expected conditions

Disables waitForAngular   You need to wait for the initial page load.

```
it('should open the dialog with expected conditions', () => {
  browser.waitForAngularEnabled(false);
  let feedButton = element(by.css('button.feed-button'));
  browser.wait(EC.elementToBeClickable(feedButton),
    3000, 'waiting for feed button to be clickable');
  feedButton.click();
                                           When you click the feed button, you'll
                                           need to wait for the dialog to show.
  let dialogTitle =
      element(by.css('app-contact-feed h2.mat-dialog-title'));
  browser.wait(EC.visibilityOf(dialogTitle),
    1000, 'waiting for the dialog title to appear');
  expect(dialogTitle.getText())
      .toContain('Latest posts from Craig Service');

  let closeButton = element(by.css('button[mat-dialog-close]'))
  closeButton.click();
  browser.wait(EC.stalenessOf(dialogTitle), 3000,
      'wait for dialog to close');
  expect(dialogTitle.isPresent()).toBeFalsy();
});
```

Clicking the close button also requires a wait.

Waiting after every action that could cause a page update can be a drag, and it makes the test harder to read. It would be better if you could write a test that used Protractor's automatic waitForAngular behavior, but doing so will require understanding how browsers run asynchronous code, and how Angular knows when to update the page.

To get there, you'll need to know more about zones and how JavaScript operates. The first step to learning about zones is to understand how the browser event loop works.

9.5.2 *The browser event loop*

JavaScript is single-threaded, meaning it does one thing at a time. Somewhere inside your browser is an event loop that looks something like this:

```
while(true) {
  event = waitForNextEvent()
  doJavaScriptThings(event);
  doBrowserThings(event);
}
```

In this example, `doBrowserThings()` refers to the work the browser does outside of your app's JavaScript—rendering the page, doing I/O, and so on. An event can be something like a timer firing, a mouse click event, or an XHR request changing in status. These events create tasks in the JavaScript VM, and three kinds of tasks are possible: microtasks, macrotasks, and eventtasks (see table 9.2).

Table 9.2 Types of tasks

Task type	When it runs
microtask	Run immediately, before the browser does any rendering or I/O. `Promise.resolve()` will schedule a microtask.
macrotask	Guaranteed to run at least once and in the same order that they're scheduled. Macrotasks run interleaved with browser rendering and I/O and are scheduled by `setTimeout` or `setInterval`. After a macrotask finishes, all microtasks are run before control passes back to the browser.
eventtask	Run in response to events (for example, `addEventListener('click', event-Callback)` or XHR state change). Unlike macrotasks, eventtasks might never run.

All microtasks run before control of the event loop goes back to the browser. Running a microtask might add more microtasks to the queue (for example, by making a `Promise.resolve()` call). Once the microtask queue is empty, control passes back to the browser so it can render the page, perform I/O, and wait for the next eventtask or macrotask to occur. The situation is a little more complicated than the simple `while(true)` loop we covered earlier. Now that you know a bit more about how browsers work, let's consider how this relates to Angular.

9.5.3 *What happened to $timeout?*

If you've used AngularJS, you might remember the `$timeout` service. When doing asynchronous work in AngularJS, instead of using `window.setTimeout()` or `XML-HttpRequest()` directly, you needed to use the special AngularJS services `$timeout` and `$http`. These services were wrappers around the native browser calls that would make sure change detection ran after the asynchronous task was done, so the content of your page would update if your model changed.

You don't need these special services in Angular. Instead, Angular uses a library called Zone.js to run your application's asynchronous tasks in a context called the Angular zone. Zone.js does this by patching all the browser APIs that create async calls with hooks that track which zone that task is running in. That's how Angular knows when an async callback started by your app occurs and is able to run change detection after it, which removes the need for $timeout.

> **DEFINITION**   A *zone* is an execution context that persists across async tasks—sort of like thread-local storage in Java, but for async tasks.

9.5.4   *Highway to the Angular zone*

Protractor knows about the Angular zone; it knows when tasks are pending that might cause a change detection. When you enable waitForAngular, Protractor will cause all of your WebDriver commands to wait until there are no more tasks pending in the Angular zone. Let's look at a simple example of running asynchronous tasks in a browser.

Assume that the code in figure 9.4 is running in the Angular zone. In this example, Protractor would wait forever, because the pollForever() function (in the lower-left red box) is constantly creating a task in the Angular zone.

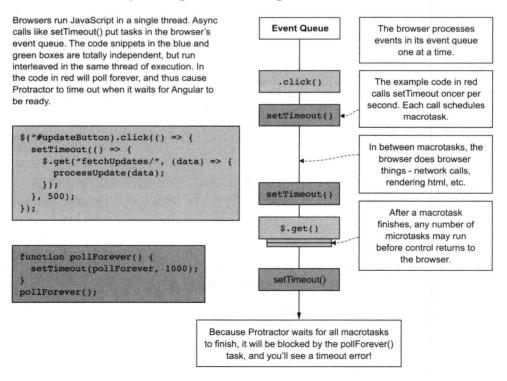

Figure 9.4   Async tasks running in a browser

> **NOTE**   A color version of this image is available in the electronic versions of this book, available free to purchasers at www.manning.com.

If you want to avoid this fate of waiting forever, you can move that code inside a call to NgZone.runOutsideAngular(), as in figure 9.5. Then pollForever() won't trigger a change detection when it runs, and Protractor won't wait for it to finish.

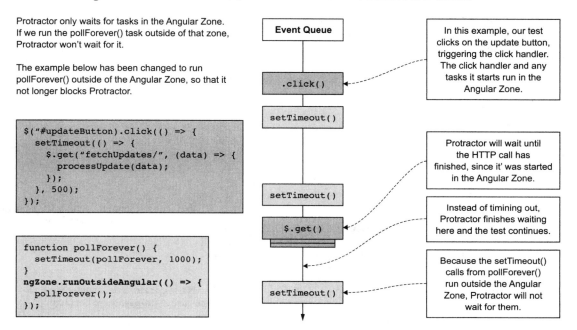

Protractor only waits for tasks in the Angular Zone. If we run the pollForever() task outside of that zone, Protractor won't wait for it.

The example below has been changed to run pollForever() outside of the Angular Zone, so that it not longer blocks Protractor.

```
$("#updateButton).click(() => {
  setTimeout(() => {
    $.get("fetchUpdates/", (data) => {
      processUpdate(data);
    });
  }, 500);
});
```

```
function pollForever() {
  setTimeout(pollForever, 1000);
}
ngZone.runOutsideAngular(() => {
  pollForever();
});
```

Event Queue

.click()

setTimeout()

setTimeout()

$.get()

setTimeout()

In this example, our test clicks on the update button, triggering the click handler. The click handler and any tasks it starts run in the Angular Zone.

Protractor will wait until the HTTP call has finished, since it' was started in the Angular Zone.

Instead of timing out, Protractor finishes waiting here and the test continues.

Because the setTimeout() calls from pollForever() run outside the Angular Zone, Protractor will not wait for them.

Figure 9.5   Running a polling task outside the Angular zone

This long-running task now runs in a way that won't cause Protractor to wait until the test times out. Next you'll apply this same technique to the Contacts app example and use it to fix the test.

9.5.5   *Fixing the test*

Now you know why your test was timing out earlier. The updates from the Contact-FeedService were scheduling async tasks in the Angular zone, and because it's a continuous stream of tasks, Protractor will wait until the test times out. You could turn off waitForAngular and use expected conditions, but you also could fix the test by changing the ContactFeedDialogComponent, as in the following listing.

Listing 9.10   Using `runOutsideAngular` in `ContactFeedDialogComponent`

```
import {Component, OnInit, OnDestroy, NgZone, Optional, Inject} from
    '@angular/core';
import {MdDialogRef, MD_DIALOG_DATA} from '@angular/material';
import {ContactFeedService} from '../shared/services/contact-feed.service';
import {Subscription} from 'rxjs/Subscription';
```

```
@Component({
  selector: 'app-contact-feed',
  templateUrl: './contact-feed.component.html',
  styleUrls: ['./contact-feed.component.css']
})
export class ContactFeedDialogComponent implements OnInit, OnDestroy {
  sub: Subscription;
  updates: string[] = [];
  name: string;
  closeDisabled = true;

  constructor(public dialogRef: MdDialogRef<ContactFeedDialogComponent>,
      private feed: ContactFeedService,
      private zone: NgZone,
      @Optional() @Inject(MD_DIALOG_DATA) data: any) {
    this.name = data.name;
  }

  ngOnInit() {
    this.closeDisabled = false;

    this.zone.runOutsideAngular(() => {          ◀── **Runs the subscription outside the Angular
      this.sub = this.feed.getFeed().subscribe((x) => {   zone, so it won't block Protractor**
        this.zone.run(() => {        ◀──
          this.updates.push(x);
          if (this.updates.length > 4) {
            this.updates.shift();                 **Adds the update in the Angular zone, so
          }                                        the change propagates to the page**
        });
      });
    });
  }

  ngOnDestroy() {
    this.sub.unsubscribe();
  }
}
```

Injects NgZone into the component

Now that the subscription is created outside of the Angular zone, it won't block Protractor. But you need to apply the update within the Angular zone so that Angular will know about the change to your model and will update the page. With only a small change to the component, the test passes! Protractor still will wait while each update is rendered in the dialog, but now it won't time out waiting for the stream of updates to finish.

Summary

- Browser tests consist of three components: your tests running in Node.js, a Selenium WebDriver server, and your application running in a browser. Protractor synchronizes your tests with your application by waiting for Angular to finish updating the page.
- Sometimes you need to disable waiting for Angular in your tests.
- Use expected conditions instead of `browser.sleep`. Tests are more reliable when they wait for a specific condition to be true, rather than pausing for an arbitrary amount of time. Protractor has many expected conditions you can use out of the box.
- If the available expected conditions don't meet your needs, you can make your own using `browser.wait`.
- Angular uses Zone.js to watch for async tasks that might cause the page to change. Protractor also uses Zone.js to wait until every async task that might modify the page has finished.
- Sometimes you'll need to change your application to run certain async tasks outside the Angular zone. If you don't, you might end up blocking Protractor from testing your page.

Advanced Protractor topics

This chapter covers

- Protractor configuration files
- Screenshot testing
- Debugging tests

Protractor is a powerful tool, and, like any powerful tool, you can use it in more creative ways than you'll find written in the manual. As developers working on Protractor, we've found that people tend to ask about certain common scenarios. Some common questions are "How do I extend Protractor's behavior with plugins?" and "How do I create screenshots when my tests fail?" We've collected our best tips for working with Protractor in this chapter to help you get the most out of your end-to-end tests. You can find the examples in this chapter at http://mng.bz/83kr.

10.1 Configuration file in depth

Protractor provides many knobs and levers that change how it launches based on configuration options. In chapter 8, you used one way to run Protractor tests. You started Protractor from the command line, using a Chrome instance running on your own machine. This configuration is fine for testing during development, but what if you need to test on a different browser or a set of browsers? How can you set up tests to run in a continuous integration environment without a GUI?

10.1.1 Driver provider options

In the Protractor examples in chapter 8, you used the `directConnect` flag to launch Chrome with the `chromedriver` binary. Protractor has other ways it can launch a new browser instance to run tests. The Protractor repository refers to these WebDriver options as *driver providers*. You can set different driver providers in your Protractor config file using the settings listed in table 10.1.

Table 10.1   Driver provider config options options

Setting	Comments
directConnect	Launching a browser with `directConnect` is great when you're developing your Protractor test suite because it allows you to work without having to start up a Selenium Standalone Server. Using `directConnect` is limited to launching tests for Chrome with the `chromedriver` binary and for Firefox with the `geckodriver` binary.
	You can limit your download to only these binaries by using the `webdriver-manager` npm package. To get these binaries, run `webdriver-manager update --standalone false`. Specifying `—standalone false` prevents `webdriver-manager` from downloading the Selenium Standalone Server jar file.
	By default, Protractor uses the binaries in the `webdriver-manager` npm folder. But if you need to bypass the `webdriver-manager` downloaded binaries, you can specify the path to your driver in the configuration file with the `chromedriver` and `geckodriver` options.
seleniumAddress	Setting `seleniumAddress` will tell Protractor to start browsers using the Selenium Standalone Server. Using the Selenium Standalone Server allows you to run tests that control browsers running on a different machine. This is helpful if the machine you're using is headless or without a desktop environment.
	The typical value for the `seleniumAddress` is `'http://127.0.0.1:4444/wd/hub'` when launching the standalone server locally using the default port.
	Typically, you run `webdriver-manager update` and then launch the Selenium Standalone Server with `webdriver-manager start`. If you need more control over Selenium, you can launch it manually like so: `java -Dwebdriver.gecko.driver=/tmp/geckodriver` `-Dwebdriver.chrome.driver=/tmp/chromedriver` `-jar /path/to/selenium-server-standalone.jar` `-port 4444`

Table 10.1 Driver provider config options options *(continued)*

Setting	Comments
`browserstackUser,` `browserstackKey`	BrowserStack is a cloud service for Selenium testing on desktop and mobile browsers. To use BrowserStack, set the `browserstackUser` and `browserstackKey` options in the configuration file. BrowserStack is a paid service and is out of the scope of this book, but you can find more information at www.browserstack.com.
`sauceUser, sauceKey`	Sauce Labs is another cloud service for Selenium testing on desktop and mobile browsers. Configure Sauce Labs by setting the `sauceUser` and `sauceKey` in the configuration file. Sauce Labs is another paid service and is also out of the scope of this book, but you can find more information at https://saucelabs.com/.
`seleniumServerJar`	If you set `seleniumServerJar` or don't set any driver providers in the config file, Protractor will start and shut down the Selenium Server for you.
	If `seleniumServerJar` isn't defined in the configuration file, Protractor will use binaries downloaded to your project's `node_modules/` `webdriver-manager/selenium` directory. To download the binaries, you need to run `webdriver-manager update`. After you have these binaries downloaded, running Protractor will also launch the Selenium Server locally.
	When the path to `seleniumServerJar` is defined in the configuration file, it will use the absolute path to launch the Selenium Server.
	In addition to specifying `seleniumServerJar`, you can specify the `chromedriver` path. Similarly, for tests using the Firefox browser, you could specify the `geckodriver` path. If you don't set the paths for either `chromedriver` or `geckodriver`, Protractor will use the default locations specified by the locally installed `webdriver-manager` module.

Note that multiple driver providers set in the same configuration file have an order of precedence. It's the same as the order shown in table 10.1: direct connect, Selenium Standalone Server, Browser Stack, Sauce Labs, a specified `seleniumServerJar` file, and then, finally, local launch. In this section, we've hinted that you can use browsers other than Chrome. In the next section on capabilities, we'll show you how to run tests against other browsers.

10.1.2 *Desired capabilities*

Let's say you want to test against Firefox instead of Chrome. All you need to do is change the `browserName` in your Protractor config, as shown in listing 10.1. You also could launch the browser using driver providers: `seleniumAddress`, `seleniumServer-Jar`, or the local driver option. In addition to Firefox, you can use browsers like Safari,

Microsoft Edge, or Internet Explorer. Only Chrome and Firefox support `direct-Connect`, so for other browsers, you should set `seleniumAddress`.

Listing 10.1   Specifying capabilities for Firefox

```
exports.config = {
  directConnect: true,
  capabilities: {
    browserName: 'firefox'
  }
};
```

TIP The only caveat when using Safari is that you need to run it on an macOS device, which comes bundled with the Safari driver. When running Safari, you'll also need to turn on Allow Remote Automation under the Develop menu. If you want to run on Microsoft's Edge and Internet Explorer browsers, you'll have to use a Windows machine. Both browsers require their own matching browser drivers. When using Internet Explorer, you can download the driver using the command `webdriver-manager update --ie` and start the Selenium Standalone Server with the command `webdriver-manager start --ie`.

You can change other browser settings beyond the browser name. But if you set a desired capability that the browser driver doesn't implement, you won't see an error during the test. When using a browser driver, it's important to check that you're using capabilities that it supports.

One good use case for desired capabilities is running Chrome in *headless mode*, which doesn't require a desktop UI. Headless Chrome is available in versions 59+ (60+ for Windows machines). Because you're running Chrome without a user interface, being able to log network traffic helps you validate that the test is working. With network traffic logging enabled, you might want to extend your test to track how long each JavaScript dependency takes to load. In the following listing, you set the headless `chromeOption` as well as `loggingPrefs`. When you enable performance logging in `loggingPrefs` to true, you'll be able to access each browser session's log in an `afterEach` method.

Listing 10.2   Configuration using headless Chrome—test_capabilities/protractor.conf.js

Sets headless option in chromeOptions

```
exports.config = {
  directConnect: true,
  capabilities: {
    browserName: 'chrome',
    chromeOptions: {
      args: ['--headless', '—disable-gpu']
    },
```

Disable GPU arg is temporarily required if running on Windows. See http://mng.bz/k5qB.

```
    loggingPrefs: {
      performance: 'ALL',          ◄──────  Sets performance logging for
      browser: 'ALL'                        each browser session
    }
  },
  baseUrl: 'https://testing-angular-applications.github.io',
  specs: ['e2e/**/*.e2e-spec.ts'],
  onPrepare: () => {
    require('ts-node').register({
      project: 'e2e'
    });
  },
  useAllAngular2AppRoots: true
};
```

After every test, you check that the browser is getting traffic and log that information to the console, as shown in the following listing.

Listing 10.3 Test using headless Chrome—test_capabilities/e2e/test.e2e-spec.ts

```
import { browser, by, element } from 'protractor';

describe('listing example', () => {
  it('load /', () => {
    console.log('get /')
    browser.get('/');
    expect(browser.getCurrentUrl()).toEqual(browser.baseUrl + '/');
  });

  it('click "+" button -> /add', () => {
    console.log('click "+" button -> /add')
    element(by.id('add-contact')).click();
    expect(browser.getCurrentUrl()).toEqual (browser.baseUrl + 'add');
  });
                                          Logs the performance values from
                                          the browser logs after each test
  afterEach(() => {              ◄───────
    browser.manage().logs().get('performance').then((browserLogs) => {
      expect(browserLogs).not.toBeNull();
      browserLogs.forEach((browserLog) => {
        let message = JSON.parse(browserLog.message).message;
        if (message.method == 'Network.responseReceived') {
          if (message.params.response.timing) {
            let status = message.params.response.status;
            let url = message.params.response.url;
            console.log('status=' + status + ' ' + url);
          }
        }                              If the response is valid, logs the
      });                              response code and URL to console
    });
  });
});
```

Checks to see if traffic is going to the browser

Instead of using a single set of capabilities to launch a browser, what if you want to run the exact same test against other browsers? To launch against multiple browsers, you'll need to use multiCapabilities. You can specify multiCapabilities as an array of desired capabilities, as shown in the following listing. Using multiple capabilities requires running against a Selenium Server, so you need to set the seleniumAddress in the configuration file.

> **Listing 10.4 Multicapabilities—test_multicapabilities/protractor-chrome.conf.js**

```
exports.config = {
  multiCapabilities: [ {
    browserName: 'chrome'         ◄───┐  Running the specs in Chrome and Firefox
  }, {
    browserName: 'firefox'        ◄───┘
  } ],
  seleniumAddress: 'http://127.0.0.1:4444/wd/hub',
  baseUrl: 'https://testing-angular-applications.github.io',
  specs: ['e2e/**/*.e2e-spec.ts'],
  useAllAngular2AppRoots: true,
  onPrepare: () => {
    require('ts-node').register({
      project: 'e2e'
    });
  }
};
```

The main reason to run tests over a set of browsers is to make sure your app is compatible with those browsers. For example, imagine some of your users have noticed navigation issues with a particular feature when they use Microsoft Edge. You might want to use a subset of tests to validate this feature with both Chrome and Microsoft Edge browsers.

It's also important to consider how many tests to run in parallel browsers. If you run your tests with multiple browsers, you could run into CPU- or RAM-resource limitations.

10.1.3 Plugins

Protractor allows you to use *lifecycle hooks* during test execution. (See chapter 7, section 7.1, for how to use them with Angular.) Lifecycle hooks let you insert custom functionality that executes at different points when you're executing a test. Some lifecycle hooks can gather test results or modify the test output. Protractor lets you use these lifecycle hooks by adding plugins to the configuration file. One such lifecycle hook is onPrepare, which is called after the test framework has been set up but before tests are run. In chapter 8, you specified an onPrepare function in your config file so you could load TypeScript spec files using the ts-node npm package. This lifecycle hook is unique in that you can specify it both as a config option and as part of a plugin.

Another good reason to use the onPrepare lifecycle hook is to create custom report artifacts. A typical report artifact is an xUnit report, which is a test report format defined in the JUnit test framework. To create JUnit-style test reports, you'll need to override Jasmine's reporter with the jasmine-reporters node module shown in the following listing.

Listing 10.5   JUnit-style reports using `onPrepare` function

```
exports.config = {
  directConnect: true,
  capabilities: {
    browserName: 'chrome'
  },
  baseUrl: 'https://testing-angular-applications.github.io',
  specs: ['e2e/**/*.e2e-spec.ts'],
  onPrepare: () => {
    let jasmineReporters = require('jasmine-reporters');
    let junitReporter = new jasmineReporters.JUnitXmlReporter({

      savePath: 'output/',                    ◀── The relative path to save the
      consolidateAll: false                        JUnit-style reports

    });
    jasmine.getEnv().addReporter(junitReporter);    ◀── Overrides the Jasmine
    require('ts-node').register({                        default reporter with
      project: 'e2e'                                      the new junitReporter
    });
  },
  useAllAngular2AppRoots: true
};
```

If true, aggregates test
results; if false, creates files

You also could define this lifecycle hook as part of a plugin definition. This setting takes an array of objects with each object defining a plugin. The following listing shows the same example as in listing 10.5 but this time using a plugin configuration.

Listing 10.6   JUnit-style reports using plugins configuration setting

```
exports.config = {
  directConnect: true,
  capabilities: {
    browserName: 'chrome'
  },
  baseUrl: 'https://testing-angular-applications.github.io',
  specs: ['e2e/**/*.e2e-spec.ts'],
  plugins: [{
    inline: {
      onPrepare: () => {
        let jasmineReporters = require('jasmine-reporters');
```

```
            let junitReporter = new jasmineReporters.JUnitXmlReporter({
              savePath: 'output/',
              consolidateAll: false
            });
            jasmine.getEnv().addReporter(junitReporter);
            require('ts-node').register({
              project: 'e2e'
            });
          }
        }
  }],
  useAllAngular2AppRoots: true
};
```

Why use one or the other? Plugins can define more lifecycle hooks than just `onPre-pare` (table 10.2). Defining multiple hooks in the same plugin allows you to share variables between them. You also don't have to define plugins in your config file—you can import them in a separate JS file and share them between multiple projects. All of these lifecycle hooks can return a promise—if they do, Protractor will wait for that promise to be resolved before proceeding.

Table 10.2   Plugin lifecycle hooks

Lifecycle hook	When it's called
`setup`	After the WebDriver session has started, but before Jasmine is set up.
`onPrepare`	After Jasmine is set up.
`teardown`	After tests have run, but before the WebDriver session is stopped.
`postTest`	After each `it()` block completes.
`onPageLoad`	After the page loads, but before Angular bootstraps.
`onPageStable`	After the page has loaded and Angular is ready and stable.
`waitForPromise`	After every WebDriver command. You can use this hook to change how Protractor waits for Angular to be stable.

Until now, all your tests have run on a single machine, but you might need to change the behavior depending on your testing environment. In some situations, for example, you might not want to create JUnit-style reports using plugins. In the next section, we'll look in depth at how to set environment-specific configurations.

10.1.4   *Environment variables*

In previous sections, you created configuration files with different options. For example, you might have Chrome installed on one machine and Firefox on another. Or in some environments, you might need to produce JUnit-style reports, whereas in others you might not want to have reports generated.

How can you change Protractor's behavior based on the environment in these use cases? One way is by setting environment variables. In listing 10.7, you set environment variables to determine which browser the test will use, and whether to use `directConnect` or Selenium Standalone Server. Remember that if you set `DIRECT_CONNECT` to `true`, as in the following listing, and `SELENIUM_ADDRESS` to `http://127.0.0.1:4444/wd/hub`, the test will launch with `directConnect` based on how Protractor handles these driver providers.

> **NOTE** If you export the variables in the bash terminal session, the variables will exist only for that terminal session. If you need those variables to persist beyond the terminal session, you can set them in your ~/.bash_profile on macOS or Linux.

Listing 10.7 Setting environment variables

Uses Selenium Standalone Server if defined and if DIRECT_CONNECT is false

Uses directConnect when set to true

```
export BROWSER_NAME='chrome'
export DIRECT_CONNECT=true
export SELENIUM_ADDRESS=''
```

Now that you've exported the environment variables, you can modify the Protractor configuration file to change behavior based on them. In listing 10.8, you set `direct-Connect` and `seleniumAddress` based on environment variables Node.js makes available in `process.env`. If you don't define `process.env.DIRECT_CONNECT` and `process.env.SELENIUM_ADDRESS`, Protractor will launch the Selenium Standalone Server using a local driver. When you set the `browserName`, if you don't set `process.env.BROWSER_NAME`, Protractor will default to using Chrome.

Listing 10.8 Using environment variables—test_environment/protractor.conf.js

Uses directConnect if the DIRECT_CONNECT environment variable is true

Uses seleniumAddress if the SELENIUM_ADDRESS isn't equal to an empty string

Uses the browser environment variable set in BROWSER_NAME

If the browser is 'chrome', creates JUnit-style reports

```
exports.config = {
  directConnect: process.env.DIRECT_CONNECT,
  seleniumAddress: process.env.SELENIUM_ADDRESS,
  capabilities: {
    browserName: (process.env.BROWSER_NAME || 'chrome')
  },
  baseUrl: 'https://testing-angular-applications.github.io',
  specs: ['e2e/**/*.e2e-spec.ts'],
  onPrepare: () => {
    if (process.env.BROWSER_NAME == 'chrome') {
      let jasmineReporters = require('jasmine-reporters');
      let junitReporter = new jasmineReporters.JUnitXmlReporter({
        savePath: 'output/',
```

```
          consolidateAll: false
        });
        jasmine.getEnv().addReporter(junitReporter);
      }
      require('ts-node').register({
        project: 'e2e'
      });
    },
    useAllAngular2AppRoots: true
};
```

Instead of setting environment variables, you also can create separate Protractor configuration files. Although having multiple Protractor configuration files for each environment might be an easy solution, it requires maintenance if you need to make a change that affects all the configuration files.

Now that you know how to configure Protractor in depth, let's use this knowledge to create a new kind of test. In the next section, you'll create a custom plugin and config that will let you compare browser screenshots in your tests.

10.2 Screenshot testing

You write tests to prevent your mistakes from becoming user-facing issues. Up until now, you've been testing only the logic of your application. But the appearance of your web app is also important. One way to verify that the appearance of your app is correct is to have a test that fails when a screenshot changes.

You might think that such a test would be fragile, and you'd be right. This test will fail whenever the look of your app changes, intentionally or not. But it's a useful safeguard to catch unintentional CSS regressions, which can be easy to introduce and hard to check. After all, who wants to spend all day before a release clicking through each page in your app, verifying that no awkward CSS errors have slipped through? This test will guard against unintentional style errors, but the price is that you need to update it whenever you intentionally change your app's CSS.

10.2.1 Taking screenshots

Taking screenshots in Protractor is easy; you can call `browser.takeScreenshot()` to take a screenshot. Unlike the other WebDriver commands you've seen so far, `takeScreenshot()` returns a promise. As mentioned in earlier chapters, a promise represents the future value of an asynchronous operation. The important thing to know is that to get the screenshot image, you need to call `.then()` on the result of `takeScreenshot()` and pass it a function that does something with the data. The following listing is an example of taking a screenshot in a test.

> **Listing 10.9   test_screenshot/e2e/screenshot.e2e-spec.ts**

```
describe('the contact list', () => {
  beforeAll(() => {
    browser.get('/');
    browser.driver.manage().window().setSize(1024,900);    ◄──┤ Sets the window size
                                                               │ before taking a screenshot
```

```
    });

    it('should be able to login', (done) => {
      const list = element(by.css('app-contact-list'));
      browser.waitForAngular();

      browser.takeScreenshot().then((data) => {
        fs.writeFileSync('screenshot.png', data, 'base64');
        done();
      })
    });
  });
```

Lets Jasmine know the test is done

**Waits for the page to load
before taking a screenshot**

Also unlike other WebDriver commands, Protractor won't automatically wait for Angular before executing `takeScreenshot()`—it'll take a screenshot immediately, which is useful when using screenshots for debugging. If you want to take the screenshot after Angular is done updating the page, you'll have to manually call `browser.waitForAngular()`.

This test is different from the previous Protractor tests in a couple of ways. As mentioned, the `takeScreenshot()` command returns a promise. In fact, all WebDriver commands return promises, but Protractor has some hidden magic that lets you ignore that and write your tests as if they were synchronous.

The other important difference is that the test is now asynchronous; it needs to wait until Node.js has written the screenshot to disk before finishing. You can make any Jasmine test asynchronous by accepting a `'done'` callback in the function you define for your `it()` block. Jasmine will wait until you execute that callback before finishing the test. This allows you to write tests with asynchronous behavior, like calling `setTimeout()` or making network calls—or, in this case, waiting for the screenshot data.

10.2.2 *Taking screenshots on test failure*

Previously, you saw how you can use plugins to extend Protractor's behavior. The plugin API provides hooks that you can use to add custom logic to your Protractor tests. Next you'll use the plugin API to take a screenshot of the browser when a test fails. First, you can add a plugin to your test's config by adding a plugin section, like this:

```
plugins: [{
  path: './screenshot_on_failure_plugin.ts'
}],
```

This loads the plugin, which you define in a separate TypeScript file. Protractor calls the plugin's lifecycle hooks at different points in the test process. In your case, you need to define a `postTest()` function, as shown in listing 10.10. Protractor calls the `postTest()` function after each `it()` block finishes. The function receives two arguments—whether the test passed and an object containing a description of the test. If the test fails, you take a screenshot and save it to a file based on the name of the test that failed. This produces a screenshot at the moment of failure for each failing test in your test suite.

Listing 10.10   test_screenshot/screenshot_on_failure_plugin.ts

```
import {browser} from 'protractor';
import * as fs from 'fs';

export function postTest(passed: boolean, testInfo: any) {
  if(!passed) {
    const fileName = `${testInfo.name.replace(/ /g, '_')}_failure.png`
    return browser.takeScreenshot().then((data) => {
      fs.writeFileSync(fileName, data, 'base64')
    });
  }
}
```

Tests name as the file name for the screenshot

Writes new screenshot synchronously to disk

Calls the postTest function after each it() block.

You can find this plugin and config file in the Chapter 10 code repo on GitHub (http://mng.bz/0OPs). Try it for yourself—make a failing test and verify that you get a screenshot of the browser at the time of failure. If you want to learn more about writing plugins, check out the official docs in the Protractor repo (http://mng.bz/bSLE). This simple plugin will help debug why a test failed, but you also can use screenshots as part of your tests, as you'll see in the next section.

10.2.3 *Comparing screenshots*

It can be hard to make an automated test that verifies how an application looks. But you can make a simple screenshot test that will fail when any major, unintended changes show up in your application's appearance. You can use the looks-same npm package to compare a screenshot of the browser against a reference image.

Listing 10.11 shows a couple of helper functions that use the looks-same library to compare a screenshot to a reference image. The writeScreenshot() function encapsulates some of the boilerplate around writing a screenshot to disk. The compare-Screenshot() function takes the callback-oriented API of looks-same and wraps it in a promise that's resolved with the value of the screenshot comparison.

Listing 10.11   test_screenshot/e2e/screenshot_helper.ts

Helper function that writes the screenshot to disk

```
function writeScreenshot(data) {
  return new Promise<string>(function (resolve, reject) {
    const folder = fs.mkdtempSync(`${os.tmpdir()}${path.sep}`);
    let screenshotFile = path.join(folder, 'new.png');
    fs.writeFile(screenshotFile, data, 'base64', function (err) {
      if (err) {
        reject(err);
      }
      resolve(screenshotFile);
    });
```

```
    });
}

export function compareScreenshot(data, golden) {
  return new Promise((resolve, reject) => {
    return writeScreenshot(data).then((screenshotPath) => {
      if (process.env['UPDATE_SCREENSHOTS']) {          ◄──────
        fs.writeFileSync(golden, fs.readFileSync(screenshotPath));
        resolve(true);
      } else {
        looksSame(screenshotPath, golden, {}, (error, equal) => {
          if (!equal) {
            looksSame.createDiff({        ◄────────
              reference: golden,
              current: screenshotPath,
              diff: 'diff.png',        ◄────────
              highlightColor: '#ff00ff'
            }, function (error) {
              resolve(equal);
            });
          } else {
            resolve(equal);
          }
        })
      }
    });
  });
}
```

> **You can use an environment variable to control the helper.**

> **If the screenshot is different, create an image highlighting those differences.**

> **The difference image is written to 'diff.png'.**

The compareScreenshot() helper has a couple of useful features. First, you can easily update the golden image if you set the environment variable UPDATE_SCREENSHOTS. For example, if you run your tests with UPDATE_SCREENSHOTS=1 protractor screenshot_ test.conf.js, the test will run, but instead of comparing the screenshot to the reference, it overwrites the reference image with the new screenshot. You can then commit the updated reference images in your git repo. It's helpful to keep these screenshots in version control along with your source code so you can track how they change.

If the images are different, compareScreenshot() automatically calls looksSame. createDiff(). This creates an image showing the difference between the current screenshot and the reference image so you can easily see what went wrong.

Listing 10.12 shows a test that uses these helpers. Note that in the test you need to explicitly call browser.waitForAngular(). Usually, when you turn on waiting for Angular with browser.waitForAngularEnabled(true), Protractor waits for Angular to be ready before executing each WebDriver command. But screenshots are taken immediately, so you'll need to manually wait for the contact list to load.

Listing 10.12 An example screenshot test

```
it('should be able to login', (done) => {
  const GOLDEN_IMG = path.join(__dirname,'contact_list_golden.png');   ◄──────
  const list = element(by.css('app-contact-list'));
  browser.waitForAngular();
```

> **Saves the golden image in the same directory as the test, so you can check it in to git**

```
browser.takeScreenshot()
  .then((data) => {
    return compareScreenshot(data, GOLDEN_IMG);
  })
  .then((result) => {
    expect(result).toBeTruthy();
    done();
  })
});
```

Returns the promise from compareScreenshot to chain it into the next then() block

Result will be true if screenshots matched

You call then() on a promise to handle the result—the callback you pass to then() will be invoked when the asynchronous operations the promise represents finish. If, when handling the result of a promise, you need to make a new asynchronous call, you can return a promise and add another then() block. This is called *promise chaining* because you chain your then() blocks together, one per asynchronous operation. In listing 10.12, you chain together two asynchronous operations—taking the screenshot and comparing the screenshot to the reference—so you have two then() blocks.

Let's look at an example showing screenshots. Say your contacts list looks like figure 10.1.

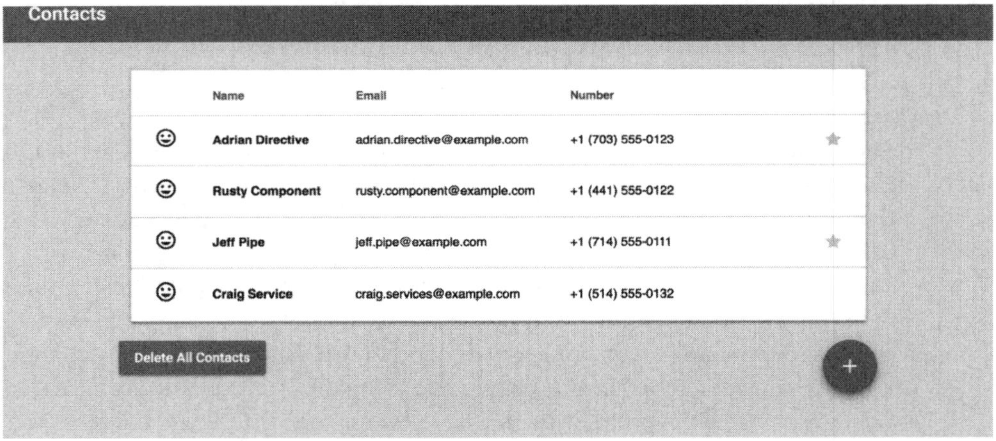

Figure 10.1   The reference screenshot image

Suppose you accidentally broke your application's CSS by adding the following to contact-list.component.css:

```css
.add-fab {
  float: right;
  cursor: pointer;
  position: absolute;
}
```

Now the list looks like figure 10.2.

Figure 10.2 The contact list with broken CSS

Your tests might still pass, despite the page being obviously broken. But your screen-shot test will fail and produce the diff image in figure 10.3.

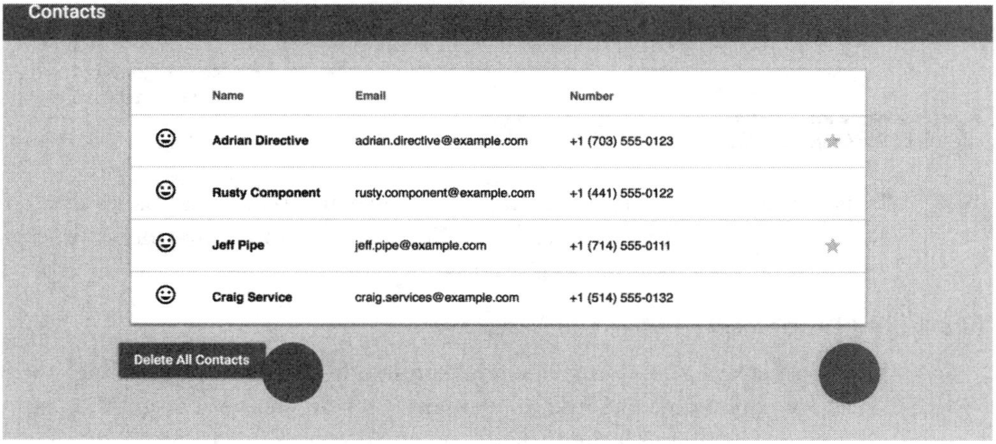

Figure 10.3 The difference image highlighting where the current screenshot differs from the reference

Notice how the diff image highlights the part of the screenshot that changed. You can change the highlight color if pink isn't your thing. The important part is that when your screenshot test fails, you can check the diff image to see what went wrong. If the change is expected, you can rerun the test with UPDATE_SCREENSHOTS=1 to update the reference image.

10.3   *Experimental debugging features*

It can be hard to know what might have caused a Protractor test to fail. Fortunately, some experimental features recently added to Protractor can make it easier to debug failing tests. In this section, you'll use these new features to debug a test in the chapter10/test_experimental directory of the book's repository (which, as mentioned, you can find at http://mng.bz/z22f).

The following listing shows the test you'll be working with in this section.

Listing 10.13   test_experimental/e2e/add-contact.e2e-spec.ts

```ts
import {browser, by, element, ExpectedConditions as EC} from 'protractor';

describe('contact list', () => {
  beforeAll(() => {
    browser.get('/');
  });

  it('should be able to add a contact', () => {          // Clicks the Add Contact button
    element(by.id('add-contact')).click();

    element(by.id('contact-name')).sendKeys('Ada Contact');
    element(by.css('.create-button')).click();

    expect(element(by.css('app-contact-list')).getText())
          .toContain('Ada Contact');
  });
});
```

Clicks the Add Contact button

Types in a name for the contact and clicks the Create button

Verifies that the new contact shows in the contact list

This is a simple test, but because it moves between two different pages (the contact list and the add contact view), it can be a little difficult to debug when things go wrong. Let's look at some tools to help with that.

10.3.1   *WebDriver logs*

When a Protractor test runs, it sends commands to the browser telling it what to do. These are commands like find an element, click an element, or get the text of an element. Even if you watch the browser as your test runs, it can be hard to know exactly what's going on. Instead, you can have Protractor create a log of the WebDriver commands it sends using the –webDriverLogDir option.

NOTE   The WebDriver protocol is a W3C specification. If you're interested in seeing all the details of the protocol, they're available at www.w3.org/TR/webdriver/.

This option specifies a directory where Protractor will create a log of the WebDriver commands it sends during a test run. Protractor will name each log file `webdriver_log_<sessionId>.txt`, with a different `sessionId` for each test run. Each line of the log file shows when the command was sent, how long it took, and what the command was. It looks like figure 10.4.

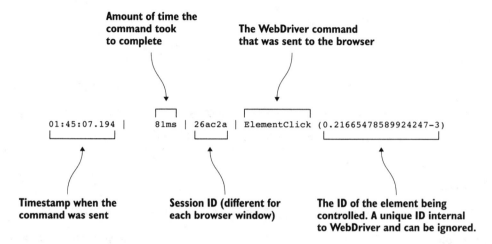

Figure 10.4   The structure of a WebDriver log line

Now run your add contact test with WebDriver logging. Unlike the other examples so far, logging WebDriver commands requires running a Selenium Server. (We'll explain why in a bit, don't worry.) To run the test in chapter10/test_experimental and generate a WebDriver log, first start a Selenium Server:

```
webdriver-manager start
```

Then, in another terminal, start the test like so:

```
protractor --webDriverLogDir ./
```

After the test runs, Protractor will create a log of WebDriver commands in the current directory. The entire log is a bit long, but the following listing shows a sample of the end of the log after running the example test.

Listing 10.14   Excerpt from WebDriver log

Typing Ada Contact into the contact name field

```
01:45:06.984 |   520ms | 26ac2a | Waiting for Angular
01:45:06.984 |    14ms | 26ac2a | FindElements
   Using css selector '*[id="contact-name"]'
   Elements: 0.21665478589924247-2
01:45:07.009 |     9ms | 26ac2a | Waiting for Angular
01:45:07.009 |   131ms | 26ac2a | ElementSendKeys (0.21665478589924247-2)
   Send: Ada Contact
```

```
01:45:07.165 |    23ms | 26ac2a | Waiting for Angular
01:45:07.166 |    18ms | 26ac2a | FindElements
   Using css selector '.create-button'
   Elements: 0.21665478589924247-3
01:45:07.194 |     8ms | 26ac2a | Waiting for Angular
01:45:07.194 |    81ms | 26ac2a | ElementClick (0.21665478589924247-3)
01:45:08.306 |  1028ms | 26ac2a | Waiting for Angular
01:45:08.306 |    15ms | 26ac2a | FindElements
   Using css selector 'app-contact-list'
   Elements: 0.21665478589924247-4
01:45:08.331 |     9ms | 26ac2a | Waiting for Angular
01:45:08.331 |    47ms | 26ac2a | GetElementText (0.21665478589924247-4)
   Name Email Number
mood Adrian Directive adrian.directive@example.com +1 (703) 555-0123 edit
➡delete
mood Rusty Component rusty.component@example.com +1 (441) 555-0122 edit
➡delete
mood Jeff Pipe jeff.pipe@example.com +1 (714) 555-0111 edit delete
mood Craig Service craig.services@example.com +1 (514) 555-0132 edit delete
mood Ada Contact edit delete

Delete All Contacts
add
01:45:08.388 |    54ms | 26ac2a | DeleteSession
```

After clicking the Create button, Protractor waits about a second for the contact list to load.

Finding and clicking the Create contact button

Getting the text of the contact list

You might have noticed all the Waiting for Angular log lines. What do they mean? Remember from chapter 9 that Protractor waits for Angular to be stable before sending a WebDriver command—every time it does so, it adds Waiting for Angular to the log. The log also shows the amount of time that each step takes to complete—you can see that after clicking the Create button, Protractor waits for Angular for 1028 ms while the contact list loads.

The WebDriver log is handy for knowing after the fact what happened in a test, but sometimes it would be nice to be able to watch the browser while the test runs. Usually, the test runs too quickly for you to see what's happening, but you can slow it down using highlight delay.

10.3.2   *Highlight delay*

When Protractor tests run, they execute WebDriver commands as fast as possible. If you've ever tried to debug a Protractor test by watching the browser window, you've seen what this looks like. Buttons are clicked so fast, it's as if the browser is being controlled by a hyperactive poltergeist. It's normally impossible to follow what's happening.

You can fix this with the –highlightDelay flag. This tells Protractor to add a delay, specified in milliseconds, before sending WebDriver commands to the browser.

Protractor also will highlight the element it's about to touch with a light blue rectangle, so you can tell which element is about to be clicked. For example, if the test is about to enter text in a field, first it'll highlight the text field with a blue rectangle (figure 10.5), then it'll wait the specified delay time before proceeding.

The name field is highlighted becuase
the test is about to enter the name there.

Figure 10.5   Protractor highlights the name input field before entering a name.

Adding a highlight delay can be a quick and easy way to see what's going on during a Protractor test. You can slow things down as much as you like, and the highlight lets you know which part of the page Protractor will touch next.

10.3.3 *Blocking proxy*

A new component in Protractor called blocking proxy makes experimental new features like highlight delay and WebDriver logs possible. This proxy sits between your test and the browser driver. This proxy can intercept and optionally delay any command that your test sends to the browser. As a result, it can create a log of commands or delay them.

One benefit of having this functionality in a proxy is that you can use it with any WebDriver test. This means you don't have to be using Protractor to use it—even if you have WebDriver tests written in Java or Python, you could still use blocking proxy to add a highlight delay to your tests. It even implements the same `waitForAngular` logic that Protractor uses. If you don't feel like writing your tests in TypeScript and running them on Node.js, you could write them in any language that WebDriver supports and use blocking proxy to get the same `waitForAngular` behavior as Protractor.

Blocking proxy is still an experimental feature in Protractor. If you'd like to learn more about it or use it in other projects, check it out at https://github.com/angular/blocking-proxy.

10.4   *The control flow and debugging with Chrome DevTools*

Debugging a failing Protractor test can be frustrating, mainly because there's no obvious way to step through the test and see what it's doing. Fortunately, recent changes to WebDriver, Node.js, and Protractor can make debugging Protractor tests as easy as debugging any traditional application. To better understand how important these changes are, and why Protractor tests are difficult to debug, you need to understand asynchronous programming in JavaScript, specifically how the `async`/`await` feature added in ES2017 makes asynchronous programming easier.

If you're already familiar with asynchronous programming in JavaScript, feel free to skip to the last section, where you'll see how easy it is to step through Protractor tests using Chrome DevTools.

10.4.1 *Asynchronous functions and promises*

In a language with threads, like Java or C#, you can write code that will block until an I/O operation (reading from the file system, sending data over the network, and so on) finishes. But in JavaScript, when you have an I/O operation, you typically pass a callback that will be invoked when the operation finishes.

Let's imagine a simple function that makes two API calls and writes some result to disk based on the responses. In Java, your imaginary function might look something like the following:

```
responseA = callServiceA();
responseB = callServiceB(responseA);
resultFile = writeResponseData(responseB);
doSomethingWithResult(resultFile);
```

Each function blocks until it finishes, running line by line in an *imperative* (or some might say *synchronous*) manner. In JavaScript, you can't make blocking calls; instead, you pass a callback that will be invoked when the function is done. The preceding imaginary example might look like the following in JavaScript:

```
callServiceA((responseA) => {
  callServiceB(responseA, (responseB) => {
    writeResponse(responseB, (resultFile) => {
      doSomethingWithResult(resultFile);
    })
  })
})
```

Depending on when the JavaScript runtime invokes your callbacks, your code may not execute the same way it reads. Asynchronous programming is kind of like being a time traveler; things don't necessarily happen in the order you expect. This can be confusing for people learning about callbacks for the first time.

For the code in listing 10.15, the first line that prints something to the console is the last line in the listing. The order in which the callbacks are invoked and printed to the console depends on when the different `setTimeout` calls are scheduled. This code may not necessarily run in the same order you see when reading it from top to bottom.

Listing 10.15   Asynchronous program flow example

```
setTimeout(() => {
  console.log('Event C');          ◄─────┐  After 1 second, this timer fires.
},1000);

                                          ┌  After 500 ms, this callback
setTimeout(() => {                        │  runs and sets another timer.
  console.log('Event B');          ◄─────┘
  setTimeout(() => {
    console.log('Event D');        ◄─────┐
  },1000);                               │  A second after Event B
},500);                                  └  happens, this timer fires.

                                          ┌  Executes first
console.log('Event A');            ◄─────┘
```

Having to pass a callback every time you want to do something with the result of an asynchronous call can lead to the *pyramid of doom*; a long list of nested callbacks can end up yielding deeply indented code that's hard to read. One fix for this is to use promises. Instead of passing a callback to be invoked when the operation is done, you can return a promise that eventually will resolve to the result of the operation. The result is much easier to read:

```
callServiceA().then((responseA) => {
  return callServiceB(responseA)
}).then((responseB) => {
  return writeResponse(responseB)
}).then((resultFile) => {
  doSomethingWithResult(resultFile);
});
```

The WebDriver commands in Protractor tests are asynchronous calls; your test is making an API call to Selenium to send the command to the browser. But you normally can write Protractor tests without worrying about callbacks and promises, thanks to a helpful feature of WebDriver called the control flow.

10.4.2   *The WebDriver control flow*

Most of the tests you've written so far seem to be synchronous, even though they execute WebDriver commands. How is this possible? The trick is that WebDriver commands return a special kind of promise (called a *managed* promise) that's executed later. Unlike a normal promise, a managed promise doesn't run an asynchronous task. Instead, it schedules a command to run on Webdriver's control flow. At the end of your test, the control flow runs, and all the scheduled browser commands execute. As a result, you can write your tests as if you were writing asynchronous code, without worrying about promises. The following listing shows how you might write a test relying on managed promises.

10.16 Test using control flow

```
it('should open the dialog with waitForAngular', () => {
  let feedButton = element(by.css('button.feed-button'));
  let closeButton = element(by.css('button[mat-dialog-close]'));
  let dialogTitle =
      element(by.css('app-contact-feed h2.mat-dialog-title'));

  feedButton.click();
  expect(dialogTitle.getText())
      .toContain('Latest posts from Craig Service');
  debugger;

  closeButton.click();
  browser.wait(EC.stalenessOf(dialogTitle), 3000,
      'Waiting for dialog to close');
  expect(dialogTitle.isPresent()).toBeFalsy();
});
```

Schedules a click command on the control flow

None of the commands have executed yet.

The test commands run when the it() block is complete.

Unfortunately, using the control flow prevents you from debugging Protractor tests with standard Node.js tools. If you've ever used the debugger keyword in a Protractor test, you've seen this. When the debugger hits the breakpoint, the browser isn't executing commands; instead, the test synchronously defines a list of commands to run (the control flow). As a result, in listing 10.16, when you hit the debugger breakpoint, the Feed button hasn't actually been clicked yet. Instead, Protractor automatically runs those commands after each it() block, which is why you don't see the commands running if you set a breakpoint in your test.

You don't have to use the control flow. You also can treat managed promises as if they were regular promises. You can schedule callbacks to run when the command is executed using .then(), as in the following listing.

Listing 10.17 Explicitly using WebDriver promises

Adds a breakpoint after the Feed button is clicked

```
it('should open the dialog with waitForAngular', (done) => {
  let feedButton = element(by.css('button.feed-button'));
  let closeButton = element(by.css('button[mat-dialog-close]'));
  let dialogTitle =
      element(by.css('app-contact-feed h2.mat-dialog-title'));

  return feedButton.click().then(() => {
    return dialogTitle.getText();
  }).then((dialogText) => {
    expect(dialogText).toContain('Latest posts from Craig Service');
    debugger;
```

```
      return closeButton.click();
  }).then(() => {
    return browser.wait(EC.stalenessOf(dialogTitle), 3000,
        'Waiting for dialog to close');
  }).then(() => {
    return dialogTitle.isPresent();
  }).then((dialogTitleIsPresent) => {
    expect(dialogTitleIsPresent).toBeFalsy();
    done();
  });
```

Notice that any interaction at all with the browser is an asynchronous action—this includes clicking buttons, getting text, waiting on expected conditions, or waiting for elements to be present. Without the control flow, you'll need to chain all of these promises; otherwise, the browser actions won't run in a defined order. Also, because the test is now asynchronous, you need to call done() to signal to Jasmine that it's done. Because you're not using the control flow in listing 10.17, the debugger breakpoint works as expected—when you hit it, the Feed button has been clicked.

Even though the tests in listings 10.16 and 10.17 do the same thing, the test that uses the control flow (in listing 10.16) is much easier to read. You can see why the authors of Selenium WebDriver added the control flow. But the new async/await feature coming to JavaScript (and available in Node v8) makes asynchronous code that uses the feature much more readable than code that uses promises. That's why the Selenium team has decided to deprecate the control flow (see GitHub issue: https://github.com/SeleniumHQ/selenium/issues/2969), and why they won't use the control flow in Selenium 4.x and greater. When using these versions of Selenium, you'll no longer be able to write tests as in listing 10.16. Instead, you'll need to explicitly write asynchronous tests. But without the control flow, your tests also will be much easier to debug.

10.4.3 The future: async/await

The async and await keywords are a new addition to JavaScript that makes asynchronous code much more readable. The details of async/await are beyond the scope of this book. All you need to know is that it's a special syntax that makes waiting on promises easier.

You can disable the WebDriver control flow by adding SELENIUM_PROMISE_MANAGER: false to your Protractor config. As of Selenium 4.x, running without the control flow will be the only option, but setting this flag gives you a way to get your tests ready for control flow deprecation. Using async/await, you can rewrite the test from the example, as shown in the following listing, to be much more readable, even though it doesn't use the control flow.

Listing 10.18   Test using `async/await`

Uses await to get the result
of the promise

Declares function as async

```
it('should open the dialog with waitForAngular', async () => {
    let feedButton = element(by.css('button.feed-button'));
    let closeButton = element(by.css('button[mat-dialog-close]'));
    let dialogTitle =
        element(by.css('app-contact-feed h2.mat-dialog-title'));

    await feedButton.click();
    let dialogText = await dialogTitle.getText();
    expect(dialogText).toContain('Latest posts from Craig Service');
    debugger;

    await closeButton.click();
    await browser.wait(EC.stalenessOf(dialogTitle), 3000,
        'Waiting for dialog to close');
    let dialogTitleIsPresent = await dialogTitle.isPresent();
    expect(dialogTitleIsPresent).toBeFalsy();
});
```

Adds a breakpoint just before
the Close button is clicked

In listing 10.18, you declare the body of your test to be `async`. This lets you wait for and get the results of each promise using `await`. Adding a breakpoint with `debugger` works as it did in listing 10.17 with promise chaining. Also, because your test body is `async`, Jasmine knows to wait for it—there's no need to explicitly call `done()`. Notice how using `async/await` makes your test much more readable, compared to waiting on promises using `.then()`. That's why the Selenium team feels comfortable removing the control flow in Selenium 4.x—JavaScript has finally evolved to the point where writing asynchronous code is easy. Disabling the control flow lets you do something that hasn't been possible until now—debug your tests using the Chrome Inspector!

10.4.4 Using Chrome DevTools

Node.js v6 added the ability to debug Node.js programs using Chrome DevTools. The test in listing 10.18 has a debugger statement to set a breakpoint right before the Close button is clicked. You can debug your test by starting Protractor with the following command:

```
node --inspect --debug-brk \
  ./node_modules/protractor/bin/protractor  ./debugging_test.conf.js
```

> **NOTE** You need to disable WebDriver control flow by adding `SELENIUM_PROMISE _MANAGER: false` to your Protractor config.

If you start Protractor with Node.js debugging enabled, you'll see something like figure 10.6.

Figure 10.6   Starting Protractor with debugging enabled

In Chrome 60 or later, you can debug Node.js programs by opening about://
inspect. Any Node.js programs ready for debugging will automatically appear in a list.
Figure 10.7 shows what this looks like.

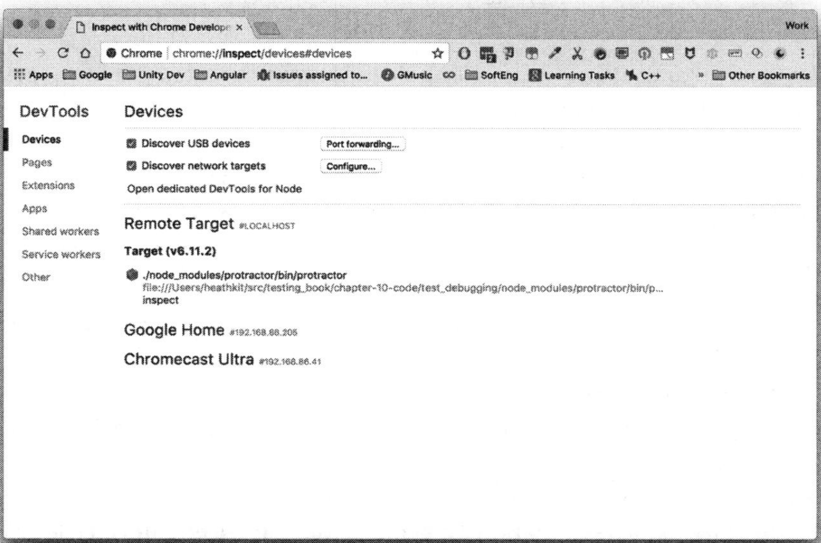

Figure 10.7   Opening DevTools in Chrome

If you select Open Dedicated DevTools for Node, you'll get a debugger attached to your Protractor test. You can step through to the breakpoint you set with the `debugger` statement. Figure 10.8 shows what this debugger looks like.

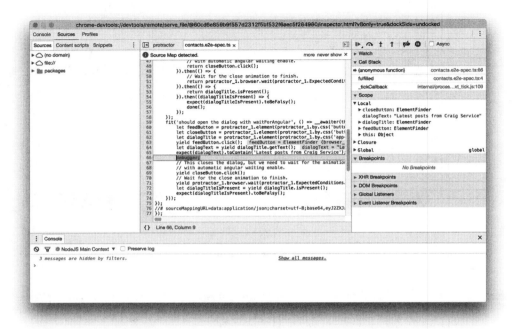

Figure 10.8   Debugging a Protractor test with the Chrome Inspector

If you have some experience writing Protractor tests, you might have seen old debugging tools like ElementExplorer or `browser.pause()`. These tools were necessary when WebDriver's control flow prevented debugging a Protractor test like a normal Node.js program. But now that the Selenium team has deprecated the control flow, you can use the much more powerful Chrome DevTools and throw away the old tools.

Summary

- You can pass command-line flags to the browser using the capabilities section of your Protractor config. For example, you can pass `'--headless'` to Chrome to start it in headless mode.
- Plugins let you add features to Protractor, like changing how test results are reported or taking screenshots on test failure.
- Protractor can take screenshots of your application during a test, and you can use them to create tests that verify if your application web interface looks right.

- New Protractor features like `highlightDelay` and `webDriverLogDir` make it easier to understand what your test is doing as it runs.
- The WebDriver control flow is deprecated and won't be in Selenium 4.x, so you should start using `async`/`await` in your tests.
- It's easy to debug tests using Chrome DevTools.

part 3

Continuous integration

This last part of the book is small but important. The other chapters show you how to write a variety of tests for your application. But what good is a test if you never run it? Continuous integration (CI) systems automatically run your entire test suite with each change, allowing you to catch issues effortlessly as soon as they're introduced.

Chapter 11 shows you how to set up two different kinds of CI systems. For the DIY-minded, we cover in depth how to configure Jenkins, a popular open-source CI tool, to run your unit and E2E tests. We also show you how to use CircleCI, a popular commercial CI service.

Continuous integration

This chapter covers

- Setting up Jenkins
- Running both unit and E2E tests on Jenkins
- Configuring CircleCI to run your unit and E2E tests

Writing tests for your Angular application is only half the battle. You need to remember to run those tests to make sure you catch regressions as you continue to add features. Running tests manually can be tedious. It's better to set up a continuous integration (CI) system that will integrate with your source repository and automatically run all the tests for each change.

In practice, you develop your Protractor tests on a desktop, where you can watch the browser and see if your tests are passing. One big stumbling block people run into when setting up their tests in a CI system is that the server doesn't normally have a GUI. (It's a *headless environment.*) In this chapter, we'll show how to set up your tests to run automatically in a headless environment. First, we'll cover setting up your own CI system using the open source Jenkins server; then we'll show you how easy it can be to set up testing with CircleCI, which is a hosted CI service that has a free tier.

11.1 Jenkins

Jenkins is an open source CI server with a powerful web interface. It was originally created for testing Java applications, but, thanks to a rich ecosystem of plugins, Jenkins can now test almost any project in any language. You're going to set up a Jenkins server that will run your tests on Node.js.

11.1.1 Setting up Jenkins

Jenkins is a large, complicated project, and the full details of installing it are beyond the scope of this book. The example in this chapter assumes you're running Jenkins on an Ubuntu server, but you also can install it on macOS and Windows. Follow the official instructions for installing Jenkins on your server at https://jenkins.io/doc/book/installing, and then come back here when you've set up the first admin user.

You need a browser to run both unit and end-to-end (E2E) tests; you'll use Chrome for this example. Chrome needs a GUI to run, and your server is headless, so you'll install Xvfb. You also need Node.js to run the tests.

> **NOTE**   In Linux, the GUI is provided by an X server. Xvfb is an X server that uses a *virtual framebuffer* (vfb) for display. This means that the graphical display is entirely in memory. Xvfb is a good tool to use if you need to use graphical programs on a Linux server that may not have a display attached.

The following listing shows how to install the prerequisites for this setup on Ubuntu. You can use `apt` to install Xvfb, but you should manually install Google Chrome and Node Version Manager (nvm) to get their latest versions.

Listing 11.1   Install prerequisites: Chrome, Xvfb, and Node

```
sudo apt-get update
sudo apt-get install Xvfb -y              ◀── Installs Xvfb

sudo sh -c 'echo "deb [arch=amd64] \
  http://dl-ssl.google.com/linux/chrome/deb/ stable main" >> \
  /etc/apt/sources.list.d/google-chrome.list'       ◀── Installs Google Chrome

wget -q -O - https://dl-ssl.google.com/linux/linux_signing_key.pub \
  | sudo apt-key add -

sudo apt-get update
sudo apt-get install google-chrome-stable -y
```

```
curl -o- \
  https://raw.githubusercontent.com/creationix/nvm/v0.33.2/install.sh \
  | bash
nvm install 8
```

Installs a node version manager

Uses node version manager to install node version 8

Now that you have your prerequisites, you're ready to install the plugins you need using Jenkins' browser-based admin interface. In the browser window, you can install plugins by navigating to Manage Jenkins and then clicking the Manage Plugins link. The plugins you need for your Jenkins job are the JUnit plugin, the Xvfb plugin, and the nvm wrapper plugin, all shown in figure 11.1. The JUnit plugin will interpret and show a trending history of your test. The nvm wrapper plugin will allow your test to launch Protractor with Node.js, and the Xvfb plugin will allow you to run your test in a browser.

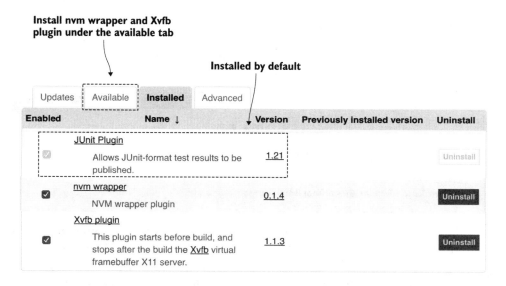

Figure 11.1   JUnit, nvm wrapper, and Xvfb plugins

You'll also need to set some configuration options for Jenkins. In the same browser window, you can configure Jenkins by clicking Manage Jenkins, then navigating to Global Tool Configuration. From there, you need to set a valid path for both JAVA_HOME and Xvfb, shown in figure 11.2. Jenkins requires Java to be set in the path to launch the Selenium standalone server and Xvfb to run the virtual desktop environment.

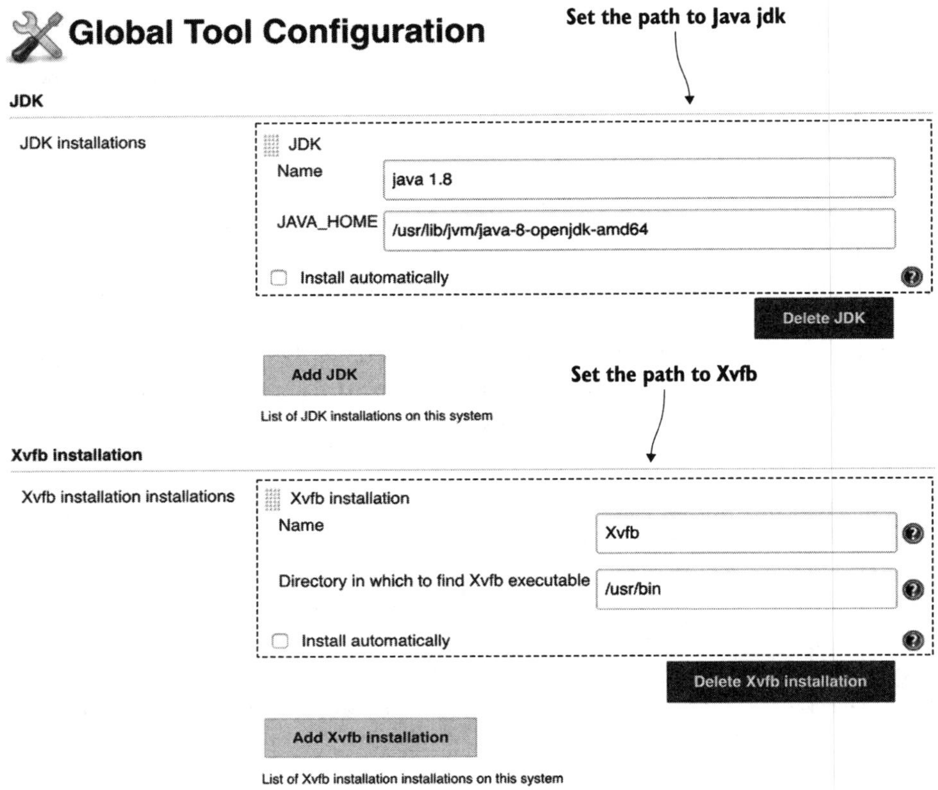

Figure 11.2 Jenkins Global Tool Configuration

Now that you have all the components required to run a Protractor test, let's review the test in the GitHub repository (http://mng.bz/z22f). In Jenkins, create a new free-style project, go to the Source Code Management section, and add the git repository as https://github.com/testing-angular-applications/testing-angular-applications.git.

11.1.2 *Unit tests*

You use Karma to run your unit tests. Karma takes care of starting a browser, connecting to it, and running your tests there. Because Karma runs your unit tests in a real browser, your tests have access to a real DOM and your client code runs exactly as it will in production. In fact, you can use Karma to run your unit tests on other browsers, like Firefox and Safari, to make sure your application is compatible with them. To keep things simple, for this example you'll run the unit tests for your project on Chrome.

Jenkins expects test results to be in an XML file with the same format the JUnit would use to report Java test results. This format has become a de-facto standard, and test frameworks in a variety of languages can now report test results in this JUnit-XML style. Karma has a plugin called `karma-junit-reporter`, which outputs the results of running Karma in this format so that Jenkins can understand them. To run your unit tests on Jenkins, you'll create a separate configuration for Karma that uses this plugin.

As noted earlier, Chrome's headless mode starts Chrome without a display. Your unit tests don't need a GUI, so even though you've already set up Xvfb, go ahead and use headless Chrome to run your unit tests. Don't worry; you'll be using Xvfb soon.

The `karma-chrome-launcher` plugin will start headless Chrome if you specify the browser as `ChromeHeadless`. The following listing shows the Karma config for your CI server, using headless Chrome and JUnit XML reporting.

Listing 11.2   Karma configuration for CI server—chapter11/karma-ci.conf.js

**Uses the JUnit reporter to create
JUnit-style XML**

```
module.exports = function (config) {
  config.set({
    basePath: '',
    frameworks: ['jasmine', '@angular/cli'],
    plugins: [
      require('karma-jasmine'),
      require('karma-chrome-launcher'),
      require('karma-jasmine-html-reporter'),
      require('karma-junit-reporter'),
      require('@angular/cli/plugins/karma')
    ],
    reporters: ['junit'],
    junitReporter: {
      outputDir: 'karma-results',
      outputFile: 'karma-results.xml'
    },
    angularCli: {
      environment: 'dev',
    },
    port: 9876,
    logLevel: config.LOG_INFO,
    browsers: ['ChromeHeadless'],
    autoWatch: false,
    singleRun: true
  });
};
```

**Outputs the results in the
'karma-results' directory**

Runs the tests in headless Chrome

**In CI, only runs the tests once and
doesn't watch for changes**

This is a Karma configuration separate from the one you use during development. For the rest of this book, we've kept the test cases and website in separate directories, so you can follow along as you write tests in each chapter.

> **NOTE** In practice, it's best to have unit tests next to the code they test. The `chapter11/run_unit_ci.sh` script in the project repo (http://mng.bz/z22f) copies the tests and Karma config to the website/ directory before running Karma.

Create a new project in Jenkins by clicking New Item on the main page. Create a new Freestyle project. In the configuration for the new project, select Git under Source Code Management. The build config for your unit tests is shown in figure 11.3.

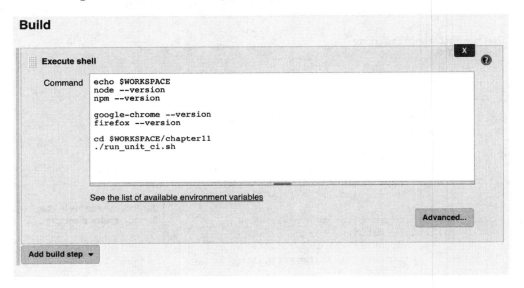

Figure 11.3   Build configuration for the unit test Jenkins job

All this config needs to do is call the `run_unit_ci.sh` script. In general, it's better to keep as much of your CI process as possible in a script in your source repo, where it's easy to debug and track changes. This also keeps your Jenkins config simple, because all it needs to do is call that script. Your Jenkins job config also prints out the versions of npm, Node, and Chrome. Jenkins saves the console output for each run, and it can be helpful to see exactly which versions of these tools were used in an old run.

You also need to tell Jenkins where to find the JUnit XML output for your test run. You do that configuration in the Post-Build Actions section, as shown in figure 11.4.

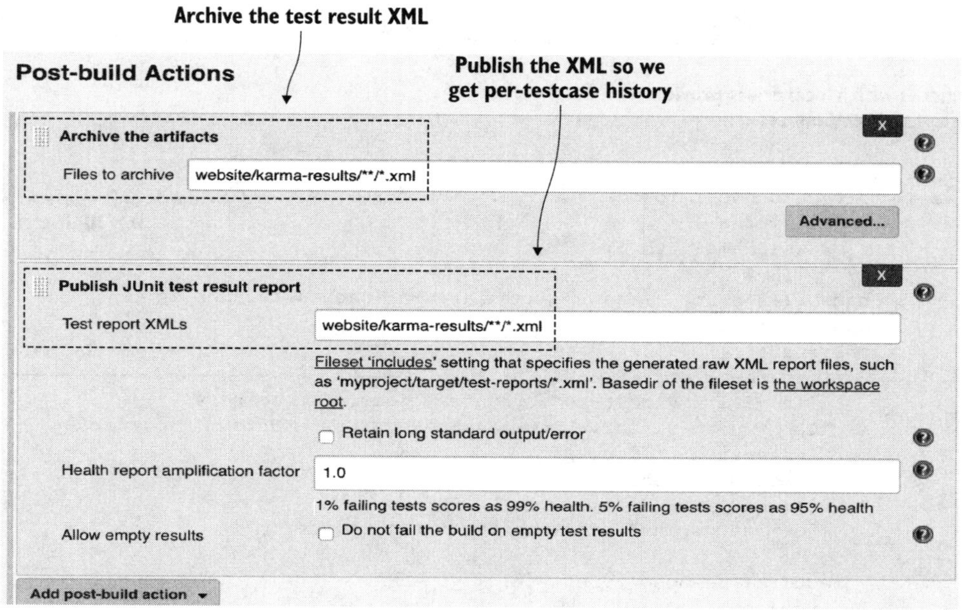

Figure 11.4   Post-build actions for the unit test Jenkins job

Note that you both archive the XML and publish a JUnit test report based on it. Publishing the JUnit test report will create a chart of test pass/failure over time, and it gives you detailed information about which test cases failed. Archiving the XML means that Jenkins will keep the file around, which can be helpful later for debugging purposes.

11.1.3   E2E tests

Setting up Jenkins to run E2E tests is quite similar to setting it up to run unit tests. You could use headless Chrome again, but for instructional purposes, you'll try something different and use regular Chrome and Xvfb. Also, instead of using `directConnect` as you've done in previous chapters, you'll use a local driver provider, which will tell Protractor to launch the Selenium server on a random available port. You'll use this option because you might not have a Selenium standalone server running in the background. As before, you'll turn on JUnit-style reports so you get detailed information about test runs in Jenkins.

Before you set up Jenkins, let's look at the Protractor configuration file (listing 11.3). You want to set up your tests to behave differently when running on Jenkins. In the configuration file, you'll set an `IS_JENKINS` environment flag. When your tests aren't running on Jenkins and that flag isn't set, the default behavior will be to use `directConnect`. In your Jenkins environment, you'll set the `IS_JENKINS` environment variable to `true`. When the flag is set, the test won't launch with `directConnect`, and Protractor will handle starting and stopping your Selenium standalone server for you. The `IS_JENKINS` flag also guards the `onPrepare` function to generate only JUnit reports on Jenkins.

Listing 11.3   Protractor configuration file—chapter11/protractor.conf.js

**Launches with a local driver provider
instead of directConnect**

```
exports.config = {
  directConnect: !process.env.IS_JENKINS,
  capabilities: {
    browserName: 'chrome'
  },
  baseUrl: 'https://testing-angular-applications.github.io',
  specs: ['e2e/**/*.spec.ts'],
  onPrepare: () => {
    if (process.env.IS_JENKINS) {
      let jasmineReporters = require('jasmine-reporters');
      let junitReporter = new jasmineReporters.JUnitXmlReporter({
        savePath: 'output/',
        consolidateAll: false
      });
      jasmine.getEnv().addReporter(junitReporter);
    }
    require('ts-node').register({
      project: 'e2e'
    });
  },
  useAllAngular2AppRoots: true
};
```

**Guards onPrepare to generate
only JUnit-style reports**

When you configure the Jenkins job for your E2E tests, you'll need to first set up the build environment. In the Build Environment section shown in figure 11.5, select these two options: Start Xvfb Before the Build and Run the Build in an NVM Managed Environment (with Node Version 8).

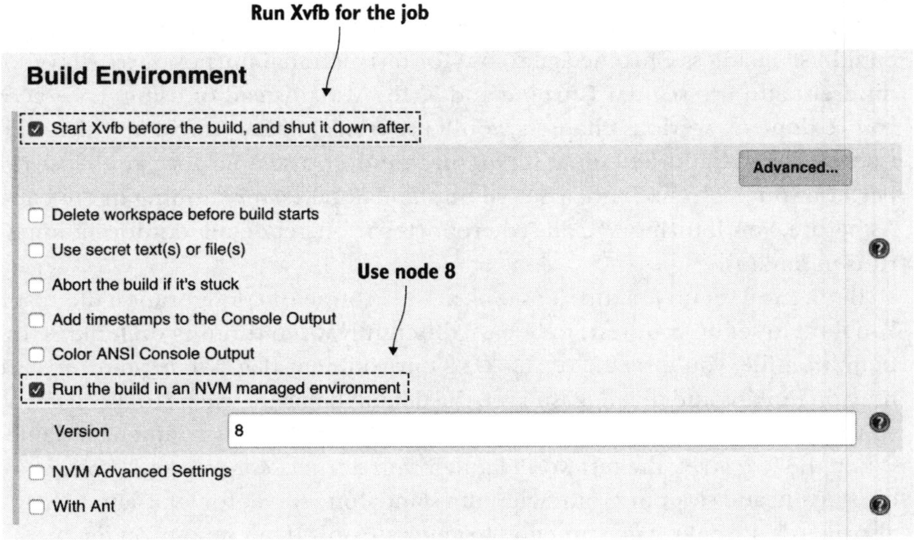

Figure 11.5   Build environment for the E2E Jenkins job

Next, set up an execute shell build step with the snippet shown in listing 11.4. In the shell commands, you specify the environment variable that your Protractor configuration file is using. You won't be using `directConnect` and you'll be generating JUnit style reports because you've set `IS_JENKINS` to `true`.

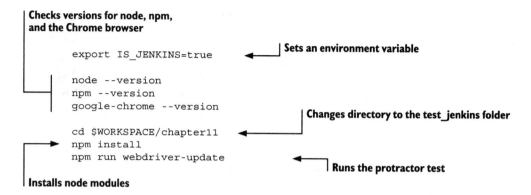

Listing 11.4   Jenkins execute shell

Checks versions for node, npm, and the Chrome browser

```
export IS_JENKINS=true          ◀── Sets an environment variable

node --version
npm --version
google-chrome --version

cd $WORKSPACE/chapter11         ◀── Changes directory to the test_jenkins folder
npm install
npm run webdriver-update        ◀── Runs the protractor test
```

Installs node modules

Finally, in the Post-Build Actions section, you'll specify Archive the Artifacts for the JUnit reports. You'll also use Publish JUnit Test Result Report with the same file set you're planning to archive (figure 11.6).

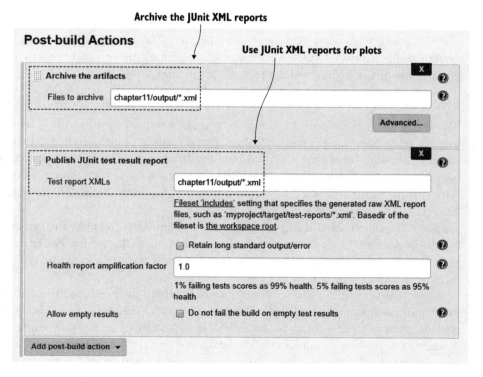

Figure 11.6   Post-build actions for the E2E Jenkins job

Publishing a JUnit test result report will create a history in Jenkins of your test runs. After more than one build occurs, the Jenkins job will display a plot of failed and passing tests along with a set of the last successful artifact outputs. Figure 11.7 shows the summary plot and artifacts for your test job.

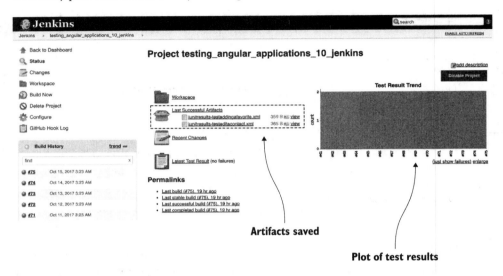

Figure 11.7   Jenkins test results display

As previously mentioned, you could have used headless Chrome instead of Xvfb, and you also could have used `directConnect` instead of launching the test with the local driver provider option. In the next section, you take the same test and run it on CircleCI, but with headless Chrome and `directConnect` instead.

11.2   *CircleCI*

CircleCI is another continuous integration service that integrates with GitHub and is free for open-source projects; it also has a paid enterprise tier. The neat thing about CircleCI version 2.0 is that it's optimized for Docker images. Docker is a container-based system for Linux virtualization, so when you use a Docker image, it's a virtual Linux distribution running preinstalled software. You can use a container to install Node.js and Chrome in your CI environment.

CircleCI makes it easy to run your tests more often. This gives you the option of testing things automatically that you might have tested manually before. For example, you can use your new Protractor CI setup to automatically test the appearance of your app using tests that take screenshots.

Before you set up your CircleCI configuration, add to the previous Protractor configuration file with a new environment variable, `IS_CIRCLE`, in listing 11.5. This additional environment variable will run your CircleCI tests with headless Chrome using `direct-Connect`. On Jenkins, it will run with a local launch of the Selenium standalone server with JUnit-style reports. Finally, in your development environment, you'll use `direct-Connect` without headless mode so that you can see what's happening in your E2E tests.

Listing 11.5   Protractor configuration for CircleCI

```
exports.config = {
  directConnect: (!process.env.IS_JENKINS && true),
  capabilities: {
    browserName: 'chrome',                         Uses headless Chrome because
    chromeOptions: {                                    IS_CIRCLE is set to true
      args: (process.env.IS_CIRCLE ? ['--headless'] : [])   ◄───
    }
  },
  baseUrl: 'https://testing-angular-applications.github.io',
  specs: ['e2e/**/*.spec.ts'],
  onPrepare: () => {
    if (process.env.IS_JENKINS) {
      let jasmineReporters = require('jasmine-reporters');
      let junitReporter = new jasmineReporters.JUnitXmlReporter({
        savePath: 'output/',
        consolidateAll: false
      });
      jasmine.getEnv().addReporter(junitReporter);
    }
    require('ts-node').register({
      project: 'e2e'
    });

  },
  useAllAngular2AppRoots: true
};
```

Next, you need to set up CircleCI by creating a configuration file, ./circle/config.yml.
You can use a CircleCI-maintained docker image that includes Node and browsers. Then
you need to specify the shell commands to run your tests. The only difference between
the shell commands in the following listing and the Jenkins shell commands is that in
CircleCI, you need to change to the website directory and run the npm command.

Listing 11.6   CircleCI configuration file .circle/config.yml

Specifies the working directory that will be
used to check out the git repository

```
version: 2        ◄───  Specifies to use CircleCI version 2.0
jobs:
  build:
    working_directory: ~/workspace
    docker:
      - image: circleci/node:8-browsers   ◄───
    steps:                                        Downloads the CircleCI docker
      - checkout                                  image for Node 8 with browsers

      - run: export IS_CIRCLE=true
```

Sets the environment variable IS_CIRCLE so
your tests will run with headless Chrome

```
- run: node --version
- run: npm --version
- run: google-chrome --version

- run: cd website && npm install
- run: cd website && npm run karma start karma-ci.conf.js
- run: cd website && npm run e2e protractor.conf.js
```

Runs the E2E tests

**Changes directory to the website folder,
then runs the unit tests**

Note that running unit and E2E tests in CircleCI is easy: you specify a shell command to run. As with Jenkins, CircleCI can take test results in JUnit XML format to give detailed test information. Unlike Jenkins, CircleCI will automatically search your project and try to interpret any test output XML files that it finds. If you don't care about detailed results, you don't have to produce a JUnit XML file. CircleCI will consider the test failed if any of the steps return a nonzero exit code, which Karma and Protractor both do if a test fails.

Summary

- If you need to set up your own CI, use Jenkins server. It requires some additional setup steps for you to be able to run your unit and E2E tests.
- If your tests can produce a JUnit-style XML test result, Jenkins can use that information to create detailed reports of your test runs.
- CircleCI is an easy to use hosted solution for CI with a free tier, and it's good if you need a quick solution for setting up a CI system.

appendix A
Setting up the sample project

This appendix covers

- Installing prerequisites
- Installing the Angular CLI, along with Jasmine, Protractor, and Karma

In this book, you'll use the Angular CLI to run tasks, execute tests, and manage dependencies. In this appendix, we'll look at the Angular CLI, and you'll install the tool itself. By installing the Angular CLI, you'll also install Jasmine, Protractor, and Karma. When you're finished with that, you'll get the sample project up and running. Let's dive in!

A.1   *Introducing the Angular CLI*

One of the major pain points in the past was that setting up an Angular project could be challenging and time-consuming. In March 2017, the Angular team launched a tool called the Angular command-line interface (CLI) to address that issue. The Angular CLI greatly cuts the time it takes to set up an Angular project.

At the time of this writing, the Angular CLI gives you access to about a dozen commands that are useful when creating and maintaining Angular applications. In this book, you'll mainly use a few of those commands for testing purposes. Table A.1 shows the commands you'll use and their respective description that we'll use throughout the book.

Table A.1 Angular CLI commands that you'll use

Command	Description
ng test	Runs your unit tests
ng e2e	Runs your end-to-end tests

For a full list of commands, visit https://github.com/angular/angular-cli/wiki. If you want to learn more about the Angular CLI in general, visit https://cli.angular.io/.

A.2 Installing prerequisites

Before you install the Angular CLI, you need to make sure you have two prerequisites installed:

- Node.js version 6.9.0 or higher
- npm version 3 or higher

To make sure you have a version of Node.js that's 6.9.0 or higher, run the following command in your terminal:

```
node -v
```

You should see output similar to the following in the terminal:

```
v8.7.0
```

If you need to update your version of Node.js, visit https://nodejs.org/en/ to install the latest version, or at least version 6.9.0. If you would like to choose which version to install, you can go to https://nodejs.org/dist/ to select the version you'd prefer.

> **TIP** If you need to switch versions of Node.js frequently because of compatibility issues with different projects, we highly recommend that you use nvm. nvm is the Node Version Manager that makes maintaining versions of Node.js a snap. You can have multiple versions of Node.js installed and switch between the versions whenever you need to. To install and use nvm, visit https://github.com/creationix/nvm.

Now that you have Node.js installed, you need to make sure you have a version of npm that's higher than 3. Run the following command:

```
npm -v
```

If you've installed npm correctly, you should see something like this in your terminal:

```
5.4.2
```

If you don't see a version higher than version 3, try reinstalling Node.js by downloading a fresh copy of Node.js at https://nodejs.org/en/. Because npm ships with Node.js, it should give you the most up-to-date version of npm by installing Node.js. If that doesn't work, try updating npm using npm (that's not a typo) by running the following command:

```
npm install npm@latest -g
```

That's it in terms of prerequisites. You can now install the Angular CLI. Follow the steps we describe to get it up and running.

A.2.1 Installing the Angular CLI the first time

If you've never installed the Angular CLI, run the following command to install it globally:

```
npm i -g @angular/cli@latest
```

That's it! You're good to go! After it's installed, go to "Verifying the installation" in section A.2.2.

A.2.2 Updating an old version of the Angular CLI

If you have an old version of the Angular CLI already installed, you may have to take a couple of steps, depending on which version you have. The difference is that after version 1.0.0-beta.28, the name of the project, and its scope, was changed from angular-cli to @angular/cli. To find out which version you have installed, run the following command:

```
ng -v
```

In your terminal, you should see the current version of the Angular CLI that's installed.

UPDATING VERSIONS EQUAL TO 1.0.0-BETA.28 OR LOWER

If you have a version installed equal to or lower than 1.0.0-beta.28, run the following commands:

```
npm uninstall -g angular-cli
npm cache clean
npm install -g @angular/cli@latest
```

Once you're done, you can skip to "Verifying the installation."

UPDATING VERSIONS HIGHER THAN 1.0.0-BETA.28

If you need to update from a version higher than 1.0.0-beta.28, run the following commands:

```
npm uninstall -g @angular/cli
npm cache clean
npm install -g @angular/cli@latest
```

VERIFYING THE INSTALLATION

Now that you have the Angular CLI installed, make sure it's installed properly before going any further. Run the following command:

```
ng -v
```

If all goes well, your output should look something like figure A.1.

Figure A.1 The Angular CLI version screen

> **NOTE** If you don't see output like figure A.1 or any type of verification saying that the Angular CLI is installed, visit the installation section of the Angular CLI README at http://mng.bz/WjIS or the updating section at http://mng.bz/jq0v. Otherwise, check out the Testing Angular Applications forum at http://mng.bz/9i4M. There, you can post questions, or you may find that someone else has asked a question about the same issue and already gotten an answer.

A.3 *Installing the sample project*

Now go ahead and clone the sample code for the project. First, navigate to a directory in your terminal where you would like to store the sample code for your project—for example, at ~/Software/GitHub. Clone the repo by running the following command:

```
git clone https://github.com/testing-angular-applications/testing-angular-
    applications.git
```

After you've cloned the site, run the following command to navigate to the directory with your app:

```
cd testing-angular-applications/website
```

A.4 *Installing dependencies*

You need to make sure you have all the necessary dependencies that the application requires by running this command:

```
npm install
```

TIP You're going to do a lot of typing in this book and throughout your career. Knowing aliases will save you valuable time and increase your efficiency. For example, you can use npm i instead of npm install. In this book, you'll get the chance to practice using some aliases. If you want to learn more about possible shortcuts and aliases, run the following command:

```
npm <command> --help
```

You also can use the --h flag (shorthand for --help). If viewing the help menu on your console is a little challenging, check out the npm documentation online at https://docs.npmjs.com/ under the "CLI Commands" section.

A.5 *Running the application*

To run the application, run the following command in your terminal:

```
ng serve
```

You also can abbreviate that to ng s. After running the command, you should see something like the screenshot in figure A.2.

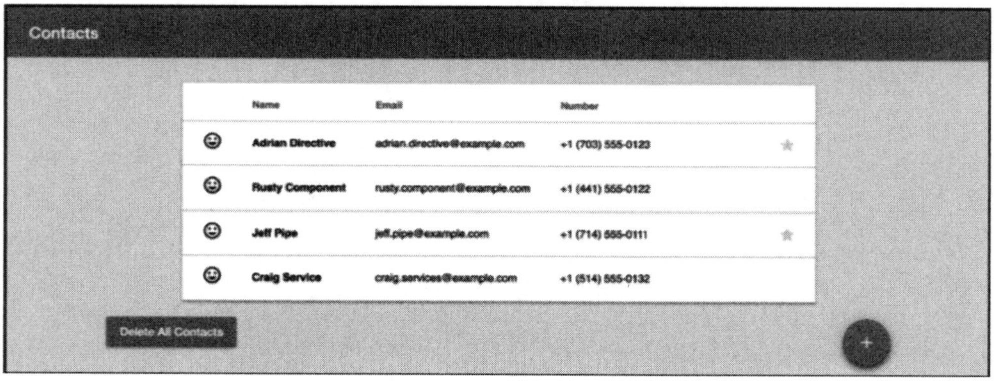

Figure A.2 Contacts app screen

The sample project is now up and running, and you're ready to write some tests!

NOTE If you have issues compiling the project, you can try reinstalling the npm packages. First, delete the existing node_modules folder by running [start code]rm -rf node_modules[/end code]. Then run [start code]package -lock.json[/end code], and finally run [start code]npm i[/end code] to reinstall the npm packages.

Otherwise visit the Testing Angular Applications forum at http://mng.bz/9i4M for help as mentioned earlier.

appendix B
Additional resources

If you're looking for more testing resources for additional learning, then you're in luck! The following collection of books and other resources will help you to further sharpen your testing skills.

B.1   Angular testing

Resource	Description	Link
Website	Angular official testing documentation	https://angular.io/guide/testing
Online video	End-to-End Testing Angular Applications	https://www.coursera.org/lecture/angular/end-to-end-testing-angular-applications-atcs6
Blog post	Angular Unit Testing performance	https://blog.angularindepth.com/angular-unit-testing-performance-34363b7345ba

B.2   General testing

- *The Art of Unit Testing with examples in C#, Second Edition,* Roy Osherove, Manning Publications, 2013
- *Effective Unit Testing: A guide for Java developers,* Lasse Koskela, Manning Publications, 2013
- *Test Driven: Practical TDD and Acceptance TDD for Java Developers,* Lasse Koskela, Manning Publications, 2007

- *Test Driven-Development: By Example*, Kent Beck, Addison-Wesley Professional, 2002
- *Growing Object-Oriented Software, Guided by Tests*, Steve Freeman and Nat Pryce, Addison-Wesley Professional, 2009
- *Agile Testing: A Practical Guide for Testers and Agile Teams*, Lisa Crispin and Janet Gregory, Addison-Wesley Professional, 2009
- *More Agile Testing: Learning Journeys for the Whole Team*, Lisa Crispin and Janet Gregory, Addison-Wesley Professional, 2014
- *Developer Testing: Building Quality into Software*, Alexander Tarlinder, Addison-Wesley Professional, 2016

index